PRAISE FOR

BEHIND NAZI LINES

"Filled with secret missions, Nazi villains, and daring escapes that actually happened, *Behind Nazi Lines* is thrilling, epic, inspiring—and have we mentioned true? Andy Hodges is a real hero whose story must never be forgotten."

—Eric Metaxas, *New York Times* bestselling author of
Miracles and *Bonhoeffer*

"One of the most intriguing books I have read on World War II . . . Captivating and nearly impossible to put down. I recommend it with enthusiasm to professional historians, history buffs, and anyone who wants to be inspired and entertained."

—Lyle W. Dorsett, author of *Serving God and Country*

"What a page-turner! It reads like a good novel, but it is all true."

—Private First Class Bernard Rader,
K Company, 301st Regiment, 94th Division

"Fascinating . . . Andy's story is one of great courage, risks, sacrifice, and commitment to a transcendent cause."

—Lt. Gen. William "Jerry" Boykin,
former commander, U.S. Army's Delta Force

"Superbly written and extensively researched, Andy Hodges's story . . . brings a human dimension to an underappreciated heroic episode . . . This informative, enjoyable and excellent work exemplifies a labor of love and courage one man had for his country."

—Lt. Gen. Ronald L. Burgess Jr.,
former director of the U.S. Defense Intelligence Agency,
senior counsel for National Security Programs, Cyber Programs
and Military Affairs, Auburn University

BEHIND NAZI LINES

My Father's Heroic Quest to Save 149 World War II POWs

ANDREW GEROW HODGES JR.
and
DENISE GEORGE

CALIBER

□
———

DUTTON CALIBER
An imprint of Penguin Random House LLC
penguinrandomhouse.com

Ⓟ

The Library of Congress has catalogued the hardcover edition as follows:

Hodges, Andrew G.
Behind Nazi lines : my father's heroic quest to save 149 World
War II POWs / Andrew Gerow Hodges Jr., Denise George.
p. cm.
ISBN 978-0-425-27646-4 (hardback)
1. Hodges, Andrew Gerow, 1918–2005.   2. World War, 1939–1945—Prisoners and
prisons, German.   3. American Red Cross—Biography.   4. World War, 1939–1945—War
work—Red Cross.   5. Prisoners of war—United States—Biography.   6. Prisoners of
war—France—Saint-Nazaire—Biography.   7. Saint-Nazaire (France)—History,
Military—20th century.   8. United States. Army. Infantry Division, 94th—Biography.
9. France—History—German occupation, 1940–1945.   I. George, Denise.   II. Title.
III. Title: My father's heroic quest to save 149 World War II POWs.
D805.5.S27H66 2015
940.54'7243092—dc23
2014045820

PUBLISHING HISTORY
Berkley Caliber hardcover edition / August 2015
Berkley Caliber trade paperback edition / August 2016
First Dutton Caliber trade paperback edition / December 2021

Dutton Caliber trade paperback ISBN: 9780593184806

PRINTED IN THE UNITED STATES OF AMERICA

2nd Printing

Cover: U.S. prisoners of war reenter American lines at Pornic, France, on November 29, 1944.
(Signal Corps photo courtesy of the National Archives)

To my mother—one of my two heroes—
Mary Louise Shirley Hodges,
who, like millions of WWII brides,
stood by her man while he was overseas,
doing his part for America and the world.

AUTHOR'S NOTE

The story's dialogue came from statements made by Andrew Gerow Hodges, Michael R. D. Foot, and the POWs that attended the Samford Reunion on January 25, 2002. These were video-recorded and included in the award-winning documentary *For One English Officer.* Other dialogue came from POW diaries, newspaper articles, military records, recorded statements, letters, telegrams, correspondence, and conversations with living participants and family members of participants. Some of the dialogue was created in a logical sequence to match documented stories and events.

All stories and events in this book happened just as they are described and can be documented by records, newsreels, military information/records, etc. All characters in this book are real, and appear in the story as they did in the real life events. The names of Schmitt's nephew, *Walter,* and sister, *Greta,* were created. Schmitt had a sister and a nephew, but their names could not be found. The German sentry in Lorient, *Klaus,* was a created name/person.

The names Léon Spanin (his birth name) and Léon Rollin (his pseudonym) are used interchangeably throughout the book. He is also referred to by his nickname, Leo.

CONTENTS

PART ONE: THE FIRST EXCHANGE 1

PART TWO: THE SECOND EXCHANGE   129

PART THREE: THE REST OF THE STORY 269

BEHIND NAZI LINES

PART ONE

THE FIRST EXCHANGE

There was one man . . . on the Allied side, armed only with his wits and a Red Cross badge.

—HARLAN HOBART GROOMS, JR.,
COLONEL, U.S. MARINE CORPS RESERVE (RETIRED),
PAST PRESIDENT OF THE BIRMINGHAM BAR ASSOCIATION,
BIRMINGHAM, ALABAMA, USA

ONE

A CROSS, A FLAG, AND A DANGEROUS JOURNEY

Thursday, 23 November 1944, Thanksgiving Day,
94th Infantry Division Headquarters, Châteaubriant, France

Andy Hodges had been handed a job no one else dared to accept—a direct order from Major General Harry J. Malony, commander of the 94th Infantry Division, headquartered in Châteaubriant, France.

"It's a suicide mission," Malony's chief of staff, Colonel Earl Bergquist, had told him. But Andy had his orders, even if he'd most likely become the target of a German bullet.

However dangerous the assignment, deep down Hodges welcomed the opportunity to serve his country. He thought about the lives that were depending on him—men with families in America, France, and Britain—mothers, fathers, wives, and siblings who waited for a word of hope about their loved ones recently declared missing in action. He hoped he could save the POWs held in the St. Nazaire prison camp. The prisoners were cold, hungry, and becoming deathly ill. They needed help, and quickly.

On that dismal predawn morning in late November, a cold rain spattered the sleeping French countryside. Andy placed a white flag in the jeep's front holder, climbed inside, and began his trek toward enemy lines. Probably, no one expected his arrival on this day. In his hand, he carried a copy of a letter, dated November 21, 1944, typed in German on American Red Cross stationery. It was addressed to the camp's *Kommandant*—whoever he was.

"*An den Deutschen Kommandanten, St. Nazaire,*" it said. That's all. No specific name.

I hope the Kommandant *has already received the original letter I sent beforehand. But I have no way to know.*

The letter he held was his protection, his only defense, if he were stopped, questioned, and searched. But he knew it would provide little security against so brutal an enemy.

In seven or eight hours, back home in Geneva, South Alabama, Thanksgiving Day would dawn. He wanted to be there, sitting in his chair around the big family table, with his new bride and toddler son, his parents, brothers, aunts, uncles, cousins, and longtime friends. He could almost smell and taste the traditional oven-baked turkey and cornbread dressing, marshmallow-crowned sweet potato casserole, last summer's homegrown canned tomatoes, and pumpkin pies his family would feast on that day. But the whole world was at war, and he had his orders.

Dinners at home will have to wait—till next year, or the year after that. I sure hope I get to sit at my family's Thanksgiving table again one day.

As he drove slowly down the narrow path from Châteaubriant, he shined his flashlight on the old, crinkled map of France, the only one he could find. When he reached Chauve, he stopped and checked the tangle of thread-like roads that branched out like a spider's web from the small Allied-occupied village southeast of St. Nazaire on the western coast of central France.

Only about four miles to Saint-Père-en-Retz. That is, if I take the right road.

He picked up a pen and carefully marked the route he had been advised to take. It was in the French language and was confusing.

Northwest along Les Epinettes. Les Epinettes becomes Le Bourg. Stay left along the Rue de Nantes.

Andy's sense of direction wasn't so bad, but, except for a few words, he knew no French.

Maybe if I'd played less football and studied more languages in college, I'd be better equipped for this mission. At least I could read this map.

He worried about the accuracy of the faded map for the Vannes-Angers region of France, and how much the area had probably changed during the years of war. He ran his hand through his thick brown hair and sighed.

Must trust the map. No other choice.

Alone in the foggy, wet darkness, the twenty-six-year-old, tall, slender Alabamian continued his journey toward enemy territory. As he drove, his stomach knotted and burned. Bile rose and stuck in his throat. He swallowed hard but couldn't dislodge it. He clutched the steering wheel tighter with each mile he traveled.

As he inched forward toward St. Père-en-Retz, he moved farther away from the Allied-controlled countryside, and closer toward the barbed wire blockade that ushered him into the German-occupied seaport pocket of France. He was thankful for the jeep's canvas top that protected him from the rain—a perk granted to him by Malony. He shivered as the west winds blew in from the Atlantic and made the eerie fog twist in surreal shapes across the still dark countryside.

The German lines can't be much farther.

Andy's heart beat faster. He wondered how a German sentry would react to a lone American, wearing Red Cross insignias, driving a jeep sporting a large white flag, appearing ghost-like and unexpected at the opening in the concertina wire fence separating the combatants.

He'll shoot me. That's how he'll respond.

Before he was ready, he was there. He saw the wire barrier within a few yards of him. He stopped the jeep and sat still, quiet, his eyes closed. In his mind, Andy envisioned the faces of the people he loved, as they would gather later that day around the family's table. He saw his young bride, Mary Louise Shirley, the popular campus beauty who had fallen in love with him—Andrew Gerow Hodges, Howard College's rising football star. Number 15.

Mary Louise Shirley—beautiful, brilliant, educated, from a good family—how did I, a poor country boy from South Alabama, ever get such a fine girl?!

Andy shook his head, smiled, and thought about the baby boy born to them a year after they married—Andrew Gerow Hodges, Jr. "Little Gerry" was almost two years old the summer Andy left Alabama to join the war effort in France.

The faces of Andy's father and mother appeared next in his mind. He felt unusually thankful for his dad at that moment, a poor horse trader with little or no education, but a loving father who had taught his three sons great lessons in moral ethics, wisdom, honest hard work, and good common horse sense. He thought about his mother, kind, selfless, loving, and dedicated to her boys.

Poor Mom. I wonder if she'll be able to handle emotionally receiving the missing-in-action telegram—or something worse—that might come before Christmas—if I don't make it back from this mission.

For a brief second, a feeling of helplessness overwhelmed him. He'd never felt so alone and so far away from those he loved, from those who had always offered him unconditional love and support.

I had a choice. I could've stayed home. I chose to come and serve.

Andy rubbed his left shoulder. The old college football injury still caused him pain. A teammate's violent blow had ruptured his biceps tendon. But the suffering caused by a damaged deltoid didn't hurt nearly as much as the military's 4-F classification that came as a result of it. Andy was in excellent physical shape—a well-built, trim, muscular college athlete. But when the army medics had examined his left shoulder, they declared him unfit for military service. The news was unexpected, shocking, and caused Andy deep grief. He watched his buddies eagerly march off to war, and he agonized over his humiliating 4-F status. Finally he could bear it no longer. He knew the physical injury could keep him out of the United States military, but it could not keep him out of the American Red Cross. If the U.S. Army forbade him to come in the front door with his college friends and other recruits—well then, he could just join the American Red Cross and come in through the back door. And that's exactly what he did.

He had chosen to come, leaving a wife and son, and a good-paying job, so that he could serve alongside his comrades, and help win this war against Hitler. The 94th Army Infantry Division, stationed in France, was glad to have him, gave him the rank of captain, and made him their ARC senior field director. Andy's dedication to duty, dependability, and courage in difficult situations quickly earned the confidence and respect of Malony as well as Bergquist. The commanding officer had given him critical missions he'd entrust to no one else. Andy was doing his part, even if a small one, and inside he felt real good about it.

As Andy faced the wire barrier, he pondered how to proceed. He had witnessed firsthand the depth of German cruelty toward Allied soldiers. He felt the urge to turn the jeep around and go back to headquarters—back to the safety of Châteaubriant and the 94th Division. But he knew he couldn't. If he'd learned anything from his father, it was determination and duty, not backing down when the going gets tough, and doing the best job you can do—even if it kills you.

And this trip might do just that.

Checking the security of his ARC collar pins and the Red Cross badge on his left shoulder, he licked his lips, took a deep breath, and somehow found the courage needed to move forward. He had no weapon, no protection—other than his wits, a letter, a white flag, and the Red Cross insignias.

I hope it's enough.

Driving slowly to the wire, Hodges stopped abruptly when he saw a surprised German sentry running from the woods, pointing his automatic weapon and screaming: *"Achtung! Halt! Achtung!"* ["Look out! Stop! Your attention!"]

Here it comes. This ballgame may be over.

TWO

THE SPY

24 August 1944, St. Nazaire Sector, Brittany, France

Captain Michael R. D. Foot had proved himself a skilled assassin. As a member of Britain's Special Air Service (SAS), whom Hitler called the "terror troops," he had participated in many demanding and dangerous missions. This one, however, would be his first foray into German-occupied France. In the summer of '44, Britain's SAS commander ordered the young Foot to infiltrate the St. Nazaire sector of Brittany to hunt down a particular vicious German officer.

"A certain German, by the name of Oberleutnant Bonner, in the Sicherheitsdienst [SD], is causing us much trouble. He has been especially cruel to our POWs. Find him. Capture him if you can. If you can't, then kill him," the commander ordered Foot.[1]

Michael knew about the Sicherheitsdienst—the Nazi Party's intelligence and security body, created by Heinrich Himmler in 1931. He'd personally seen the results of their unlimited power—given to them by Hitler himself—to deal with all opposition to the Nazi government. Foot eagerly accepted the assignment, and parachuted into Normandy, ready and eager to begin his secret mission. On August 22, he secured a jeep, hired a French SAS driver named Caplan, and together they wormed their way along narrow roads and set out to infiltrate enemy lines.

"Make haste, Caplan," Foot ordered his driver. "We don't have much time. Let's get this job done and get out of here."

Foot and Caplan spoke little as they sped down dirt roads toward St. Nazaire. As Foot saw the countryside pass by, he thought about the long list of military heroes sprinkled throughout his prominent British family—his great-great-uncle, the Royal Navy's first sea lord, Jackie Fisher; his paternal grandfather, who had achieved the rank of major general; his father, Brigadier General Richard C. Foot, head of London's air defenses; and himself, an SAS captain. He held his head a little higher. He felt proud—of his family, of his father, and of himself. He knew he had a legacy to uphold, and that he could never fail. He'd rather die than face embarrassing his distinguished father, or disgracing his celebrated British ancestors. Military failure was not an option for Michael Foot.

Foot watched closely for German machine gun nests hiding along the roadsides. He had been warned about Jerries crouching and hiding beneath and behind the thick hedgerows that grew in this part of France. He knew the Germans feared the SAS, the elite United Kingdom forces, one of the toughest in the military worldwide. He had heard of the unfortunate fates of SAS members when captured by the enemy, and the fact that few SAS men had ever seen the inside of a German POW prison camp. Most had been shot on sight, no questions asked.

As Caplan drove in the area near Savenay, the English officer thought about the recently failed Operation Bulbasket—a military disaster.[2] He remembered that just the month before, a group of SAS members had been captured near Poitiers, France.

That was a bloody mess, a really bad show. Those mucking Jerries. They should all be shot for what they did to those SAS members.

Foot instinctively winced when he envisioned how thirty of these SAS men had been savagely tortured and executed by a German firing squad. He scanned the area around him, feeling an uncharacteristic moment of fear.

If I'm captured, I'm dead.

Suddenly, without warning, Caplan slammed on the brakes. The jeep's wheels skidded to a stop at the edge of a steep drop-off in the middle of the road.

With his right hand, Foot grabbed hold of the windshield to keep from falling out.

"Caplan! What the blazing . . . !"

"The bridge! Sir, the bridge across the canal is gone!" Caplan shouted. "We're lucky we didn't go over!"

"Go around another way, mate!" Foot ordered, straightening himself in his seat and checking his wristwatch.

"Sir, there is no other way. We'll have to go back. I'll turn the jeep around. It might take a moment."

"Do what you must!" Foot scowled. "Just chivvy on and hurry it up!"

Foot climbed out and stretched his long legs. It took several tries for Caplan to reposition the jeep between the tight hedgerows bordering the road. Foot checked his watch again and began to pace.

Hurry up, Caplan! Turn the sodding jeep around!

While he waited, Foot thought about his grandfather, a commanding officer in the Territorial Army Hartfordshire Artillery Regiment, who, in 1912, had told Michael's father, Richard, it looked as if a war was going to occur. He suggested that young Richard enlist. Of course, he did. He fought throughout World War I, and made his father proud.

And that's exactly the same thing that Richard, my father, told me in the winter of 1938–39, while I was still in university.

Michael had taken his father's advice, enlisted, and was assigned to a searchlight battalion in an anti-aircraft command. He spent eighteen months in North Africa and Sicily, and was promoted to major in January 1944. He, too, made his father proud.

And I will make him even prouder as an intelligence officer with the esteemed SAS. I don't dare make a muck out of this assignment.

Michael had requested the mission. He wanted to get closer to the enemy.

I've spent only six months with the SAS. They assured me I would get much closer to the daft Germans, and they were certainly right!

Back and forth, back and forth, Foot paced, waiting for his driver to turn around. Then he heard a terrifying shout.

"*Halt! Hände hoch! Halt! Hände hoch!*" ["Stop! Put your hands up!"] a harsh, deep voice shouted from behind him.

Foot felt his heart race. He stopped and raised his arms high. Then he turned around slowly, and looked straight into the barrels of machine guns. The camouflaged blouses and pot-shaped helmets instantly identified the enemies as German paratroopers. The weapons were no surprise, the deadly, rapid-firing MG42s. They proved a nasty combination. He held his breath and waited for a paratrooper to fire.

Go ahead. Shoot me. Get it over with. I am not afraid to die. But I had hoped for a more spectacular demise!

Foot, well bred, brilliant, and wealthy, felt he deserved a more sensational end to his mission, to his life.

His head held high and his face showing no expression, he mentally prepared himself to be shot.

One bullet to the head and it's over. Finished. A life lived well, but cut short.

Michael Foot should prove a prized catch, one the Germans could brag about for a very long time. A handsome young intelligence officer, he had been well schooled before his military career, studying at England's foremost universities, including Winchester College and Oxford University. His father had boasted of his son's distinguished involvement in North Africa's Operation Torch and Sicily's Operation Husky.

"My boy also helped plan certain phases of the D-Day landings," Michael had heard his father tell important friends.

My father will be disappointed; I've mucked up and let him down. He expected more from me.

The Germans kept their weapons focused on him. For the first time, he wanted to make the prestigious SAS insignia on his sleeve disappear. It was no longer a symbol of pride and honor, but a death sentence. Not only did it identify him as a member of the British Army's most renowned special forces unit, but it proudly boasted the SAS's pompous motto: "Who Dares Wins."

They'll see the insignia, and I'm dead. My new motto? "I dared. I lost." I hope Father knows I did my best.

Foot kept his eyes on the machine guns. In the distance, he heard the gunning sound of the jeep's motor, and the squeal of spinning tires, as his driver escaped down the road.

Good for Caplan! He's nobody's fool. At least one of us has been saved.[3]

The captain let out the breath he had been holding, exhaling a bit more loudly than he meant to.

A German lieutenant approached Foot, speaking in English.

"You are with the SAS? Impressive!" the lieutenant said, noticing the insignia on the captain's left shoulder. A rare find. Not too many of you men left."

Foot remained silent, ignoring the remark.

"You remember, of course, last month's Poitiers incident?" the lieutenant asked Foot.

Upon hearing the name "Poitiers," the surrounding soldiers nodded and some grinned.

Foot clenched his jaw, narrowed his eyes, and focused on the woods far in the distance.

Yes. I remember. Some of those mates were my friends.

The officer, who then introduced himself as Lieutenant Bernstein, walked up close to Foot's face and pulled a penknife from his pocket, the sharp blade extended. Foot didn't flinch, as he expected to be stabbed or his throat to be cut. With one swift, unexpected move, Bernstein sliced at the SAS insignia on the captain's shoulder. When two threads held the badge in place, the lieutenant ripped the insignia off with his fingers. With a smirk, he stuffed it into his pocket.

"For my son! He'll appreciate it one day. Thanks for the nice souvenir," he told Foot.

The captain could hardly believe his stroke of luck—on two counts.

I'm still alive! And you just saved my life, old Jerry! Without knowing it, you removed the one visible piece of evidence linking me to the SAS. Now, if you don't see the SAS cheque book in my pocket . . . Foot struggled to hold back a smile of relief.

Bernstein then added: "I have decided to let you live. For the moment."

Just like I thought—all mouth and no trousers! Well, Bernstein, you've lengthened my life much longer than you know! And thank you for not checking my clothes. Had you searched me, you'd have found my compass and MI

9 hacksaw. Now you think you can imprison me? I've got news for you, mate. I'll escape! The SAS has taught me well!

The Germans hauled Foot to their POW prison camp, Camp Franco, a former French Air Force facility in the Fortress St. Nazaire. Michael told no one of his membership in the SAS. To the Germans at the prison camp, the young captain was no one special, just another captured Tommy.

Brigadier Foot received the SAS's telegram one evening in early September 1944, advising him that his son, Michael, had been reported "missing in action, and believed killed." He fell back into a chair and read the telegram again.

Missing in action? Maybe. But I refuse to believe my son is dead.

Brigadier Foot stood, walked to his dresser, and picked up the framed photograph of his son. A friend had snapped the shot the spring before, as Michael stood in full uniform in the brigadier's garden in Hampstead. Young, tall, dignified, his hands clasped together in front of him, Michael fit like the perfect puzzle piece into the long line of military heroes that had so elegantly graced the Foot family tree.

I hope this won't be the last snapshot of Michael I will ever see.

Even though the hour was late, Foot telephoned the SAS commander. Positioning his stiff-upper-lip military British posture, in a well-controlled voice he explained the telegram, and after a while ended the conversation:

"I know Michael is alive. I don't care what it takes, find my son."

The commander informed Foot of Michael's last mission and the delicate war situation in France.

"Brigadier Foot, we believe Michael was captured by the Germans on 24 August on a mission in France—in the St. Nazaire sector. As you know, the enemy still holds a total of eight hundred square miles there—the Atlantic coastal ports: Fortress St. Nazaire and Fortress Lorient. The Americans have sealed more than sixty-six thousand Germans within those ports. The enemy is highly trained and well equipped. The Allies are frequent targets of their ambushes around those areas."

"Do you have any evidence Michael could possibly be imprisoned in the St. Nazaire area, in a German POW camp?" Foot asked.

"We have no way to confirm that." The commander paused. "Let me be frank with you, sir. After the incident at Poitiers, we must expect and prepare for the worst. You and I both know the Germans do not imprison SAS members. They usually . . ."

"Sir," Foot interrupted: "My son has been shot at, parachuted over enemy lines, helped plan raids, taken part in air operations and in sea commando attacks, and organized daring escapes. I cannot believe he is dead. He's too smart to get himself killed!"

"I am sorry for your loss, Brigadier Foot. Michael was one of our best. He will be greatly missed."

Richard Foot coldly and formally expressed his gratitude for any offered help from the SAS commander, and said a proper British goodbye. But inside his gut, a volcano rumbled and threatened to erupt.

I'm sorry for your loss?! Michael WAS one of our best? He will be missed?! That idiot talks as if Michael is dead! Did he not hear a word I said?! It certainly sounds like I can expect little or no help from the SAS to find and rescue my son!

The brigadier poured himself a drink from his small sterling silver flask, plunked down in his chair, and tapped his right foot hard on the floor. Late that night, three whiskeys later, Foot lay in bed and thought about his son. He envisioned the sparkle in his eyes; his love for learning, for education; the intense way he conversed with others about stimulating ideas; his remarkable fund of anecdotes, his quick wit; his dreams of great things he hoped to accomplish in life. But he forbade himself to shed a tear. Proper British military fathers did not cry when an heir fell on some distant battlefield—no matter how loved. They understood the risks of duty, of serving one's beloved country. They knew the many generations of blood sacrifices that had been paid—and would yet be required—by Britain's native sons.

Michael had such a promising future. And . . . and now this tragedy. My only son. So young. Such great potential lost. Lost . . . forever.

Foot stared at the bedroom ceiling for the rest of the night. He dared not admit it, not even to himself, but his old, tough warrior heart was broken.

THREE

A WARM SEPTEMBER MORNING

13 September 1944, St. Nazaire Sector, France

Sergeant Harold Thompson and his twelve-man patrol were returning from an intelligence mission behind German lines in Festung St. Nazaire. Thompson, the young Gary Cooper look-alike from Alabama, and his comrades laughed and joked as they enjoyed the warm September morning. Thompson wished the girls back home could see him now—handsomely uniformed, solely responsible for the lives of a dozen men, and, at the early age of eighteen, already leading an important, dangerous mission.

Suddenly the quiet moments were rent by the zipper-like sounds of enemy machine guns. Thompson gasped as he watched his men drop like ninepins, their bodies ripped apart. He heard their cries and calls for help, and saw German soldiers take them prisoners. Then Thompson caught a glimpse of one of his most courageous men, Corporal Onald Nelson, throwing down his rifle and quickly raising his arms.

In the midst of the melee, Thompson, and one of his infantrymen, scampered to an old rotting woodshed nearby.

"We'll hide here till dark," Thompson whispered to his frightened comrade. "Then we'll sneak back to Allied lines."

Huddling down behind a stack of long-forgotten firewood, Thompson closed his eyes and shook with fear. *Failure! Failure! Failure!* As hard as he tried, he couldn't shut out the devilish voices that condemned him for his lack of caution, and for the deaths and capture of his men.

You just couldn't wait until you turned eighteen to join the army! You think this is a game? It's not! It's war and it's serious. You think you're a man? Ha! Don't fool yourself! You're still a boy—and a murderer. Those men are dead because of you!

Thompson thought about the day he arrived in Normandy, less than two months before—on July 4, 1944. He was filled with excitement, and ready for battle. He had hoped the war wouldn't end before he could join up, see some front line action, and make his mark as a war hero. Not much happened back home in Mobile, Alabama, and at eighteen, he was ready for some real adventure.

Assigned to the 31st Regiment, 83rd Infantry Division, Thompson wasn't satisfied to be one GI among many infantrymen stationed in France. He yearned for a front row seat in the European theater of war. So when his CO asked for volunteers to lead a dangerous information-gathering assignment at enemy front lines near the St. Nazaire pocket, Thompson's hand shot up first. Only a few other hands followed.

"Thompson," his commander told him, "this is a dangerous and extremely important mission. Be on your constant guard. You and your men try to find out what kind of soldiers and artillery the Germans have in the St. Nazaire sector, whether the bridges and roads are mined, and anything else you can bring back."

"Yes sir," Thompson said and saluted.

The CO continued: "Try to locate the U-boats at the Keroman sub base. We think they have thirteen or fourteen U-boats. We've bombed St. Nazaire to bits, but we haven't been able to touch those subs they've hidden beneath twenty feet of reinforced concrete. See if you can find a way we can get at them in their pens—assuming you can get that close. That's all, Sergeant, give it your best shot."

That morning Thompson's patrol sneaked single file through the quiet French countryside. The temperature reached a pleasant seventy degrees as they stayed close to the woods, trying to avoid hidden and ever-watching enemy eyes.

Thompson and his men had gathered some useful data, and had somehow gone unseen. But as they headed back to base, the Germans spotted them and attacked. Now half his men were dead or captured, and the sergeant and his comrade were hunkered down in hiding, waiting for dusk, and hoping to escape with their lives.

Thompson heard a slight noise outside the woodshed.

Footsteps?

He sucked in his breath and grasped his rifle tighter. The footsteps were followed by men's whispers.

The enemy! They know we're in here.

Before Thompson could decide whether to fight or flee, he heard a deafening blast, felt a searing hot pain in his shoulders, and saw black.

When the young sergeant regained consciousness, he painfully opened his bloated eyes. His comrade was gone. Standing on all sides of him he saw gray-clad helmeted Germans pointing rifles with bayonets. He tasted blood and saw torn flesh on his chest. Pain overwhelmed him as he was loaded onto a litter and taken to a makeshift first aid station. After German medics removed some of the largest pieces of shrapnel from his face, neck, shoulders, and chest, they trucked him to the St. Nazaire POW camp. At first glance, Thompson thought it looked like an abandoned aircraft factory.

One of his captured men, Corporal Nelson, saw Thompson arrive at the camp.

"Sergeant, we didn't know if you had survived or not," Nelson said. "They killed six of our men. I am one of the four men from our mission they captured and imprisoned here."

"What is this place?" Thompson asked.

"It's a compound with about a dozen Americans and several British prisoners," Nelson said. "I'm told it's completely surrounded by barbed wire and located between a large swamp and the Loire River. The water here is undrinkable, and they say the chow's pretty bad, too. So far we've had some soup, black bread, a bit of cheese, and ersatz coffee—that's about the size of it."

"Any way to escape from this place?" Thompson asked.

"Must be," Nelson said. "I heard someone got away about a week ago."

Late that night, Thompson lay flat on his back, trying to sleep, writhing in pain. He put his hands to his face. No longer did his fingers feel the smooth youthful skin of a teenager. The finely tuned features that had once turned girls' heads and made him the most sought after guy in Mobile, had swollen to a monstrous size.

After several days of limited food, Thompson noticed his weight dropping. He found some scraps of paper and wrote in his makeshift diary:

"A typical day's rationing: weak coffee for breakfast, a cup of thin clear liquid soup—filled with sawdust—for lunch, and a piece of black bread, about the size of a small paperback book, that had to be divided by five men.

"The camp: a narrow building that includes bunk beds with bug-infested straw mattresses and a thin blanket.

"The latrine: a shared bucket."

Thompson put down his pencil, hid the diary under the straw mattress, and thought about the men killed on the mission he had led. And, for the first time in his young life, his heart's feverish yearning for adventure and action seemed to lose its tight grip, arousing little, if any, stirring in his soul.

FOUR

THE PILOT

19 September 1944, St. Nazaire Sector, France

Ground flak hit the Massachusetts-born pilot's P-51 Mustang over Paim-boeuf, some five thousand feet above northwest France on the Loire River. From the cockpit, Second Lieutenant James L. Silva saw coolant spewing from the plane's tail. The ear-deafening engine overheated, sputtered, then stalled. Smoke filled the cockpit, so thick that Silva could no longer see the instrument panel. Caught in a high-speed stall, he tried unsuccessfully to turn the plane around. He was falling, losing altitude. Fast.

The twenty-year-old Northeastern University freshman held his breath. His first solo mission, he'd never bailed out of a plane before. Not even a practice jump. He struggled to remember the proper procedures.

Shot down. Gotta cross over. Upper left for a turn down the coast. Like thrown rod. No other flak. Ugh, rough. Less throttle. I'm okay. Increase a little. OKAY. White smoke. Other flak low and right. Climb and turn. Stall. Dark brown smoke. Gotta turn, stall and . . . whoa . . . half spin. Something's broke. Smitty cross bow. Here we go. Turn north. Stall. Broke. See nothing. Gotta bail. Now.

He had had nightmares about this situation—alone in a plane, an inexperienced pilot, shot down, having to parachute out for the first time ever.

Silva jerked back the canopy of his cockpit and prepared to bail out. But . . . he couldn't move. He was leashed to the panel. *Stuck! Brilliant!* He had forgotten to disconnect his head-and-throat radio set. Still losing altitude, he tried frantically to free himself from the tangle of cords. *Finally free!* Just as he started to exit, his knee hit a pin—the pin that held back the canopy. It closed as Silva, halfway in and halfway out, got caught in the middle and tried not to panic.

Climb half out. Canopy closed. Free cords. Squeeze out little more.

The ground came closer.

Too close. Seconds count now. Too late! Less than one thousand feet from ground. Too close to bail out. Going down with plane.

In a second of renewed strength, he forced back the canopy and jumped out.

Dive. Slipstream dragged out. Plane lower left in eye. Rip cord.

He began the 350-mile-an-hour dive, and not a second too soon. Pulling his rip cord, he waited for the expected jerk he'd been told would happen when his parachute opened.

At least, I hope my chute will open.

Jerk. Chute opens. OKAY. Look up. Beautiful canopy. Strange, quiet, heavenly sensation.

Silva exhaled a breath of relief when the chute opened and slowed his dive. *I'm still alive!* As he drifted down, he looked at the ground. *Oh no!* The burning plane lay just beneath him. *Plane burning center of field.* To his horror, he saw he was positioned to land right on top of it.

He watched the burning plane as it, and the ground, raced closer and closer to him.

No! No! No! I'll burn alive. Not death by fire!

Seconds before he landed on the burning wreckage, he felt a slight wind blow in from the Atlantic. It blew him a few yards off course, and beyond the flames. He missed the burning plane, hit the ground hard, rolled over, and stood up.

OKAY! Safe. Don't believe it! Alive! Unhurt!

The sound of gunfire blasted nearby. He turned his head to figure out its location.

German fire?

He ducked and looked around.

No Krauts within sight. Who's shooting at me? Pucker factor very high!

He glanced at the nearby burning plane.

For crying out loud! It's the ammunition exploding in my own plane!

He wiped the sweat from his face.

Now take off chute. Carry canopy and drag shrouds.

Silva wrestled with his chute. It tangled up in the thick bushes beside him. He struggled to free the chute, and then quickly balled it up, knelt down, and hid it under some branches.

Chute under leaves. Well hidden. Good. Now, where am I?

As Silva stood up, German soldiers sprang from the hedgerows, surrounded him, and aimed their rifles at his chest. Suddenly the young pilot was living the second part of his nightmare: capture by the enemy. Silva raised his hands high in surrender.

German guards placed him in a car and drove to a nearby anti-aircraft station in the St. Nazaire sector. On the way, as he traveled through small villages, Silva saw French citizens walking down the roads, farmers working in fields, and women shopping in outdoor markets. Each time French civilians saw the handsome young Yank, and recognized his American uniform, they held up their hands and, with two fingers, secretly flashed the "V" sign, as if encouraging him to victory. Silva, somewhat surprised at their friendly gestures, gave them a nod. To the pretty young French girls, who swooned at his movie star looks, he gave a wink and an Elvis half smile.

Silva wanted to shout out loud to the French citizens: *We're winning this war! It's just a matter of time!*

But instead he kept his words hidden in his heart and his gaze glued on the girls.

When he arrived at the station, Silva noticed a huge-bellied German corporal wearing a decorative pin on the left upper pocket of his uniform—an oval-shaped silver wreath of oak leaves, crowned by a flying eagle clutching a swastika. Beneath it an 8.8 cm anti-aircraft gun pointed skyward, its barrel breaking through the top right of the wreath. Silva had never before seen such a pin.

Impressive! I wonder what it means!

Noticing Silva's admiration of his badge, the well-fed corporal approached him, pointed to the pin, and boasted in limited English: "It . . . the Luftwaffen Kampfabz. I am . . . the one . . . that shoot you . . . down." The German smiled and, with his meaty fingers, patted the silver wreath pinned to his pocket.

Silva acknowledged the corporal with a nod. *Enjoy your fancy pin now, Kraut. It won't mean much after Germany loses the war.*

German guards delivered Silva to an old stone warehouse near the St. Nazaire submarine pens.

I joined up for some adventure! I think I'm getting it now!

Guards searched him thoroughly. Somehow they overlooked the French one-hundred-franc-bill he had hidden deep in his pants' secret pocket. They took him to an English-speaking *Hauptmann* for interrogation. Silva towered over the short, slight German, and even offered him a smile. The German ignored him.

Silva gave his name, rank, and serial number. Nothing else.

"I can take you out and shoot you if I want to," the *Hauptmann* told Silva, and tapped a gun hard on the table.

This guy's not kidding around. He's little, but he's deadly.

"I know you can," the pilot responded, erasing his smile and swallowing hard. *My award-winning smile doesn't work with short, mean Krauts.* Silva refused to give the German any additional information.

The first week Silva stayed at the warehouse in solitary confinement. He slept on a pile of straw in one corner of the cell. Rats gnawed nearby. He lay awake at night watching the rodents, making sure they kept their distance.

Rather rats than Krauts. Rats are safer.

He heard taps coming from the other side of the wall and assumed they were POWs like himself trying to communicate with him. But he wasn't sure.

Might be a trick.

He decided not to respond. In the morning, someone shoved his breakfast through a small opening in the door—a bowl of thin soup mixed with straw, and a slice of dark, coarse bread.

Not exactly Boston's Parker House. What I'd give for a bite of their Boston cream pie right now.

Day after dreary day passed in solitary confinement. Silva began to lose weight. His once strong, muscular frame became weaker and thinner. After one lengthy interrogation, he gave the German officer his parents' names and home address. He saw no harm in it. It seemed to satisfy the interrogator. In appreciation, the German released him from solitary confinement. In his new quarters, he met other allied POWs, including Harold Thompson, a mysterious English captain named Foot, and a reclusive prisoner who introduced himself as Frenchman Lieutenant Léon Rollin. Within Silva's first few days there, he heard Spanin speak several different languages, all with flawless accents: English, German, French, and Russian.

Thompson seems normal enough. But a weird accent. Southern, I think. Can't understand half of what he says. Seems kind of sad. Face swollen; black and blue, but healing. Hard to believe he's only eighteen. Seems much older.

But Foot and Spanin? Foot's English. Seems educated. Arrogant bird. Proud, too. Looks lots like nobility. Blue blood, for sure. No doubt from a long line of redcoats—probably fought my ancestors during the Siege of Boston.

Spanin? Not sure where he's from. He's strange. Punchy. Distrusting. Dangerous? Maybe. Think I'll keep my distance.

Silva noticed that Foot and Spanin spent a lot of time conversing together secretly. They spoke in whispers, discussed nothing with anyone else, and remained distant, private, and aloof. Once Silva thought he overheard Foot say the word "escape." But he couldn't be sure. And he dared not ask.

FIVE

AMBUSH!

2 October 1944, Lorient Sector, France

Second Lieutenant David Devonald briefed K Company's Third Platoon on their assignment that day.

"Pack some rifles and cartridge belts," he said. "No need to take mortars, machine guns, steel helmets, or combat boots. We have orders to go to a meadow in the Lorient vicinity, near German lines, pick up some deserting German soldiers that want to surrender, and bring them back to headquarters. We expect no enemy resistance."

Devonald led the fifty-four men as they marched toward the French village.

"Harden, Brady, Trachtenberg!" he called. "Stay alert! Watch for snipers behind these bushes."

Devonald had warned his men many times about the dangers posed by the hedgerows that lined both sides of the roads.

"Great for farmers," he had told them. "Protect their animals, mark their property lines, keep their farm soil from eroding. But," he cautioned, "deadly for allied patrols. Give the enemy ideal cover for surprise ambushes."

Privates First Class Kermit Harden, George Brady, and David Trachtenberg trained their eyes on the tangled branches and watched for the slightest movement. Private First Class Thomas Richards walked ahead, scouting the area a few yards in front of the others.

"I'm glad this mission will be uneventful," Sergeant Roy Connatser said to Devonald. "And I hope this will be one of my last assignments."

"The war can't last much longer, Roy," Devonald said. "Surely we'll all be home by Christmas."

"I've seen about as much action as I can take," Connatser continued. "Two-and-a-half years of constant combat with General Patton, and I'm ready for it to end!"

Devonald wasn't too keen on marching into the no-man's-land—the border between Allied and Axis boundaries near the German-manned Fortress Lorient. He knew how well Hitler had equipped the seaport: twenty-five thousand German troops and some five hundred pieces of artillery.

En route, Devonald turned to radio operator Private Harry Glixon. He liked Glixon, the quiet, respectful young man who left a good-paying job at New York's Brooklyn Navy Yard to join the army. He appreciated the way Glixon took orders, got along with others, and never made waves.

"Harry," he said. "I haven't seen a single French civilian on the streets since we started out. I find that highly unusual."

"Yes, sir," Glixon said. "That is kinda spooky. They're usually on the roads and in the villages this time of day. I don't understand it either."

About noon, when they reached a high plateau, Devonald told several men to walk ahead and scout out the meadow below them, the designated meeting place for the surrendering Germans.

"Richards, Rader, Boyd, Shulman, Stewart," he ordered. "Check out the meadow. We'll come along behind you."

Privates First Class Richards, Rader, and Boyd, along with Privates Shulman and Stewart, walked down the plateau. They arrived at the bottom and looked around the large, open meadow.

"Sir! There's no one down here," Richards shouted.

"Glixon, set up the radio, call headquarters, tell them our situation, and ask for instructions," Devonald said.

"Yes, sir." Glixon set down the forty-pound field radio, raised the antenna high, put the receiver to his ear, and talked to Colonel Hagerty, the regimental commander. After a few minutes of conversation, Glixon reported the conversation to Devonald.

"Sir," Glixon said, "Colonel Hagerty ordered us to keep going until we find the surrendering Germans."

"That's all?" Devonald asked. "Just 'keep going'?"

"Yes, sir, that's all he said."

Devonald ordered the men to walk deeper into the meadow.

"Something's just not right here," he told Glixon at 1255, after his men had spent several more minutes inspecting the area. "Something's going on. I don't like—"

Devonald heard the first shot. He saw Richards crumple to the ground, blood flowing from the hole in the center of his forehead.

"Take cover!" Devonald shouted. The soldiers hit the ground and scrambled into the twisted hedgerow branches for protection from flying bullets. The Germans opened up their machine guns.

"We've been tricked!" Devonald screamed. In the distance, he saw hundreds of German soldiers dressed in full combat gear, firing as they advanced toward them.

Bullets tore into three more K Company men.

"We're outnumbered!" Devonald shouted. "We're not prepared to fight them! Let's go back! There's no place to go but back!"

The patrol turned around at their leader's command. But Devonald and the men saw that they couldn't retreat. The Germans had surrounded them, firing from all sides. They scurried back into the bushes and returned fire.

Seeing they were surrounded, Devonald shouted to Glixon: "Radio headquarters. Ask for reinforcements!"

Devonald waited for Glixon's report as he dodged bullets and counted the passing minutes. *Men are dead and wounded. Ammunition is running low. If we don't get help, and fast, we're all dead!*

"Glixon!" he shouted. "What's the dope?! Are they sending reinforcements?!"

"They said they've sent them, sir!" Glixon shouted back.

Devonald looked east, west, north, and south. He saw no reinforcements.

"Then where are they?" he shouted.

"Wait, sir!" Glixon called out. "They are telling me the reinforcements can't get through German lines! That we are completely surrounded!"

Devonald watched his men drop all around him, victims of German bullets. Trachtenberg was hit. He saw George Boyd, backed deep into a tangled hedgerow, trying to dodge the bullets that bounced off the ground around his lanky legs.

"The Kraut's gonna cut off my legs!" he heard Boyd scream out.

He watched the steady barrage of mortars, grenades, and bullets bombard his men. He heard explosions, mixed with shouts and screams of pain—the deafening noise of combat he knew so well.

"Sir!" Brady shouted from a nearby hiding spot deep in the bushes. "We have four men down: Rowe, Button, Dyer, and Richards."

Devonald looked around him and saw the four dead, as well as dozens of his men unconscious and wounded, sprawled on the ground. He also watched hundreds of fresh, strong reinforcements join the German troops as his men tried in vain to hold their small circle of ground.

Time to make a decision. Hagerty won't like it. We've got to surrender. We have no choice.

He glanced at young Glixon, still manning the radio and squatting behind a thin tree now fewer than one hundred yards from the advancing enemy.

"Glixon!" he shouted. "Call Hagerty! Tell him—"

Devonald felt a sharp intense pain in his forehead.

A mortar explosion. I'm hit. Hurt. Hurt bad.

He felt his knees weaken and bend. Desperately trying to hold on to consciousness, he slowly sank to the ground. He saw Glixon leave the radio and run to his side.

"Glixon," Devonald whispered. "Before I lose consciousness . . . tell Harrington to take over. Give him my permission to surrender if he thinks the situation calls for it. . . ."

Devonald felt his body go limp. He closed his eyes, and his world went dark.

Sergeant Ames Harrington, upon receiving Glixon's message from Devonald, assumed immediate charge of the patrol.

"Glixon," Harrington said. "Go ahead like Devonald advised and radio Hagerty. Tell him we must surrender."

Glixon obeyed orders and ran back to the radio. A minute later, he shouted back: "Sergeant! Hagerty said NO! NO surrender! Keep fighting!"

Harrington watched German soldiers advance forward, coming closer and trying to tighten and choke off the circle around K Company's men. He saw a mortar shell hit the ground beside Bernie Rader, a short distance away. Rader fell backward and lay bleeding, faceup in the dirt. Another shell followed, hitting George Boyd, who fell down beside Rader.

Harrington turned to Corporal John Atkinson, who crouched down beside him.

"Atkinson! Take a message to Glixon. Have him radio Hagerty again. Make sure Glixon tells Hagerty we have no choice but to surrender, we've got four men dead, a dozen or more wounded, we're running out of ammo, and we're surrounded by the enemy! Tell Glixon not to take no for an answer!"

"Yes, sir," Atkinson responded. He spread-eagled his body on the ground and crawled to Glixon, who was now fewer than fifty feet from the advancing enemy.

From the distance, Harrington watched Atkinson give Glixon the message, and then saw Glixon shouting into the radio, an angry frown on his face.

What's taking so long? Is Glixon arguing with Hagerty? Mild-mannered Glixon? Is the colonel refusing to allow us to surrender?

Harrington saw a frantic expression appear on Glixon's face, and a hurried attempt to reconnect the radio call.

Oh no! The radio went dead! I hope Hagerty said "surrender" before . . .

Harrington saw Atkinson signal back to him the hand sign "okay to surrender." Harrington motioned for Atkinson to raise the white flag.

Atkinson pulled a white bandage from his first aid pack. Harrington took a deep breath of relief when he saw the young corporal attach the large bandage to the tip of his bayonet, stand up, and wave it high in the air.

Now maybe I can get the rest of these men out of here alive and back to their families.

For a split second, Harrington envisioned the face of his wife at their home in Wisconsin.

The love of my life. I can't even imagine her pain if I didn't come home.

"We surrender! We surrender!" Harrington heard Atkinson shout to the enemy, and he saw him as he stood and waved the bandage flag.

Suddenly, the Germans let loose a string of machine gun bullets that stitched the young corporal's groin, almost cutting him in half. The mutilated body dropped to the ground, the white bandage flag falling on top of him. Harrington started to vomit.

No! No! No! They didn't understand Atkinson! Maybe they don't speak English! Who can speak German? Trachtenberg—he knows some German! But Trachtenberg's been hit. Is he dead? Don't think so. Maybe alive . . .

"Trachtenberg! Trachtenberg! Tell the Krauts we surrender!" Harrington screamed, and hoped Trachtenberg was still conscious, had the mental capability to remember the German words, and the physical strength to shout them out with enough volume to be heard above the sounds of combat.

He heard nothing.

Trachtenberg must be unconscious . . . or dead. Must try again.

"Trachtenberg! Trachtenberg! Tell the Krauts we surrender!" he screamed again.

After several seconds, he heard Trachtenberg's voice call out, faint at first, then becoming louder and louder—German words with a distinctive New York accent.

"Wir Kapitulieren!" ["We surrender!"] *"Wir Kapitulieren!" "Wir Kapitulieren!" "Wir Ergeben Uns!"* ["We give ourselves up!"] *"Wir Ergeben Uns!" "Wir Ergeben Uns!"*

Trachtenberg shouted the German words until the firing stopped. The enemies showed themselves, and ordered Harrington's men to drop their weapons and come out single file. It was finally over.

Private First Class Rader was conscious, but barely. He stared at the sky, dazed, bleeding badly, every part of his thick, muscular body riddled with shrapnel. He could barely move; the pain proved almost unbearable.

Out of the corner of his eye, he saw his buddy, Boyd, lying next to him.

"Boyd, Boyd," he whispered. "Are you okay?"

"I've been hit. But not bad. I'll make it," the tall, lanky North Carolinian told him in his familiar Southern drawl. "Thought they were gonna take off my legs there for a while. But you, buddy, you don't look so good."

"I don't feel 'so good' either, Boyd," he said. "Why has the firing stopped?"

"Looks like we've surrendered, Bernie. Our men have put down their weapons and are lining up."

"Do me a favor, Boyd. Take my dog tags—both of them. Put them in the ground. The Krauts can't find out I'm Jewish."

"I'll do it, Bernie," Boyd said, his words coming out as slow as cold molasses.

Boyd pulled Rader's "H"(Hebrew)-marked dog tags from the native New Yorker's neck, dug a hole in the ground with his fingers, and covered them with black earth.

"I've done it, Bernie. Buried your identity and your religion—all in the same hole."

"Thanks, Boyd! I owe you one."

"You don't owe me nothing, Bernie. You'd do it for me."

Rader felt Boyd's long, skinny arms slip under his back and legs, and heard Boyd audibly strain as he tried to lift him.

"You can't lift me, Boyd. I'm too solid—I weigh twice as much as you do, buddy."

Rader looked in the distance and saw an abandoned wheelbarrow stranded on a nearby roadside.

"Boyd, maybe we can use the wheelbarrow—over there, on your left."

Boyd ran the short distance and retrieved it. Somehow he was able to scoop up Rader, put him inside, and wheel him away with the rest of the surrendering K Company men.

Rader watched as Boyd and the other able-bodied men stepped onto a bus and were driven away. He and Trachtenberg, both seriously wounded, were transported to a nearby building that looked like the front of an old hospital.

THE FIRING SQUAD

October 1944, Lorient Sector, France

Bernie Rader heard deafening screams as he and Trachtenberg were carried on stretchers into the old building in Lorient.

"Trachtenberg," Rader whispered. "Ask the nurse beside you where we are and why all the screaming?"

After a brief conversation in German with the talkative young nurse, Trachtenberg reported his findings.

"She says we're in a former French naval hospital the Germans now use as a hospital. And the people are screaming because doctors have run out of anesthesia. They're performing surgeries without it. And they're out of everything else, too."

Before Rader could respond, a German patient lying beside him cried out for water. The nurse put cider to his swollen lips. "*Kein wasser*" ["No water"], she told him.

Before the day ended, Rader had discovered the grave seriousness of the medical supply shortage. With Trachtenberg's help, mainly from casual conversations with German nurses and patients, Rader found out the hospital staff had run out of hydrochloride and cocaine, as well as morphine, sutures, hypodermic syringes, and bandages.

German medics bandaged Rader's wounds with bloodied dressings. Both he and Trachtenberg lay on unchanged bedsheets, soiled by the patients who left before them—patients either recovered and dismissed, or dead and buried. They quickly learned that clean water was severely scarce, whether for drinking, bathing, or washing soiled bedclothes.

"We must be careful what we say around here," Rader told Trachtenberg, as he glanced at the suffering German patients surrounding them. He was well aware they lay beside wounded German soldiers, their makeshift beds crowded and touching one another, their faces close enough to smell the blood and breath of the ones who'd put them there.

As Rader lay still, almost afraid to move—even if the pain allowed him to—he thought about his home in the Bronx, about his mother and father, and his sister, Gloria.

"Trachtenberg," he asked as he stared at the hospital's white ceiling, "do you believe a person can transmit his thoughts across the miles to people he loves?"

"Don't know, Bernie," he answered. "Maybe. Some people believe that stuff."

I hope so. I also hope I live to see my twenty-first birthday in December. I guess I won't be celebrating my birthday or Chanukah at home this year. Little chance of that now. I wonder when Mother will receive the "missing in action" telegram. When she does, I hope she won't worry too much. That would be my greatest sorrow—to cause her that terrible grief.

Bernie Rader had seen a lot of action for a twenty-year-old after he joined the army in '43 as a rifleman and was assigned to the 94th Division. *I wonder if . . .*

A fight between two patients in the hospital room interrupted his thoughts. He saw a German doctor pull a pistol from his belt and aim it at a soldier's head. That seemed to quell the violence. Trachtenberg saw it, too, and with wide brown eyes, he shot a hard glance at Rader.

"The doctors carry weapons?" he asked. "This is a scary place. I hope we survive it."

"Me, too," Rader whispered, and then added: "Trachtenberg, I'm sorry you got hurt, but I'm sure glad I'm not here alone in this hospital. Maybe we can help protect each other."

"We can sure try," Trachtenberg responded.

Oberleutnant Alfons Schmitt greeted K Company's captured when they stepped off the old bus and arrived at the large building in German-occupied Lorient. The Oberleutnant was the epitome of poise and confidence, and a rare blend of self-assured boldness and daring that he saw immediately commanded K Company's respect and fear.

In excellent English, Schmitt ordered the prisoners to stand in formation. They shot to rigid attention, their eyes staring straight ahead. No one moved.

Straight and dignified, the muscular thirty-nine-year-old man with dark hair and thick eyebrows glared at each prisoner, one by one.

"Name! Rank! Serial number!" he demanded, stopping and peering deeply into the face of each man with his penetrating black eyes.

When Schmitt reached Glixon, he paused. He studied the young private's dog tags.

"H," he said. "A Hebrew. Most interesting."

Schmitt stared for a long time at Glixon's round boyish face, soft smooth skin, and wavy brown hair.

"Just a boy," he said. "A Hebrew boy."

He gave a thin smile, and moved on.

"Bring these boys some lunch!" he ordered a German Army cook. A few minutes later, the cook delivered a tray of sandwiches and a pot of ersatz coffee, made of pulverized acorns soaked in bad water. The men seemed hungry, and Schmitt watched them wolf down the food with gusto.

When they had finished their lunch, Schmitt handed each prisoner a sheet of blank paper—at least one side was blank—and a pencil stub.

"Write a letter to your family," he ordered them.

The men took the paper and pencils, and glanced at each other with bewilderment.

"Dear Mom and Dad," Schmitt watched each one write. As he read over their shoulders, he noticed they kept their words vague and impersonal, and volunteered no names or addresses.

When they finished, Schmitt collected the letters, and then disappeared for the next four days.

Harry Glixon had felt strange and unusually vulnerable after guards captured him in the meadow following the ambush. Riding on the bus with his captured comrades on the way to Lorient, Glixon had been surprised to see the city's ruins and bombed-out buildings. He saw the huge concrete submarine pens and felt shocked that, with the exception of a few bomb pockmarks, the subs had been undamaged.

Looks like the Americans destroyed the city but couldn't damage the sub pens. Concrete's too thick, too well constructed. But looks like they sure tried to.

Glixon was also surprised to see French farmers transporting apples to market with makeshift carts drawn by mules and dogs.

Looks like we've stepped back into another century.

The young radio operator noticed that the German soldiers peered at the American POWs with great curiosity, but that the French citizens simply ignored them.

While marching through the city, one of the captured Americans had turned to Glixon and asked: "Which telegram do you think the War Department will send our folks?"

"They will send one of the standard three," Glixon said. "We are sorry to inform you that your son or husband or brother was 'wounded in action,' or 'missing in action,' or 'killed in action.' I hope the War Department knows we're still alive and sends the right telegram!"

Sergeant Harrington and his K Company captives were incarcerated on the second floor of the building in Lorient.

"Keep quiet," he told his men. "And find out everything you can. Report all you learn directly to me."

Harrington thought about his wife, and wondered how she would react to the War Department's "missing in action" telegram.

I wish I could let her know I'm alive and well.

Over the next few days, the sergeant gleaned bits of information gathered from his men. He discovered that Polish and Dutch prisoners were housed on the first floor of the building, and that they had been forced to serve in the German Army. He also learned the enemy suffered from a severe food shortage—worse than he could have ever imagined. They lacked enough rations to feed their own wounded troops, much less the captured Allied prisoners. The sergeant discovered firsthand the meager fare when he and the other men received only one bowl of thin soup and a small piece of bread each day. He wasn't surprised when his men began to lose weight.

"Sergeant," Boyd said one day, voicing aloud the thought the sergeant had heard almost every K Company man mumble under his breath at least once during the past few days:

"We're nothing but 'hay burners'—old horses that can't work. We eat up what little food the Krauts have. We're no good to them. I'm wondering how long they're gonna let us live."

"Wouldn't surprise me," Glixon said, "if they lined us up and shot us. I know Schmitt doesn't like Jews. Did you see the way he looked at me after he saw the 'H' on my dog tags?"

"Makes sense to me," Shulman said. "Put us in front of a firing squad. That'd be a sure way to make the chow go further. Maybe that's why the Oberleutnant ordered us to write our families."

"Our last will and testament maybe?" Connatser asked. "Yes, Shulman, it certainly makes sense."

"I agree, Sergeant," Stewart said. "I think they're planning to shoot us. Hard to figure these birds."

"These goons are all heart," Harden sneered. "Letting us say goodbye to our families before they shoot us!"

George Brady chuckled. But his gaiety evaporated when no one else laughed.

"The not-knowing's the worst part, isn't it?" Harrington said. The men nodded.

On the fifth day of captivity, Harrington and the men sat on the floor, hungry and thirsty.

"Next month's Thanksgiving back home on the farm," Boyd said. "I sure hate to miss that Thanksgiving feast my mother always cooks for us!"

"What does your mama cook on Thanksgiving Day down South there, Boyd?" Brady, from Baltimore, asked in his best Southern accent.

"Fried turkey and dressing, fried potatoes, fried apple pies—all that good stuff—and all fried!" he recalled.

Harrington laughed as the others joined in, each naming what his mother would cook for the holidays: "Potato kugel and candied sweet potatoes, ricotta pie and minestrone, baked ham and apples, chocolate fudge cake and vanilla ice cream, and . . ."

The sergeant leapt to his feet when an armed guard burst through the open door and shouted: *"Kommen! Jetzt!"* ["Come! Now!"] *"Kommen! Jetzt!"*

"What's going on?" Harrington asked the guard.

Ignoring the sergeant, the German counted the men—*"Eins, zwei, drei, vier . . ."* ["One, two, three, four . . ."]—until he reached *"zwanzig"* ["twenty"], and pushed them hard toward the door with the barrel of his rifle.

Again he shouted *"Kommen! Jetzt!"* and motioned them toward the stairs.

Brady looked at Harrington, and whispered: "The firing squad! We guessed right."

Harrington had no chance to respond. He led the men downstairs in single file, armed guards on all sides. A guard took the sergeant into a nearby room and closed the door.

A German holding a straight razor waited for the sergeant when he entered the room. Harrington closed his eyes and paused in place.

He's going to cut my throat. Maybe that will bring death quicker than a bullet to the heart. I just wish I could tell my wife one more time how much I love her.

Nothing happened. Harrington opened his eyes and saw the German motioning for him to sit in a large leather chair. The sergeant obeyed. Without saying a word, the German then gave Harrington a straight-razor shave and a high-and-tight haircut. The barber inspected his handiwork, brushed a few stray hairs from his trousers, nodded stiffly to the sergeant, turned on his heels, and beckoned his next "customer." Harrington returned to the waiting room, and told the men what had happened.

One by one, each man was led into the room. After a few minutes with the barber, he was returned to the waiting room, having been clipped, shaved, and cleaned up. After a while, Harrington saw the twentieth POW return. The guards then told the men to go upstairs, fetch their helmets, and come back and walk outside. It made no sense to the POWs, but they followed orders. They covered their new haircuts with their helmets and ventured outside, as ordered. The guards led them down a narrow road, stopping them when they reached a French cemetery—a large open field dotted with cedars and small trees.

Segeant Harrington saw them first, the row of German soldiers lined up side by side in the cemetery, rifles at their shoulders as if waiting and ready to fire. He glanced back at George Brady, and with his eyes, he confirmed Brady's previous suspicions.

Yes, Brady, you're right. This is a firing squad. It all adds up. I'm sorry it has to end like this.

In the front of the cemetery, beside the firing squad, Oberleutnant Schmitt stood erect, back straight, and head high, waiting for the arrival of K Company's POWs. He looked impressive in his baggy pants, knee-high polished boots, and officer's cap—so stylishly adorned with the Nazi Party's eagle grasping the swastika in its sharp talons. A brass-buckled, wide leather belt showed off his trim waist and well-tended physique. He tried to put on a good act—the enthusiasm, the Hitler salutes, the gung-ho spirit. But even with the prestigious rank, position, and title, and the respect and fear they evoked from those around him, the Oberleutnant was a sad man. He seldom smiled. Except for a widowed sister and a young nephew back in Germany, he had no family, friends, or loved ones. He missed his old life, the one he gave up to serve Hitler on this lonely forsaken seaport. Deep in his heart, he knew Germany was losing the war. He was just marking time, wondering how in the world it would all end.

Schmitt ordered K Company's men to move forward and stand in formation in front of the firing squad. He then positioned himself on the right and stood beside them. When the men were in place, they looked down at the ground, and most of their mouths dropped open in surprise.

Directly in front of them, in the narrow space between the men and the firing squad, were freshly dug graves. Beside the deep holes lay five rough wooden coffins, each topped with a small bouquet of flowers.

In a loud voice and in perfect English, Schmitt told the men: "This is the final resting place of K Company's five men KIA [killed in action]."

He put his hands behind his back, and looked into the nearby camera lens stationed on his left. The German photographer captured his photograph, as well as the rest of K Company's men, the chaplain, graves, coffins, and flowers.

Schmitt nodded to the German naval officer chaplain, who stepped up before them, opened a Bible, and read Scripture from the twenty-third Psalm. He read a line in German, and then repeated the same line in English.

"*Der HERR ist mein Hirte, mir wird nichts mangeln.*"

"The LORD is my shepherd; I shall not want."

"*Er weidet mich auf einer grünen Aue und führet mich zum frischen Wasser.*"

"He maketh me to lie down in green pastures: he leadeth me beside the still waters."

"*Er erquicket meine Seele. Er führet mich auf rechter Straße um seines Namens willen.*"

"He restoreth my soul. He leadeth me in the paths of righteousness for his name's sake."

"*Und ob ich schon wanderte im finstern Tal, fürchte ich kein Unglück; denn du bist bei mir, dein Stecken und Stab trösten mich.*"

"Yea, though I walk through the valley of the shadow of death, I will fear no evil: for thou art with me; thy rod and thy staff they comfort me."

When finished, the chaplain closed the Bible and stepped back into his place.

Schmitt then read aloud, with great respect, the names of Sergeant Frank F. Rowe, Corporal John Atkinson, Private Jack C. Button, Private First Class Winfred Dyer, and Private First Class Thomas Richards.

Schmitt asked Harrington to say a few words, and then gave the signal to the firing squad.

Schmitt watched as the POWs almost jumped out of their shoes when the squad of soldiers fired the customary volley over the graves of the fallen soldiers.

They are still so tense. I did not expect that reaction from them. Perhaps they thought I had planned to shoot them! Could it be?

Schmitt looked at his feet and shook his head from side to side as if in disbelief.

Cut their hair, shave their faces, and then shoot them? They must think we Germans are uncivilized savages!

"You have my permission to salute your fallen comrades," Schmitt told the POWs.

After the salute, he ordered the five coffins lowered into the graves, and motioned to the German cameraman to take more photographs. He allowed K Company's men to help bury their slain buddies, and then he ended the service.

Shall I tell them that we suffered casualties in this skirmish, too? Eight dead. Eight missing. Nine wounded. And that we, too, as human beings are grieving for our dead?

The Oberleutnant commanded the guards to return the prisoners to the building where he planned to keep them for several more days of confinement before relocating them to Île de Groix, the prison camp eight miles off France's Atlantic coast.

Before the day ended, Schmitt ordered the photographer to develop extra copies of the funeral photographs. He planned to take them to Devonald at the Lorient Naval Hospital.

"When Lieutenant Devonald gets home to the United States," Schmitt told the photographer, "I hope he will show the photographs to the Yanks so they will know we Germans are not all barbarians."

. . .

That evening, after the unexpected funeral of his comrades, Harrington noted in his diary:

"At the burial . . . the German Chaplain conducted the last rites with a .25 on his hip. I said a few words and then the firing squad—the first volley almost caused me to jump out of my shoes. Still very jumpy."

11 October 1944, Lorient

Sergeant Harrington received the message from the Oberleutnant that the able-bodied American prisoners among them would be transferred to Île de Groix. Guards took Harrington and the other POWs to the port of Lorient, and loaded them onto an old boat.

"Where are they taking us?" Private First Class Harden asked Harrington.

"To the POW camp," he said, "on an island in the Atlantic."

Harrington and the Americans watched as a group of strong young Germans loaded the vessel with beds, bales of straw, and cords of firewood. After they had finished and left, Harrington saw two elderly guards board the boat. Then it pulled away from the dock.

At first, Harrington wondered why the Germans would put so much trust into just two old guards for so many prisoners. After a few moments, he understood.

Harrington looked to his left, and saw Harden nudge Brady, and then the two men whispered to each other.

Those boys are up to something. And I think I know what it is.

Harrington moved closer and strained to hear their conversation.

"This is our chance," Harden said to Brady. "We can easily take on those old guards—we far outnumber them."

"I agree," Brady said. "We can overpower them, throw them overboard, and escape. Let's do it!"

Harrington watched as Harden and Brady moved slowly toward the German guards. He darted forward and grabbed the two GIs by the arms.

"Roll up your flaps, boys, and don't even think about it," Harrington said, tightening his grip to emphasize his words.

"But Sergeant," Harden said, "this is our chance."

Brady agreed: "Sergeant, it's too easy! It may be our only chance to escape!"

"Think about that," Harrington said calmly, still holding on to their arms. "Why would the Germans put thirty-six young, strong American POWs on a boat with two stooped-over guards that could be easily overtaken?"

"You got me, sir," Brady said.

"It makes perfect sense to me," Harrington said. "I doubt there's a GI on board who knows beans about piloting a boat in the Atlantic. Besides, the Germans have planted mines everywhere in these waters protecting all coastal approaches to Lorient, and we don't know where they are or how to bypass them."

Harden looked down at his feet: "That never crossed my mind."

Brady nodded. "I never thought about that. I guess we'd never make it out of here . . . alive . . . would we?"

Harrington released the two, then raised his voice above the boat's loud engine and announced: "Don't any of you birds get any ideas about escaping! It's not an option! It won't work."

From the looks on the men's faces, Harrington knew he'd spoken just in time.

The rest of the guys were thinking the same thing. I'm surprised they waited this long to try something stupid!

When the boat docked, Harrington and the Americans disembarked at Port Tudy. Under the guards' watchful eyes, they climbed a hill and then marched through the treeless countryside. They followed a narrow path, passed under a stone archway, and arrived at a massive stone building with steel bars on the windows. The POWs filed through a heavy wooden door into their new home: Fort Surville. When he stepped into the large second-floor room, Sergeant Harrington saw twenty-two dirty, bushy-bearded Allied prisoners living there. When the old POWs saw the new arrivals, their questioning faces looked anxious to hear everything going on beyond the craggy shores of the bleak island. The sergeant prepared himself to answer a lot of questions.

POW Sergeant James Sarsfield welcomed K Company's men to Fort Surville when, cold, hungry, and exhausted, they entered the old castle-like structure.

"Welcome, fellow prisoners!" he said in a lighthearted manner, in an effort to relieve the men's inevitable tension when they saw their new home— a giant stone fort complete with massively thick walls, grassy moat, and drawbridge.

"I'm Sergeant James Sarsfield, 6th Armored Division, originally from the coal-mining section of Pennsylvania, a little town called Luzerne."

"How long have you been here, Sergeant?" Kermit Harden asked.

"Since 19 September," he responded. Sarsfield flashed a warm smile. "Let me show you around.

"Île de Groix is a small island about two miles wide and eight miles long. The French have a few small farms here. The Germans keep a large artillery emplacement and a rehabilitation center for their wounded on the island," the sergeant told them, and led the men inside a large room with a window at the end wall.

"Each of us has a wooden bunk bed, straw mattress, and one blanket. See the metal container by the wall? That's our urinal at night. During the day we can use the outdoor latrine, provided a guard agrees to go with us."

"What's life here like?" Stewart asked.

"Not bad. But not great either," Sarsfield said. "The lice come out at night and those little suckers can bite. You might want to go to sleep before they come out. The food is awful and there's not much of it. Dark bread, lard, watery bean soup, and that horrible fake coffee. Not like your mother's cooking! Nobody has much to eat here, not the Germans or the POWs. The Krauts raise a few rabbits or sometimes buy food from French farmers—if they have any to sell. The fishermen might swap them a few fish. And we've seen an occasional cow or pig.

"What about drinking water?" Connatser asked.

"Not much clean water here," Sarsfield responded. "We haul water from an old farmhouse well about a third of a mile away. Usually twice a day, six of us volunteer to go there with the two-wheeled cart and wooden barrel to collect it. A guard always goes with us. Some of the French girls hand us an apple or something to eat when the guard's not looking. That's nice—and generous! They don't have much food themselves."

"What will happen if the French are caught giving us food?" Connatser asked.

"They'll be in trouble," Sarsfield said. "The Germans have strict regulations for farmers and their crops. The farmers are required to sell half their apple crops to the Germans. The French usually obey the rules, and their relationship with the Germans is fairly good. So when a farm girl gives you an apple or a slice of bread, she is risking severe punishment. The French residents also pay a stiff price for any resistance or sabotage."

"What do you mean?" Connatser asked.

"The Germans execute five French civilians for each German casualty they cause," Sarsfield said.

"As far as morale goes," Sarsfield told them, "you'll find the German morale here is zilch. The guards believe Germany is already kaput. They'd probably desert and go home if they didn't fear what Hitler and his goons might do to the rest of their families. They are constantly threatened. They hate it here as much as we do."

Sarsfield glanced at K Company's flimsy summer uniforms.

"You're gonna get cold in those rags, fellas! There's no heat in this place, and winter's coming. I hear the winters here are long, and it's always cold with that Atlantic wind blowing. Not much coal on this island either. A Kraut was shot not long ago for stealing a few lumps of it. We probably won't survive the freezing temps without more blankets or coats or something to keep us warm. We're all dreading winter."

"Does anybody know we're in this place?" Stewart asked.

"Nope. Don't think so," Sarsfield said. "We've probably been classified MIA or presumed dead. No doubt, your family and mine have already received the army's telegrams telling them that."

"Any way we can escape from this island?" Glixon asked.

"No way! Don't even think about it. It's eight miles to shore, ole buddy.

Unless you're swimmer Jack Medica and won Gold at the '36 Summer Olympics, I wouldn't suggest you even try it."

Late one night, Harrington scribbled in his diary:

"We walked outside today—about three miles. In every direction, there is nothing but debris . . . the result of aerial and artillery bombardment. . . . The German guards appear more frightened of us than we are of the German garrison . . . these poor Krauts, they have been fighting on every front for years and no relief in sight. Some of them went home to Germany on leave last spring and found their cities and homes are in ruins. Their families are scattered. Defeat is in sight. There is nothing to return to or live for."

The sergeant laid down his pencil and spent the next few minutes in deep thought. Then he made another diary entry:

"What a place for fifty-seven G.I.'s to meet and exchange experiences. The ironic fate of war has brought us together for a period of time that cannot be too short, but every moment makes it too long. Our worst enemy is time and the shortage of food . . . makes our environment almost unbearable. The filth is awful. The majority of us merely have fatigues—no jackets or caps."

Harrington looked around at the sleeping men.

With winter coming and no heat, and with unclean water to drink and little food, I doubt any of us will survive for long.

SEVEN

THE LETTER

12 October 1944, Île de Groix Prison Camp

Sergeant Sarsfield walked to the far end of the room, knelt down by the private lying quietly on a bottom bunk, and slowly began spooning the thin soup into his mouth. Glixon joined him.

"What's wrong with him?" Glixon asked Sarsfield.

"He has pellagra. See the red crusty lesions on his neck and face?"

Sarsfield pulled back the worn blanket that covered the private's hands and legs. "They're covering his hands, too. The blisters keep him from moving his fingers. He's got the same lesions on his legs, feet, and toes. See how swollen his feet are? Can't even wear his boots anymore."

Glixon laid his hand on the private's forehead as if to comfort him.

"What's pellagra?" Glixon asked.

"A disease we get here," Sarsfield told him. "It's bad. Causes stomach cramps and diarrhea. The *runs* are the worst, and they never let up."

"Looks like leprosy. Is it contagious?" Glixon asked, his hand still resting on the patient's forehead.

"No, it's not catching. It's a disease that makes you depressed, and well, crazy. The upset stomach, diarrhea, blisters, and skin lesions are all part of it.

After a while, pellagra can even cause death. It can . . . and most likely will happen to all of us, if we stay here much longer. That is, if we don't starve or freeze to death first."

Glixon pulled the thin blanket up from the private's feet and covered him to his shoulders. "What causes it?"

"It's the diet, the chow we're eating . . . or rather, the chow we're *not* eating," Sarsfield said. "From what I hear, pellagra is some kind of niacin deficiency disease, caused by malnutrition, by not eating the right things the body needs, like meat, chicken, fish, milk, eggs, fruits and vegetables."

Glixon reached over and took the spoon from Sarsfield's hand. "I'll finish feeding him," he said. "You'd better tell the others about pellagra before they see these hideous blisters and panic."

Sarsfield called the POWs together in a corner of the room and explained the disease. He watched them as they sat silently, staring in the direction of their fellow prisoner with the weird lesions—the result of the dementia-causing disease they had just heard described as pellagra. They looked afraid, helpless, and frustrated.

The men still wore the summer uniforms they had fought in when captured. The outfits had become tattered and threadbare long before their imprisonment. Now they were filthy, too. The men couldn't wash their clothes; they had no water for laundry. Their uniforms, still stained with battlefield filth, reeked of sweat, blood, and muck.

Later that afternoon, Sarsfield sat down and listened to the Atlantic's strong winds of autumn blow icy cold, pummeling hard the little island. He watched the shivering prisoners wrap up in their solitary blankets and try to stay warm in the drafty building. As days passed, he saw the soldiers become thinner, their bones beginning to protrude from their weakening frames. He also noticed the ugly red lesions of pellagra developing on some of the other POWs' necks, faces, and hands.

We won't last much longer.

When the Germans reduced the breakfast bread ration, Sarsfield knew he had to do something, or he and the prisoners wouldn't have a gnat's chance of surviving the oncoming winter.

He counted heads. *There are fifty seven of us. We need to get help. But from where?*

He made a decision and shared it with the others.

"I'm going to write the American Red Cross," he told them. "I don't know who else to turn to. If they can't help us, nobody can."

"How can we possibly get a letter to the Red Cross?!" Harrington asked. "How can we get it past the Germans on this island, to the mainland, and then to the right person?"

"It's probably impossible," Sarsfield responded, "but it's worth a try. Anyway, we have no other option."

The sergeant found a piece of scrap paper and a pencil stub. He wrote clearly and slowly, with a distinct, angled hand. Several gathered around him, looking over his shoulder and giving him advice.

"Tell them we're starving, and to send food," one POW suggested.

"And warm clothes and cigarettes!" another said.

"To the Recipient of This Letter," Sarsfield began writing. "This is a request from a group of 57 American soldiers being held as Prisoners of War by the German Army in the Isle of the Cross. We are in need of clothing for the group. In addition, we are in need of food and cigarettes. They will not allow us to communicate in person with anyone, so we are using this method of contacting you. Any help you can give us will be greatly appreciated. We would be especially grateful for food and cigarettes. I hope this letter finds you in a position to give us some help in the very near future. Respectfully, A Group of Americans."

Sarsfield folded the letter and hid it under his straw mattress. That evening they tried to think of how they could get the letter into the hands of the American Red Cross—a feat they all agreed seemed a world away and next to impossible.

By morning, Sarsfield had devised a plan.

"When six of us go to the well to draw water this morning, we'll take the letter. If the guard turns his eyes away for one second, I'll slip it to one of the French girls at the farmhouse. We can ask her to try to deliver it to an official on the mainland who can get it to the American Red Cross."

"Let me get this straight, Sarsfield," Connatser said. "A French farm girl will need to appear at the same second the guard happens to look the other way? And you'll have to somehow hand her the letter without the guard seeing it, and tell her what to do with it? And she's got to agree to sneak it to the American Red Cross, some eight miles away on the German-occupied mainland, in Lorient?"

"Yes, that's the plan," Sarsfield said. "But when you put it like that, it sounds impossible, doesn't it?"

"Yes, it does," Connatser said. The others nodded in agreement.

"And you said the French residents are punished when they help the Allied prisoners," Glixon said. "What if the farm girls are afraid and refuse to help us?"

"We'll just have to take that chance, Harry," Sarsfield said. "It's our only hope."

Later that morning, Sarsfield slipped the letter into his pocket, and he and five other volunteers, accompanied by the armed guard, rolled the cart to the farmhouse well. But they saw no French girl or civilian who could help them with the letter. Disheartened, they filled the wooden barrel with water and headed back to the prison.

"We'll try again this afternoon," Sarsfield told the POWs when he returned.

The same six men volunteered to haul water at sundown. But the farmhouse and grounds seemed deserted. They filled the barrel with water and headed back. The guard walked a few steps ahead of them. Just as Sarsfield was leaving, purposely lingering and hoping to see a friendly French face, he saw a farm girl appear at the door of the kitchen. She held a small apple and motioned for him to slip over and take it. Carefully and cautiously, Sarsfield sprinted to the door, took the apple, and delivered his letter to the girl with quick instructions.

"*Veuillez obtenir cette . . . ah . . . à la Croix-rouge américaine!*" he whispered.

She closed her hand, nodded, and, before the guard cast a backward glance in her direction, she stepped back into the house. When Sarsfield returned to the camp, he removed the apple from his pocket and attempted to chop it into fifty-seven small bits.

"I passed the letter to one of the farm girls," Sarsfield told the men. "I asked her to please try to get the letter to the American Red Cross. At least that's what I think I said. My French isn't great."

For the next several days, Sarsfield and the men waited for a response to the letter. Two long weeks passed. They heard nothing.

On all their future trips to the farmhouse well, they never again saw the girl who had slipped them the apple and accepted the note.

"The letter's probably been intercepted, lost, or destroyed," Sarsfield told the men. "But at least we tried."

"I hope the poor girl wasn't caught and punished," Glixon said. "I'd feel terrible about that."

Atlantic gales blew harder, and the cold wind swept between the large crevices of the old stone fort as Sergeant Sarsfield watched the POWs huddle together to keep warm, share their dwindling rations with the pellagra-sick, and continue to lose weight. He knew that, without help—and soon—he and the men wouldn't make it.

When we die, they'll just throw our bodies into the sea. None of our troops or families will ever know we were here or what happened to us.

Late one night at the prison camp, Sergeant Harrington had an unexpected conversation with a visiting German soldier.

"Your men fought bravely on 2 October," the soldier told Harrington. "In fact, the *Kurz-Nachrichten*—the newspaper published by the German garrison here at Lorient—gave almost a complete page commending your patrol's fighting fierceness."

"That's interesting! And surprising!" Harrington said, and then asked the blond-haired man: "How long have you been in the German Army?"

"Since the war began. And I have spent some time on the Russian Front," the soldier said.

"That must've been terrible!" Harrington said.

"Yes, it was," the soldier replied. "Fortunately, I speak Russian—that helped. I also speak English and French. I studied for many years at a London university."

"Do you think Germany has a chance of actually winning this war?" Harrington asked.

"Of course!" the soldier snapped. "I am a loyal German. I believe Hitler will win this war!"

The soldier looked off into the distance.

"If, however, the Reich is defeated?" he said, turned his head, and looked Harrington in the eye. "Well, I am keeping my gun's last bullet for myself."

EIGHT

THE ENIGMA

**24 October 1944, U.S. Army 94th Infantry
Division Headquarters, Châteaubriant**

Andrew Gerow Hodges stood quietly and at attention in his brown Red Cross uniform as Malony addressed him.

"Andy, we've just received a letter from a POW that American prisoners of war are held on an island called Île de Groix, in the Lorient pocket. They are in dire need of food, clothing, and medical supplies. I'm not entirely sure how this letter came to us, but it looks genuine, and if it's true, we need to do something about it. As the American Red Cross senior field director for this division, this is your baby. Handle it."

"Yes, sir," Andy Hodges replied and saluted.

Andy walked back to his office and closed the door. He sat down at his desk and rubbed the back of his neck.

Handle it? Just how in the world am I supposed to do that?!

He closed his eyes and tried to figure out how he could possibly help American POWs imprisoned on an island in the heart of enemy-occupied Lorient—if, of course, the letter was genuine.

Who do I contact? I don't even know how to contact the enemy! Why should the Germans listen to me? What do they care if our prisoners starve?

If I cross into enemy territory, what will keep them from using me for target practice? And if I deliver food, clothing, and medicine, how can I trust the Krauts to give it to our guys instead of keeping it for themselves?

He shook his head.

This is crazy! But what can I do? It's an order, and from the major general himself!

He grabbed a pad of paper and started making notes. Then he stopped and sighed at the enormity of the task.

I don't even know the German commander's name or address. He'll never get this letter!

Andy addressed the inquiry to: "The German Commandant, Île de Groix."

The letter was simple and to the point:

"In regard to the American prisoners now being held on the Île de Groix, the privilege is requested of allowing American Red Cross supplies be taken to the American prisoners of war and distributed by Mr. Andrew G. Hodges, Field Director, a representative of this organization."

Andy listed the supplies he thought the Red Cross had in stock and could provide immediately and that were items the prisoners might most need.

Certainly, if prisoners are really there, they probably need clothes—trousers, shirts, socks, handkerchiefs, field jackets, overcoats . . . and personal hygiene items like towels, soap, shaving supplies, toothbrushes and paste, combs . . . and I know they'll appreciate some treats like candy, pipe tobacco and cigarettes . . . and they'll also need matches . . . and we can't forget shoelaces and halazone tablets . . . I hope I'm not leaving out anything. . . .

He continued to write:

"The supplies heretofore mentioned have been procured by the American Red Cross and consist of the following:

"Trousers, shirts, socks, handkerchiefs, towels, field jackets, candles, Halazone tablets (for purification of water), soap (laundry and face), overcoats, shaving brushes, razors, razor blades, shaving cream, combs, matches, pipe tobacco, cigarettes, tooth brushes, tooth paste, candy, shoe-laces."

Then he wrote the letter's closing:

"It is desired that these supplies, which will be transported on the next trip of the Red Cross Ship, Ile de Groix, be accompanied and distributed by the representative of the American Red Cross and that the safe passage and the safe return of this representative be guaranteed by the German Commandant by endorsement hereon. Respectfully submitted, Andrew G. Hodges, FD, American Red Cross."

Andy reread the letter, and asked a translator in G-2 to type it in both English and German. Before he folded the German letter and placed it in an envelope, he scanned it:

"An den Deutschen Kommandanten, Île de Groix. In Betreff der amerikanischen Kriegsgefangenen die eich jetzt auf der Île de Groix befinden, wirt die Erlaubnis ersucht, dass Vorrate des Amerikanischen Roten Kreuzes an die amerikanischen Kriegsgefangenen von Herrn Andrew G. Hodges, Feld-Direktor, als Vertreter dieser Organisation, mitgebracht und ausgeteilt werden. . . ."

I sure hope the translator got it right! Wish I knew some German so I could check it. Doesn't matter. No Lorient German will receive it. And if he does, I doubt he'll read it or respond.

The young field director took the letter to the owner of a French fishing boat and asked him to deliver it to the German commandant in the Lorient sector. He had heard the fisherman frequently carried supplies to French prisoners held there. Meanwhile, Andy contacted an army base quartermaster depot and asked about the requested provisions.

Andy knew Malony's name opened a lot of doors. He got an immediate commitment for medical supplies, as well as outfits for each prisoner: two suits of underwear, two pairs of socks, shoes, a shirt, trousers, a field jacket, and an overcoat. Hodges also made sure he asked for plenty of food, candy, cigarettes, and the comfort articles on his list.

Several days passed without a word from the German commandant—whoever he was, wherever he was. So Hodges asked the translator to type another letter—again, an original in both English and German. This time he personally carried the German-language letter to the French maritime commissioner in Concarneau, France, a two-and-a-half-hour drive from nearby Nantes. He had heard that the commissioner might have some contact with the Germans in that sector. Then he returned to HQ and waited to receive some word.

Not long after, the 94th Division Reconnaissance relayed a message to Hodges, sent through a French priest by a German commandant from Lorient.

"German officials in Lorient will notify you on 27 October—if it would be possible for a German officer to meet you in the town of Le Magouer at 1100 on the 28th."

If it would be possible? What does that mean?

On 27 October, Hodges waited to receive some sort of confirmation from the priest about the tentative 28 October meeting that was supposed to take place in German-held Le Magouer.

While he waited, he thought about his wife and son back home. Andy tried to write her often, he missed them so much. He had been given permission to contact her on September 28, shortly after arriving in France. He recalled the letter:

"My dearest Shirley," he had written (calling his wife, Mary Louise, by her maiden name "Shirley"). "I was just informed by one of our unit censors that I could now write you some of the places I visited in England. My visits were mostly in southern England."

Andy had listed some of those places, all the while wishing his wife could have been with him during the sightseeing.

"I visited Bradford-on-Avon to see the little Saxton church built in 709 A.D. It was nice to see, but the large, Norman-type architectural church built in the twelfth century was much more impressive. I had planned a trip to Stratford-on-Avon, but our moving to France prevented that."

Andy told his wife about the beautiful and impressive cathedral that had "a leper's peep hewed into a stone to permit the lepers to walk a few feet inside the church, and see the cross."

He told her about traveling into France, visiting Rennes, and buying her some gifts.

"I bought perfume and a lace handkerchief for you. I hope you will like the handkerchief."

During his early travels in France, Andy had been amazed to see all the destruction caused by war. He wrote:

"All the towers I have seen in France were bombed, and a few almost destroyed. The people here have really suffered, and they seem to appreciate the American soldier coming into their country."

Andy waited all day on October 27 for the next day's meeting confirmation to come. But the priest never came. Hodges received no word about the meeting. That evening he contacted Division Recon about the delay.

"We were under the impression that German officials would be waiting for you at Le Magouer on the 28th," they told him.

"They promised confirmation today," Hodges said, "but I've waited all day and I haven't received it. I think I'll drive to Le Magouer in the morning and see if anyone will be there to meet with me."

"Hodges," the recon troop's leader said, "you know that if you go behind enemy lines without the proper written pass, you'll be fair game. They won't hesitate to shoot you!"

"And if I don't go," Hodges said, "the Germans will think Americans are uncaring cowards, and our POWs there will starve or freeze to death."

The next morning, October 28, Hodges jumped into a jeep and motored toward Etel, a small French town held by Americans, west of Auray and south of Nostang, and just across the Etel River from German-held La Magouer—the site of the hoped-for, but unconfirmed, meeting.

After supper at Fort Surville on the Île de Groix, an old guard, Otto, staggered into the POWs' second-floor room.

"Did you hear what happened today in the United States?" he asked in broken English.

The American POWs looked at Otto anxiously and waited for him to speak.

"I read it in the newspaper," Otto said. "And I am very sorry to have to tell you this bad news."

"What is it?" a POW asked impatiently.

"Germany has bombed New York and Detroit!" the guard said. "Also, the United States' entire Pacific Fleet has been sunk!"

"Stop lying to us, Otto!" Shulman called out.

"Is it true?!" Winn asked, his young eyes wide with shock. "My folks live in West Virginia! Did that really happen?"

"Of course not!" Shulman said.

"Don't believe it, Winn!" Stewart said. "Otto's just an old geezer, and it's hogwash German propaganda!"

After everyone had gone to sleep that night at the Île de Groix prison camp, Harrington wrote in his diary.

"Tonight the Krauts showed us a German movie titled 'Hello, Fannie.' Very appropriate. The deutsche gals were all 'fannie.' They reminded me of the feminine version of a wrestler.

"We were allowed to take a shower today. Hot dog!!! No soap. No towels. No nothing. Nice deal to put on our dirty clothes again after the bath!

"Our rations have been cut again. Two cigarettes per day and six men to a one-and-a-half-pound loaf of bread per day—one loaf gives fifteen shadows. We used to laugh at the saying: 'The U. S. Army is the best paid, best equipped, and best fed in the world.' Believe it's the truth, unless you're on the wrong side of the line. I've come to the conclusion that we're forgotten men.

"But we have some hope. There's strict orders against speaking to the French [residents] or buying foodstuff from them. However, we do receive food in 'dribbles'—go for a walk and some Frenchman will be standing in the doorway of his house—and out flashes a loaf of bread, and it is quickly tucked under a G.I.'s field jacket. Through this and similar channels comes our sustaining source of food."

NINE

THE MEETING

28 October 1944, Etel/Le Magouer, France

When Andy Hodges reached Etel, he grabbed the white flag, stepped from the jeep, and looked out over the wide river separating the warring factions. He had studied the small village on the map, located halfway between Quiberon to the south and Lorient to the north. The River Etel stretched for nine miles inland, reaching from the Bay of Biscay, and looked like fingers on a gnarled hand.

As Hodges watched the rippling water, he recalled the mysterious legends that had surrounded the river's entrance for centuries, the dangerous mouth that had swallowed many a boat and sailor. He was only twelve years old when he heard the story of the freakish storm at the river's mouth that swallowed ten large boats and devoured seventy-two fishermen. It seemed that even seasoned sailors never learned to respect the well-known sandbar that lay like a hidden predator beneath the river's entrance, hospitable only at times of high tide and low wind.

Hodges had received no meeting confirmation, and no signed papers that would allow him official entrance into the German territory. He had no boat, and no idea how he'd cross the River Etel.

How will I cross to the other side?

He focused his eyes on the water and felt the cold wind blow against his face.

And what will I do when I get there? I know no one in Le Magouer, and I don't speak German.

After some time passed, Hodges saw a boat moving slowly along the water's edge. He called to the two men inside, and after a few minutes of conversation, he discovered they were English-speaking Frenchmen, and their boat had been used, years before, by the French Red Cross.

"Can I pay you to take me across the river to Le Magouer?" Andy asked them.

"You will be going into German-occupied territory," one man said. "I would not advise an American to go there. They will shoot you."

"I know," Andy answered. "But I have a meeting."

"Yes," they told him. "We can take you. But we have warned you. And you must find your own way back across the Etel."

Andy paid the men. Then he smiled, nodded, and climbed into the boat. For safety, he draped the large white flag over the boat's side. Together the three men made the trip across the River Etel. When they arrived, Hodges thanked the Frenchmen, retrieved the flag, and stepped onto the stone wharf.

Andy saw a young German sentry posted at the guardhouse on the dock at Le Magouer. The uniformed lad stood up and forbade Hodges to pass.

"Your name?" the sentry asked in elementary English. "Your business here?"

"My name is Andy Hodges, and I have a meeting here," Hodges said and smiled. "German officials are expecting me, I think."

"I have no instructions about this meeting," the sentry said as he checked a stack of papers.

"What is your name, son?" Hodges asked.

"My name is Klaus," he said. "But why is knowing my name important to you?"

At that moment two well-dressed German officers walked up and interrupted the conversation. Hodges instinctively raised his hands in the air and smiled broadly.

"Andrew Gerow Hodges, American Red Cross senior field director," he said in a warm Southern drawl. "But you can call me 'Andy.' I wrote the letter to you. Oh, and I'm not armed," he told them. "Members of the American Red Cross don't carry weapons. Please feel free to search me."

Andy saw the two Frenchmen turn their boat around and disappear downstream.

For a long moment the two officers said nothing and studied the young field director. Then the German with deep, dark eyes and thick eyebrows responded in perfect English with a slight British accent.

"I am Oberleutnant Alfons Schmitt," he said. "And this is Hauptmann Helmut Reick."

Both Schmitt and Reick gave the *Hitlergruß* [Hitler salute].

"Ve vonder . . . ah . . . if you . . . vould come here . . ." Reick said in limited and badly butchered English. "Ve . . . believed . . . you . . . vould not." He stepped toward Hodges and extended his right hand, as did Schmitt. Hodges responded with his right hand.

"Oberleutnant Schmitt, Hauptmann Reick," Andy said as he, in turn, shook both officers' hands and smiled. "I'm pleased to meet you both."

Then the Oberleutnant said the last thing the American from South Alabama ever expected to hear from a German Nazi officer:

"Andrew Gerow Hodges. You are a brave man for coming here—without confirmation. We admire that."

Standing on the dock at the mouth of the River Etel, sworn enemies—two Nazis and one lone American—faced each other and smiled.

TEN

THE AGREEMENT

28 October 1944, Etel/Le Magouer, France

Oberleutnant Schmitt and Hauptmann Reick led Andy Hodges to a small café in the drab fishing village of Le Magouer. They chose a table in an isolated corner. The restaurant's few customers finished eating and exited quietly. When a young French girl walked toward them to take their order, Reick waved her away and said a curt *"Nein!"*

Although the Hauptmann was definitely the man in charge, he deferred to the younger Schmitt to communicate with Hodges in English. Reick filled his pipe with tobacco, stuffed it into the bowl, and lit a match to it. He took several deep breaths and blew each out slowly.

Schmitt took a cigarette from its pack and offered it to Hodges.

"Smoke?" he asked.

"Thank you, but no," Hodges replied. "I don't smoke cigarettes. Occasionally I enjoy a cigar or pipe. My wife sends my favorite cigars from the States."

The Oberleutnant lit a cigarette and drew several deep breaths. He sat straight and rigid in the chair, his head held high. His eyes fixed on Hodges, he studied the young American like a specimen under a microscope.

Let us see what you are made of, Herr Hodges.

Schmitt had interrogated many Amis, but this one was obviously different. Hodges seemed completely composed and unafraid, as he sat comfortably in the chair with the informality and casualness of visiting with old friends. A strikingly handsome man, his natural smile and kind-hearted eyes suggested a kindred spirit, not a threatening combatant.

The Oberleutnant wanted to know more about this unpretentious, unarmed American, so willing to cross into hostile territory with no official papers, and to meet with two strange German officers, not knowing how he'd be received. Schmitt took his time, finished his cigarette, and finally spoke, beginning the conversation with a soft, but self-assured voice:

"Herr Hodges, have you been to this area before?" he asked.

"No, I haven't," Hodges said.

"We've been in Fortress Lorient since the summer of 1940," Schmitt boasted. "Admiral Karl Dönitz conquered this port and organized our courageous U-boat 'wolf packs' here. Within a few months, our submarines sank more than one hundred fifty allied ships. Perhaps you have heard of it?"

Reick nodded and smiled.

"Yes," Hodges replied. He looked Schmitt in the eye. "I know about the German U-boats. And as I recall, your 'gray wolves' attacked unarmed civilian cargo ships. That took no courage."

The Oberleutnant felt miffed, but he didn't show it. He glanced at Reick. From the look on Reick's face, it was obvious he had caught the drift of the conversation. The Hauptmann frowned.

Schmitt noticed that this American was refreshingly different from others he had met. He possessed a rare intelligence and a keen wit. And he wasn't afraid to speak his mind.

Hmmm . . . braver than most Amis I have met.

Schmitt wasn't finished with the young Red Cross officer. He raised his smooth-shaven chin high and said: "You Americans tried to destroy our U-boat pens here at Fortress Lorient, but for all your bombs, no damage was done. Just a lot of Ami planes shot down, and pilots and crew killed. No matter the losses, they kept coming. Those were our 'Happy Times.'"

Andy Hodges, his smile erased and his expression serious, leaned forward in his chair and looked directly into the Oberleutnant's face.

"Oberleutnant Schmitt," he said. "War is a tragedy—for all of us. People are killed; their property is destroyed; mothers are separated from their babies; lives are disrupted, forever changed, and ruined. How can you call intended and violent death and destruction 'Happy Times' for any of us? No one wins in a war."

A clever answer. I like this man, Hodges—even if he is an American. He is no fool.

Schmitt sat up straight in his chair, nodded his head once toward the American, and said a simple "Touché."

The test was over. Hodges didn't back down. He spoke his mind with the polish and politeness of a true Southern gentleman, and seemed unafraid. Schmitt had to acknowledge that Hodges had won Round One.[1]

After a while, Hodges grew tired of playing cat-and-mouse games with the two Germans. He wanted to state the reason for his visit, leave the depressing village of Le Magouer, find a way across the River Etel, and get back to headquarters—alive and before dark.

This talk could go on forever and go nowhere!

"Hauptmann Reick, Oberleutnant Schmitt," Hodges said in his gentle drawl. "Back home in South Alabama, we, like you, always make small talk when we first meet people. We talk about the weather, or Aunt Tilda's new grandbaby, or what's going on in our community. We're taught it's just the polite thing to do, so we do it."

Hodges paused and smiled. "Well," he said, "we've had our necessary small talk. Can we get down to business now?"

Schmitt raised his thick eyebrows, seeming somewhat surprised at the American's boldness.

"Certainly," he said, and cleared his throat. "Make your request. We are listening."

"As I mentioned in my letter," Hodges began, "you are holding Allied soldiers in your POW camp at Fortress Lorient, and they badly need supplies. The American Red Cross requests your permission to bring in those provisions by boat, and to allow me, their representative, to distribute them personally to the men. I listed the requested supplies in my letter of 24 October."

"We are supplying well the needs of the prisoners," Schmitt said.

Sure you are! They're starving, freezing, and getting sick!

"I understand that," Hodges replied. "The American Red Cross wants to help you in your commendable efforts to do that."

The Hauptmann drew several deep breaths on his pipe. The odor of stale, cheap pipe tobacco filled the café, the foul-smelling smoke encircling Hodges's head and making him feel nauseated.

"On your list, you mention items . . . as trousers, shirts, socks, field jackets, and . . . other essential supplies," Hauptmann Reick said. "But the men vould not need . . . nor deserve, candy, cigarettes, tobacco, and such . . . ah . . . luxuries. Under the . . . Geneva Convention, POWs receive . . . the same rations as our troops. You . . . cannot ask for more."

"Hauptmann Reick, the American Red Cross cares for the physical, as well as for the emotional, well-being of our men," Hodges countered. "We want the men to know we care, that we haven't forgotten them. These small comfort items, that you call luxuries, will speak volumes to our troops—just as they would to a German on the Eastern Front."

"Point taken," Schmitt said in a muted voice. "It is admirable that you still care about your prisoners."

"We want our men to stay alive and healthy," Hodges said, "until we can reunite them with their families and loved ones back home—the very ones they're fighting this war to protect."

Hodges watched the stern, arrogant expression on Schmitt's face start to fade and his heavy eyebrows furrow. He seemed to grow smaller as he sunk into his chair.

But the greatest change began to happen in the face and body of the Hauptmann. Hodges noticed the many medals and badges Reick wore on the front of his uniform, and saw that the Oberleutnant wore none. And in his mind, he tried to piece together the Hauptmann's story.

Surely, probably unlike Schmitt, Hauptmann Reick has seen action—violent, bloody, battlefield combat—the horrors of war seem to be reflected in his eyes.

At just the mention of the Russian Front, Hodges saw the muscles in Reick's face start to sag. The Hauptmann seemed suddenly very tired, his broad, rigid shoulders showing the slightest hint of a slump.

Hodges sensed a heaviness overcoming the two men, and it gave him a moment of understanding into these enemy officers so far away from home.

You are prisoners, too, aren't you? Isolated, miles from your family, your homeland. You guard empty, useless submarine pens and nurse allied POWs while waiting for Germany's inevitable collapse. Then what? The French may have your names on a hit list, too. They won't forget what the Germans did to their country, to their people.

For the first time during the meeting, Hodges actually felt sorry for the two officers—obedient soldiers, surrounded by Allied divisions, ordered to hold out to the last bullet by a madman führer who was enjoying a good life, many miles away. Hodges remembered the orders given to the 94th Division: Don't attack the Germans at Lorient and St. Nazaire. Just contain them. Let them wither on the vine with no hope of escape or resupply.

And they are withering . . . actually rotting here—hungry, sick, disheartened, and facing winter's long, cold, and bleak inhospitality.

Another thought plagued Hodges's mind. *When Germany loses the war, will Schmitt or Reick have a country, a home, or a family left to return to? Or will their loved ones be gone, dead, and their homes and country destroyed?*

Sensing the moment ripe, Hodges asked Schmitt an unusual question, one that the Oberleutnant didn't seem to expect.

"Oberleutnant, do you have a family back home in Germany?"

Schmitt said nothing for a few seconds. He took a no-brand cigarette from its pack and lit it. Then he sat still in his chair, his eyes fixed and focused on the wall or door or something far behind the young Red Cross volunteer.

"Yes," he answered, then blinked several times and lowered his eyes. "I have a sister, Greta, and a nephew, Walter, in Germany. I think they are still alive and in Germany. I haven't heard from them in many months."

Now is my opportunity.

"And if your sister and nephew were imprisoned by the enemy," Hodges continued, "wouldn't you do everything in your power to keep them healthy and make them as comfortable as possible during their internment?"

A second or two passed in silence.

Schmitt pressed his lips together, nodded, and replied softly: "Certainly."

That's the answer I hoped he'd give.

Hodges turned his attention to Hauptmann Reick.

"Will you then allow me to bring supplies to our men in Fortress Lorient, Hauptmann Reick?" Hodges asked. "And Oberleutnant Schmitt, will you allow me to personally distribute the provisions to the men?"

Hodges watched the two officers. They sat still for several seconds, as if in deep thought. Finally Schmitt leaned over and whispered briefly to his captain. Reick nodded.

"Yes, Hodges, we will allow you to bring the supplies," Schmitt said. "But we will not allow you to personally distribute them to the men. I will do that myself."

I was afraid of that! Schmitt will take the supplies and give them to his own soldiers and guards. Our POWs will never even see them!

"I don't mean to question your integrity, Oberleutnant," Hodges said, "but how will I know for sure our POWs will receive the Red Cross provisions?"

Oops! Too strong. I challenged his integrity, I doubted his honesty. He'll be angry and call off the whole deal. I've got to be more careful, more tactful!

Hodges saw a certain harshness move across Schmitt's face. He stood to his feet, his back straight and rigid once more. "You have my word of honor as a German officer!" he said in a loud official voice. "Your men will receive every item! Bring your supplies here on 30 October!"

Hodges smiled: "Thank you, Oberleutnant Schmitt. That's good enough for me!"

With those words, the two Germans gave the *Hitlergruß*, and the meeting ended.

ELEVEN

THE DENTIST

28 October 1944, Lorient, Allied Sector

On that same day, First Lieutenant Dr. William Reynolds, a twenty-five-year-old dentist from El Paso, Texas, was riding the bumpy, pockmarked roads of Lorient scouting out a location for a new field hospital. He and Lieutenant Norman Le Barre, a Californian from the 94th medical personnel, had secured an ambulance and a driver, Private Orville Spencer, a native Iowan. They had orders to find, set up, and supply a new military unit site and operation.

At one point Reynolds asked the driver to stop. He adjusted his wire eyeglasses and focused on a large area of level ground several feet from the road.

"This looks like a good location for a hospital," he said. "Spencer, exactly where are we?"

"I'm, I'm not . . . uh . . . not quite sure, sir," the driver responded.

You're not sure?! Are you kidding me?!

"What do you mean?" Reynolds asked, his voice showing alarm. "You are supposed to know these roads! The Krauts have planted anti-tank mines everywhere in this area!"

"I'm afraid we're lost, sir," the driver admitted.

"Turn around! Go back!" Reynolds ordered. "Then figure out where in the world we are!"

Reynolds tried to appear calm, but he felt his heart pounding, and he struggled to breathe.

Unknown roads mean hidden mines! A vehicle as heavy as our ambulance could detonate a German Topfmine, instantly killing all three of us!

Reynolds swallowed hard, looked around all sides of him, and inwardly braced for a possible explosion.

The driver made a sharp U-turn in the middle of the narrow road and headed in the opposite direction.

"I'm keeping watch for mines," he said as he drove slowly and purposely.

"You won't see a Topfmine!" Reynolds shouted. "The enemy knows how to paint them, and bury them under the road's surface. They camouflage—"

The ear-deafening explosion instantly blew Reynolds and his companions out of the heavy Dodge ambulance. Still conscious and lying faceup in a roadside ditch, Reynolds watched the horrific scene unfold. The blast had shot the heavy Dodge ambulance high into the air, piercing its sheet metal body, blowing off its four massive tires and side-mounted spare, and ripping away its side and rear doors, grill, and front bumper. Airborne from the blast's violent force, the six-thousand-pound WC-54's chassis had crashed to the ground and landed hard on its side. A gasoline fire was burning with bright orange flames, filling the sky with dense black smoke, and quickly consuming everything within its range. Reynolds saw glass from the shattered windshield and windows littering the roadside around him. Several bunk stretchers had landed in the woods.

From the ditch, Reynolds could feel the intense burning heat. His head throbbed and his ears rang as he listened to the sounds of the crackling blaze. He lay still, on his back, staring at the sky.

"Le Barre! Spencer!" he shouted as loud as he could. But he heard no one respond to his cries. Reynolds felt his consciousness start to fade, and then . . .

When Reynolds came to, he coughed to clear the suffocating smoke from his throat and lungs, blinked his eyes numerous times, and struggled to stay conscious. He tasted blood, and wiped his flowing nose with his hand.

"Le Barre! Spencer!" he shouted again. But no answer came.

He struggled to lift himself out of the ditch and get to his feet. But he couldn't. The excruciating pain in his right foot forced him back to the ground. He lay there for several seconds, afraid to move.

I pray my foot is still attached.

Then he leaned slightly forward to examine the foot, the source of his intense pain. He slowly and carefully tried to pull his right foot from the boot, but the agonizing pain stopped him. Blood poured from the boot. Wrestling to release himself from the boot, he half expected to find his severed foot still inside. When the boot had been removed, he saw that the end of a sharp jagged bone had broken through the skin. His ankle and foot were still attached to his lower leg, but were barely hanging on by a piece of torn flesh. He knew better than to try to stand up, and he hoped he would be spared amputation.

Need medical help! Fast!

With his blood-covered hands, Reynolds felt around him in the ditch for his eyeglasses.

With my bad eyes, I can't see much of anything without them.

His fingers finally rested on a twisted wire rim, the glass gone. Glancing at the burning ambulance, he saw the fuzzy image, and figured out what had happened.

We ran over a Topfmine. I was afraid that would happen. I'm fortunate to be alive! Am I the only one who survived?

He again screamed out for his companions, but no one replied.

They're dead. Gotta be. I'm surprised I survived that blast.

Reynolds became nauseated and dizzy. He felt himself passing out. When he came to, he wondered how he could find help. Blood was pouring from his shrapnel-peppered, crushed foot and soaking into the dirt around him.

As he lay in the ditch, drifting in and out of consciousness, the lieutenant pondered his brief military career. He'd seen active duty for a year and three months as part of the U.S. Army Dental Corps. He had served with the 29th Field Hospital in Europe, assisting with D-Day invasion preparations and later accompanying troops ashore at Omaha Beach in

Normandy. He participated in the siege and capture of the Port of Brest, where nearly ten thousand American casualties were sustained.

I survived all that combat unscathed, and now this. I'll probably lose my foot. And what will I do without my eyeglasses? I can't see much without them.

Deep in thought and pain, he heard footsteps running on the ground above him. Looking up, he tried to focus his nearsighted eyes. A group of German soldiers had formed and stood circled around him. Each carried a machine pistol, and aimed it directly at him.

Forget the foot. I'm a dead man.

Two German soldiers picked up one of the ambulance's folding bunk stretchers scattered alongside the road and woods. As they scooped him up and placed him on the stretcher, Reynolds grabbed his boot. They loaded him into a camouflaged pickup truck and sped off. During the long, bumpy ride, Reynolds's foot throbbed. He worried about Le Barre and Spencer. He also felt his bladder get uncomfortably full.

My bladder's going to burst. I don't guess the Krauts will allow me to make a pit stop. How does one say, "help, I've got to pee" in German?

The best he could manage, the lieutenant positioned his bloody boot below his waist and relieved his aching bladder, much to the amusement of his captors. One of the German soldiers snickered and shouted to the others: *"Hey, pisst in den Schuh des Ami!"* ["Hey, pee in the Ami's boot!"] They put down their weapons. One by one, the German soldiers borrowed the boot, passing it around, taking turns and taking aim until the boot was full. When they finished, they returned the boot to Reynolds, overflowing with warm yellow liquid. Even in great pain from his injuries, the dentist took the boot and half chuckled inside.

I'll never wear that boot again. Wait till I tell the guys about this.

When the vehicle finally stopped, the soldiers placed Reynolds inside an abandoned farmhouse with half a dozen German soldiers. During the long night, no one examined or doctored his foot. By the next morning, Reynolds no longer felt pain stabbing his ankle and shooting up his leg. Both his foot and leg were numb. About mid-morning, a soldier grabbed

Reynolds and ran with him when U.S. artillery began shelling the farmhouse. They put him inside a concrete bunker aid station in Lorient. He discovered he was the only Allied soldier among fifteen Germans, a Spaniard, and a Russian. After a few days, the enemy took him to another bunker that had a makeshift operating room. A doctor removed the shrapnel from his foot, and most of his toenails, and wrapped the foot in a thin, dirty bandage.

After the primitive surgery came the customary interrogation. When Reynolds refused to give the officer any information, the German blurted out in English:

"I know you are with the 29th Field Hospital! I saw it on the bumper of your ambulance." Then he added: "You and your allies should join with us Germans and help us fight the Russians! Someday you will wish you had!"

Later they took Reynolds to the French Naval Hospital in Lorient, where he met David Devonald and Second Lieutenant Richard Baldwin from the 6th Armored Division.

Once settled, his foot throbbing, Reynolds laid his head down flat on his bunk, closed his now next-to-useless eyes, and yearned for the pair of spare eyeglasses he had left back in his footlocker.

That night, Kermit Harden and the other POWs took turns crowding around a wood-fire potbelly stove trying to stay warm in the old stone fort at the cold, wind-swept Île de Groix prison camp. They said little as they ate their thin half slice of brown bread and bowl of watery soup. Harden counted the bites of soup aloud as he ate them, stopping when he finished at twenty-two spoonfuls. Occasionally he found a little grain in the liquid. But not in this bowl. Once he discovered a piece of meat the size of a pencil eraser. At least he thought it was meat. He didn't much care; he ate it anyway.

"Weighed in today," Harden told a fellow prisoner. "I've lost forty pounds. That's a lot for me."

Some looked up and nodded at the thin nineteen-year-old Midwesterner, a sophomore at the University of Illinois when he left school to join the army in '43. His once full face was now hollow and his cheeks sunken.

"Not sure how much longer I can last," Harden said to nobody in particular. "The rations are getting smaller. I guess Sarsfield's letter never made it to the mainland or to the Red Cross. Otherwise we would've heard something by now."

"I'd give my left arm for an Oh Henry! candy bar," Harden heard young Private Louis Winn mumble. "Always got a bag full of them at Halloween back in West Virginia when I was a kid—we always went trick-or-treatin' 'round this time of year."

Harden took a long hard look at Private Winn. With his slight build, dark fine hair, and round smooth face, Winn looked like a kid.

He should still be back in West Virginia trick-or-treating with his brothers and sisters. That boy can't be more than twelve years old!

One of the older German guards walked into the room, bringing in two more POWs—Le Barre and Spencer. They were dirty, cut, and bruised, and walked with limps. Harden sighed.

More prisoners. Less food for us.

Le Barre and Spencer introduced themselves to the other men, told them about the ambulance, mine, explosion, and capture.

"I don't know how we ever survived the blast," Le Barre said. "Somehow we were thrown a distance from the ambulance. Our companion, Lieutenant William Reynolds, who was with us, is . . . well, was . . . a dentist. We didn't see him after the explosion. We think he must've died in the burning vehicle."

"You can take those bunks," Harden said and pointed to two nearby beds.

"I've had medical experience," Le Barre said. "I'll be glad to help out in any way I can."

The old guard joined the men around the stove. In his hand he carried a small chess set, and he gave it to Harden.

Harden smiled warmly at the guard.

"*Danke schön,*" he said.

The guard nodded and placed his rough red hands closer to the hot stove.

An hour later, and after a halfhearted game or two of chess, the men climbed into their bunk beds and snuggled deep into the straw mattresses. Unfortunately the fleas and lice, which never slept, were waiting for them.

On Sunday, Sergeant Harrington heard that the Catholic prisoners would be allowed to go to church.

"Come with us, Sergeant," they said. "Church might do you some good!"

"No, thanks," Harrington said. "I'm not Catholic."

When the Catholic men returned from the church service, they were all smiling.

"The French church people took us to their homes and fed us meals!" they said.

That night Harrington noted in his diary:

"Sunday, the catholic boys were allowed to go to church. They came back with wild stories of the French feeding them. Must be true; they all have that satisfied smile. What an argument I'll have to settle next Sunday— a sudden conversion of faith [among the other men] will most likely take place."

TWELVE

GIFTS FROM THE HEART

30 October 1944, Lorient Sector

Andy Hodges returned to enemy-occupied Lorient on October 30, the meeting day set by Reick and Schmitt. He brought with him a boat loaded with supplies for the Allied prisoners at Île de Groix.

The young German sentry, Klaus, stationed at the dock, recognized Hodges from his first visit.

"Herr Hodges," he said. "Hauptmann Reick and Oberleutnant Schmitt are waiting for you at the café."

"Thank you, Klaus," Hodges said and smiled.

When he walked into the nearby café, Reick and Schmitt greeted him with the German officers' customary *Hitlergruß*. The three men sat down at the corner table and removed their caps.

The mood seemed formal, stiff. Hodges wondered if Schmitt was still miffed at his remarks during their last meeting. Hodges had never meant to question the officer's integrity.

I'll let it go for now.

"Hauptmann Reick," Hodges said. "I have a gift for you."

He slid a small package across the table. Reick looked surprised as he removed the brown paper and found a bright red metal tin of Prince Albert pipe tobacco. He flipped open the lid, put his nose deep into the tin, and breathed in the rich aroma.

"Vonderful!" Reick said. "*Danke!* Most kind."

Reick packed some of the tobacco in his pipe's bowl, lit it several times, and breathed in the delicious fragrance. He seemed to greatly enjoy the experience.

Hodges wasted no time getting down to business.

"Oberleutnant Schmitt," he said. "I have every item on the list waiting to be delivered by boat to our men at Île de Groix. Can the supplies be delivered immediately? Will you check the provisions and sign a receipt of acceptance for them?"

"Certainly," Schmitt replied. "And as I said, you have my word of honor as a German officer that the supplies—every one of them—will be delivered to your men."

"I trust you, Oberleutnant," Hodges replied. "Your word is good enough for me. However, we are in a war, and I am responsible to answer to my superiors. I know you understand these necessary procedures."

"Yes, I do," Schmitt said. "It is the same for me."

"I want to thank you and Hauptmann Reick from the 94th Division for allowing me to bring supplies to our men," Hodges said.

"You are welcome. The supplies will be delivered to the POWs tomorrow," the Oberleutnant said.

Mission accomplished. Now back to headquarters.

"Are ve . . . finished now vith . . . business?" Reick asked. "If so, I vould suggest . . . we order lunch."

Lunch? I didn't expect that. Lunch with German officers? Oh well, why not?!

"Sounds great! I'm hungry!" Hodges said and then paused. "There is one more thing I forgot to mention."

Just to make sure our POWs not only receive the food, but can also control it themselves. . . .

"Yes?" Both officers looked squarely at Hodges.

"I'd like to ask permission for the POWs to be permitted to set up a private kitchen so they can store and cook their own food. And I'd like to return to Lorient each week with a boatload of fresh rations."

"A private kitchen? Weekly rations?" Schmitt asked. "You ask for many things, Herr Hodges."

The Oberleutnant leaned over and whispered to the Hauptmann. Reick nodded.

"Yes, you have our permission," Schmitt said.

"Now . . . may ve eat?!" Reick asked. He called the French waitress and ordered "*soupe aux haricots et pain français pour trois personnes.*"

The three men ate the lunch of thick bean soup and French bread, and talked. After a while Schmitt lit a cigarette, took a few deep breaths, and seemed to loosen up.

If Schmitt was miffed at me, I believe the bean soup and cigarette have cured it.

"I have visited the United States," Schmitt said, "but I cannot identify your unusual accent, Herr Hodges. Where do you live?"

"In the Deep South," Hodges said, smiling. "I was born in Geneva County, Alabama, a few miles from the Florida state line. We Southerners have our own way of talking—slow. Always slow. We just never seem to get in much of a hurry down there. And like I said at our first meeting, you can call me Andy. In the Southern United States, we call each other by our given names. Not much formality practiced down there."

"Ah, Andy, do you come from a wealthy Southern American family— like in *Gone with the Wind*?" he asked with a twinkle in his eye.

Hodges laughed out loud, surprised by the question.

"No, few people in the South are rich plantation owners," he said. "My daddy was dirt-poor when I was growing up. Still is. He worked as a horse-and-mule trader in a storefront stable—H. T. Holman & Sons, Horses and Mules—in downtown Hartford most of his life. Mr. Holman started that business back in 1903. My dad never made much money, but somehow my mother, two brothers, and I managed. We didn't know we were so poor. We were never hungry or without clothes and shelter. Though I can remember as a kid having only two school shirts, and Mama washing and ironing one every afternoon for the next school day."

"Did you finish school before you enlisted into the United States Army?" Schmitt asked, seeming interested in Hodges's background.

"Yes, I graduated from Howard College—a small Baptist school in Birmingham, Alabama. Went to Howard on a football scholarship—that is until I got my shoulder torn up in a practice scrimmage. Had to give up the sport. Howard offered to keep me on the scholarship until I graduated, but I couldn't do that. Just didn't feel right taking a football scholarship and not playing football. But they talked me into accepting half the scholarship so I could afford to finish college. I also worked part-time at an athletic club and sold burial policies door-to-door to help out financially. Somehow I had enough money to graduate."

"Interesting . . . to get an education . . . by playing a sport," Reick said. "Most unusual."

Then Reick added: "Vhat . . . brought you . . . to France?"

"Well," Hodges confessed, "the United States Army wouldn't take me because of my shoulder injury. They classified me 4-F—'unfit for military service.' That was a great disappointment. So I joined the American Red Cross, and was assigned senior field director for the 94th here in France."

Schmitt raised his thick eyebrows. "Admirable," he said. "You must possess a strong call to duty, Andy, as we do."

"Yep." Hodges nodded. "I guess you're right on that score."

"Most unfortunate that we are on opposite sides of this war," Schmitt said. "Germany needs men with your courage and strong commitment to country."

I wonder if he knows how bad his side is losing this war. Do these men realize they will soon face a past of regrets and a future with no hope?

Lost in his thoughts, Hodges heard Schmitt's voice interrupt with a question:

"Do you have a family back in Alabama?"

Hodges blinked his eyes several times, looked at the Oberleutnant, nodded, and smiled. "Yes. A beautiful wife and a two-year-old son. They're with her parents while I'm away. I miss my whole family very much."

Trying to turn the attention away from himself, Hodges said: "Tell me about yourselves, Hauptmann Reick, Oberleutnant Schmitt. What kind of work did you do before the war? Do you have families back in Germany?"

Reick looked down at his pipe.

"I . . . prefer not to talk about my . . . personal . . . life," Reick said. "But Oberleutnant Schmitt has . . . fascinating stories he vill, no doubt . . . be very villing . . . to share vith you."

Schmitt smiled, remembering his life as a civilian in Europe.

"I had a career in academics," Schmitt said. "I studied in Britain for six years and earned a degree in history from Oxford University. I taught English and German at the University of Rennes before the outbreak of the war. I also traveled around the world. My cousin lives in Philadelphia, so I spent some time in the United States."

Then he added: "After the war, I hope to teach again. Maybe marry a strong, beautiful German woman, and have lots of *kinder* . . . children and grandchildren. Who knows?"

Oxford University! That explains the Oberleutnant's excellent English-speaking skills, as well as the slight British accent. A degree in history?! Did Schmitt learn nothing from his studies of history about Germany's failure in World War I?! Such an educated man—what a shame to end up like this.

THIRTEEN

ALL HALLOWS' EVE

31 October 1944, Fort Surville POW Camp

After breakfast Schmitt walked unannounced into the prisoners' room at Fort Surville. Startled, the POWs jumped to their feet and stood at attention. Schmitt said nothing for a full minute as he looked out across the room at the incarcerated men.

They are quite thin. Nothing like the healthy fellows we captured four weeks ago.

He glanced at the German guards who stood quietly against the walls holding their weapons.

The guards don't look much better. They know they are stuck here until the war is over. The Americans, it seems, are not the only prisoners.

The Oberleutnant shook his head and looked at the floor, his hands clutched together behind his back.

Hodges is right. War is a terrible, senseless interruption of life. Such a human tragedy.

He took a deep breath and looked directly at the men.

"You may be at ease," he said. "I have an announcement to make."

The POWs looked at one another as if trying to guess what the Ober-leutnant might say.

"The American Red Cross has sent a shipment of provisions for you. I have given permission for immediate delivery of these supplies. The boat is docked and ready to be unloaded. If you wish to help, you may follow the guards to the dock."

The men broke out in yelps and screams, raising their arms in the air, jumping up and down. They all rushed to the door, eager to get to the dock.

As they hauled the heavy containers across the body of the grand moat, into the fort, up the stairs, and into their room, Schmitt heard the men trying to guess what each wooden box contained.

They have become boys again as if an Weihnachten *[at Christmas].*

Schmitt instructed a guard to tell the prisoners—when they calmed down—about the makeshift kitchen where they could store and cook their own food. He ordered another guard to check Hodges's supply list, making sure every item the American POWs received was accounted for and properly noted.

James Sarsfield stood back and beamed as he saw the men laugh and shout to one another: "Smokes! Real coffee! Sugar! Candy!"

The German guards watched with envy as the POWs tore into the Red Cross containers and discovered the food, clothes, and other items Hodges had secured for them.

Glixon opened a box filled with fifty pairs of new drawers. He held up three pairs, waved them like flags, and exclaimed: "Clean drawers! Now I can finally change my underwear!"

"Look!" Boyd shouted as he unpacked soap and towels. "These will come in handy if they ever let us take a Saturday night shower!"

The other men laughed as they grabbed shaving soap/cream, thirty-four razors, fifty-five packs of blades, and twenty-four shaving brushes.

"Winn!" they joked. "Now you can get that 'peach fuzz' off your face!"

Sarsfield saw the men's obvious gratitude as they excitedly slipped on their fresh trousers, shirts, socks, and jackets. Each prisoner placed a new overcoat on top of his bunk, as well as a toothbrush, tooth cream, and a new comb.

When Sarsfield saw a box filled with Oh Henry! candy bars, he handed it to Private Winn.

"Here, Winn! Caramel, chocolate, and peanuts! All the Oh Henry! bars you can eat! The whole box is yours!"

Then he added with a smile: "Happy Halloween! And Winn, you can keep your left arm!"

Harrington walked up to Sarsfield and put out his right hand.

"Thanks," he said. "Thanks for writing that letter. It did the trick. I really doubted the Red Cross would get it. Everyone appreciates what you did."

That morning on All Hallows' Eve, a room full of Allied POWs prepared a breakfast of oatmeal, canned bacon, American pancakes, bread with butter and jelly, and real coffee loaded with sugar and condensed milk.

One old German guard stood beside the door breathing in the aroma of brewing real coffee, watching the men flip pancakes and fry bacon. When Sarsfield filled a plate with hot breakfast, and a cup to brimming with coffee, and placed both in the guard's hands, the old man burst into tears, laid down his weapon, and ate between appreciative sobs.

"*Danke*, I haven't tasted real coffee in years," the guard said. The POWs invited the other guards to eat, too.

That afternoon during the routine trip to the farmhouse well to draw water, Sarsfield and the other five volunteer POWs carried bundles of food and gave them to the French islanders who had been so unselfish and generous in sharing with them from their own meager rations.

5 November 1944

Several days later Sarsfield received word from Schmitt that new supply shipments from the Red Cross would be delivered weekly. Schmitt instructed him to write down medical and other supplies they needed, and told them he'd pass on the requests to the Red Cross representative.

On a sheet of lined paper, Sarsfield scribbled the following message to the Red Cross:

"Sirs: We would like to take this opportunity to express our profound gratitude for the generous shipment of vitally needed supplies that we received on Oct. 31. Our immediate reaction was a tremendous boost in morale and a restored faith in the future.

"Our environment is the product of war but our treatment in the hands of the German authorities is very humane. Lt. Schmitt is a gracious symbol of this treatment.

"We trust that our future needs will come within the scope of your activities—whatever aid is extended us will receive our continued appreciation. Again we offer our heartiest thanks. Respectfully, Sgt. James A. Sarsfield, 6th. A.D. Behalf of American Prisoners of War, Lorient, France."

Sarsfield handed the finished letter to Connatser to read.

"What do you think?" he asked.

"Laid it on kind of thick about Schmitt, didn't you, Jim?" he asked.

"Schmitt's bound to read it, Norman. It sure can't hurt," Sarsfield said and winked.

After talking at length with Le Barre and the other POWs, Sarsfield made a long list of needed supplies: insect powder, bandages, iodine, alcohol, vitamin capsules, dressings, and other medical provisions Le Barre suggested. The men asked Sarsfield to also request field jackets, wool shirts and trousers, woolen caps and gloves. Sarsfield agreed. He knew the wind coming off the Atlantic was getting colder, and winter would be with them before long. One man asked for a pair of size 11EE shoes. After more discussion, they added additional items to Sarsfield's list: blankets, more toothbrushes, toilet paper, mess kits, canteen cups, playing cards, pencils, towels, books, and stationery.

Upon completing the list, the sergeant wrote a letter to Schmitt, recalling their October 31 discussion and thanking him for his "interest" on their behalf. Sarsfield worked hard and thought long to get every word just right:

"To: Lt. Schmitt, from: American Prisoners.

"Via: Military Channels.

"Re: Request for Listed Items through Red Cross.

"Dear Sir:

"In accordance with our conversation of the 31st of October, I am hereby requesting the supplies as itemized on the enclosed supplementary list.

"I would like to point out that the 'medical supplies' are a request of Lt. Le Barre who has made himself responsible for our physical well-being.

"Under the heading of 'food' we cannot be as brazen as to itemize it. However this is the request of the entire complement. It is needless to say that we are deeply grateful for your interest in our behalf. We will be looking forward to the pleasure of a visit in the very near future. Respectfully, Sgt. James A. Sarsfield."

A few hours before dawn, and unable to sleep, Harrington wrote in his diary:

"What a day!!! I must atone for my lack of faith. Today we were informed that supplies from the Red Cross would arrive. No Christmas present or gift will ever hold the near hysteria at seeing American cigarettes for us! The morale is so high that chatting continued until the wee-hours. Smoke is so thick that it can be cut with a knife! Morale is high because of a slight ray of hope exists! We are busy rationing our precious bundles from heaven!"

FOURTEEN

THE OUTRAGEOUS IDEA

Early November 1944, Lorient

Andy Hodges again requisitioned provisions for the POWs held in Lorient, including the extra supplies Sarsfield had requested. He had them loaded into a boat and met the young German sentry on the dock at Le Magouer.

"Good morning, Herr Hodges," the sentry said, greeting him.

"Hello, Klaus. Are Hauptmann Reick and Oberleutnant Schmitt at the café?"

"Yes, sir," Klaus said, and escorted Hodges to the small restaurant.

The men made some brief small talk and ate a light lunch. Reick took tobacco from the red Prince Albert tin, loaded it into his pipe bowl, and lit it. For the next few moments, he sat back in his chair and drew in deep breaths.

Schmitt lit a cigarette and seemed to relax. The discussion then moved to the prisoners and the provisions. With curls of smoke encircling their heads, the mood of the men around the table seemed friendly, almost jovial.

The Oberleutnant spoke even more this time about his teaching career, his worldwide travels, and about his young nephew, Walter, who would one day be a member of the *Deutsches Jungvolk* [German Young People].

Schmitt boasted: "Walter already talks excitedly about his fifteenth birthday when he can join the Hitler Youth."

Schmitt opened his wallet and showed Hodges a photograph of a blond-haired boy in shorts and hiking boots.

"He hopes one day to become an Oberleutnant like his favorite uncle." He smiled and winked.

"That's a fine boy," Hodges said. "I know you're proud of him."

Hodges couldn't help wondering about the boy's future in his war-devastated homeland.

Reick said little during or after lunch. He drew deep breaths from his pipe, filling the tiny café with the Prince Albert's rare and delicious fragrance.

When Schmitt inquired about Andy's growing up in Alabama, Hodges told how his father taught him to swim.

"Our dad—everybody called him Ole Jesse T—took my two brothers and me down to Geneva County's creek, picked up each one of us, and one at a time threw us in the water headfirst," Hodges laughed. "One by one we each found our way out of the creek. Choking up muddy water from our throats, we clawed our way up to the bank, flopped our bare backs down on the dirt, and just glared at our dad. We couldn't believe what he'd done.

"'That's how you learn to swim, boys,' Ole Jesse T told us. Then he said: 'You boys did real good.'

"I've never been so scared!" Hodges said and grinned.

The three men laughed so hard the other diners stopped eating and stared at them. Two German officers. One American Red Cross officer. Eating lunch together. Smoking. And laughing?! The baffled customers whispered to one another. Some gulped down their food and left the café.

"Ole Jesse T was something else!" Hodges continued. "Once he rode a horse up the steps of the grand old Geneva County Courthouse, galloped through the building like Wild Bill Hickok riding Dice, and came down the stairs on the other side. People may still be talking about that!"

Again the three men broke into deep belly laughs. Andy Hodges was glad to see the two German officers relax and have a good time. He wondered how long it had been since they had loosened up and laughed.

Hodges noticed that Reick still volunteered nothing about himself, his family or military career. Nothing. He remained a mystery. Whenever the conversation naturally pointed to Reick, and gave him an opportunity to join in, the Hauptmann fiddled with his pipe, refilling and relighting it and taking long, deep puffs. He would nod and smile, but nothing more.

At the end of the meeting, the trio planned the next supply delivery.

"Same time, same place next week?" Hodges asked.

"Yes," Schmitt said. "We will deliver the supplies to Fort Surville and the hospital tomorrow. You will have the signed receipt awaiting you when you return."

"Thank you, Hauptmann Reick, Oberleutnant Schmitt. I'll see you next week," Hodges said.

As the men stood to leave, Hodges stopped. Hesitating, he looked into the faces of the officers.

"You know," he began, "it sure would be a whole lot easier if you'd just let me bring the American POWs back with me to feed them, rather than for me to bring all this food over here for you to feed them!"

Schmitt and Reick stood still, staring at the Southerner with the winsome smile and the weird idea.

"Why don't you just give us back our American POWs?" Hodges asked.

Silence. Then Schmitt spoke up.

"Are you proposing an exchange?" he asked, arching his dark eyebrows.

"Sure would make things a whole lot easier. For everybody," Hodges replied.

The two German officers said nothing for several seconds.

I can't tell if they like the idea or not. But we need to get our POWs out of there before they die of disease and malnutrition.

Oberleutnant Schmitt had never heard such a proposition as Andy Hodges had just made. Due to Reick's limited understanding of English, Schmitt wondered if Reick had fully grasped the meaning of Hodges's suggestion.

Can he be serious?! Does he have the authority to suggest such a trade? If we say yes, does he have the power to carry out this plan? We certainly need battle-ready men. A swap would give us more soldiers to fight on the front lines.

"Excuse me for a moment, Andy," Schmitt said. He and Reick stepped aside and talked in low voices for a full five minutes. Then both men returned.

"Andy," Schmitt said, "if you have the proper authority to conduct this prisoner trade, Hauptmann Reick thinks our Festungkommandant, General der Artillerie Wilhelm Fahrmbacher, might look with favor on such a proposal."

"I understand, Oberleutnant Schmitt," Hodges told him. "I, too, have my channels. But it sure makes a lot more sense than hauling these supplies here every week."

Then Hodges added: "If we could make this POW exchange work, would General Fahrmbacher be willing to abide by the rules set by the Geneva Conference?"

"We shall certainly ask him," Schmitt replied.

"So should I continue to come here each week with more supplies, and hopefully, before long, we'll be allowed to discuss this matter further?" Hodges asked.

"Yes. We shall work to that end," Schmitt said.

As the two German officers walked out the door of the café, Reick asked the Oberleutnant a question:

"Schmitt," he asked. "Who . . . in the vorld . . . is Vild Bill Hickok?!"

Several worries nagged at Andy Hodges as he drove back to division headquarters that afternoon.

I spoke too soon. I should've gotten official permission before I mentioned the prisoner exchange idea to Schmitt and Reick. I'm probably in big trouble. But the timing seemed so right. I certainly went beyond my normal authority when I suggested a swap. What will Schmitt and Reick think if I can't get permission for the trade? Will they still allow me to bring supplies to our men on a regular basis? I've probably just messed up the whole arrangement. And our boys in the prison camps will suffer for my blunder.

When Hodges returned to 94th's headquarters, he immediately regretted mentioning his far-fetched proposal to the German officers. He contacted officials at the International Red Cross to tell them what he had done.

"You've overstepped your boundaries, Mr. Hodges!" they told him. "We've never heard of or dealt with such an exchange like this! Especially on such a large scale! Hodges, you are talking about exchanging seventy-nine prisoners! That's never been done before! Ever!"

"The Germans seemed open to the idea," Hodges said in his defense.

"We will think and talk about this, Hodges," they said. "But this is a unique situation. We usually deal with small prisoner exchanges, and they are conducted by the highest military levels and through neutral intermediaries. And they take a lot of time to complete. We might exchange one or two prisoners at a time, and they are usually repatriations of seriously wounded combatants. But large prisoner exchanges in the hands of a single American Red Cross representative? That's ridiculous! We don't do things that way!"

That afternoon Andy waited to be summoned to Colonel Bergquist's office. He knew Bergquist would not be happy.

Why didn't I just keep my big mouth shut?! What was I thinking when I proposed a POW swap?! I WASN'T thinking—that's the problem! I don't know if the Americans can agree with each other about it, much less work on exchange plans with the enemy—and in the middle of a war! How in the world did I think this could possibly work?!

Hodges thought about all the people that would be involved in making this decision:

Major General Harry Malony and the 94th Infantry Division, SHAEF (Supreme Headquarters Allied Expeditionary Force), the Geneva Convention, the American Red Cross, the International Red Cross, General Wilhelm Fahrmbacher, and maybe numerous others I don't even know about!

He rolled his eyes to the ceiling. *Why did I think it would ever work?! There are far too many cooks in this kitchen to make anything like this possibly happen!*

Hodges heard nothing from the colonel until the next morning, when he was ordered to come immediately to Bergquist's office.

The colonel said nothing, but he looked Hodges squarely in the face with a deadpan expression, and then shook his head from side to side.

"Hodges," he said. "What in the Sam Hill have you done?!"

"I'm sorry, sir. It just seemed like the right thing to suggest at the time. I know I should have checked with you first before I said anything. I'm truly sorry, sir. I hope I haven't done damage beyond repair."

"Well I don't know where you came up with this wild idea about a massive prisoner exchange," Bergquist said, "but Malony has just given his permission to go ahead with it!"

The young ARC representative's mouth dropped open, and for a few seconds, he just stared at Bergquist and blinked his eyes.

"Permission granted?! Major General Malony said YES?! And he said yes already?!" Hodges asked, his jaw still dropped.

"Close your mouth, Andy," Bergquist said. "Yes, he gave his permission. He also gave his requirements."

"Yes, sir," Hodges said and noticeably joined his lips.

"This exchange must be on a man-for-man, rank-for-rank basis," the colonel said. "And Andy, let me quote Malony: 'Put Andy Hodges in charge of this exchange. Tell him to make sure it goes smoothly and according to the rules of the Geneva Convention.'"

"Yes, sir," Hodges said.

"Andy, this exchange will be heavily scrutinized by people everywhere. No embarrassing mess-ups! It's not just *your* head on the chopping block, but mine, too! Just bring our boys home. Understand?! We cannot disappoint or fail Malony!"

"Yes, sir! I'll do my best, sir," Hodges said and swallowed hard.

Hodges knew that, according to Malony, it was now "his baby."

He left the colonel's office still shaking his head in disbelief.

I don't believe it! The exchange is on! Our boys will be saved!

Then Bergquist's words, quoting the general, rang in his head like a loud clanging bell:

"Put Andy Hodges in charge . . . Tell him to make sure it goes smoothly . . ."

Hodges drew in a long, deep breath and blew it out slowly, deliberately, through his lips.

What in the world have I gotten myself into?!

He then made arrangements for two more trips to meet with Schmitt and Reick to prepare for the exchange between Allied and Axis prisoners of war.

Late that night Andy wrote a letter to his wife. He wanted to tell her everything that had happened that day, but he knew he couldn't.

"Darling," he wrote, "I think you know I miss you very much, but I don't think you could truly imagine how terribly much. Honey, it will be so wonderful when we are together again. That is all I can think of lately. Goodnight darling. I love you."

5 November 1944, Lorient Naval Hospital

Dental officer William Reynolds lay in the Lorient Naval Hospital barely able to see without his eyeglasses. His crushed foot, pulsating with sharp pain, proved the least of his worries.

Six days after his ambulance was blown up by a land mine, he still had no idea what had happened to his companions, physician Le Barre and driver/corpsman Spencer.

If they survived, no doubt the Krauts captured them, too. I wonder if anyone knows I'm alive and here in this hospital.

Oberleutnant Schmitt had visited him once in the hospital and mentioned something about a Red Cross rep and a possible prisoner exchange. Reynolds was impressed with Schmitt, noticing he was an energetic individual with an assured, precise manner and excellent English.

He flagged a nurse's attention and, using hand motions, requested a pencil and piece of paper. Putting the blank sheet close to his face, he scratched out a letter to the "American Representative, International Red Cross."

Whoever that is, I hope he somehow receives this letter and will help me! I need my spare eyeglasses. And I want to know what Schmitt meant about a possible prisoner exchange. Maybe he'll know something about it.

Reynolds began to write:

"Dear Sir: I am an American Dental officer captured together with Lt. Norman Le Barre M.A.C. and Pvt. Orville Spencer Medical Corpsman. We sincerely hope that a POW exchange can be arranged.

"I am slightly wounded and am at present separated from my two comrades to receive medical care.

"If an exchange should be impossible, I would appreciate it greatly if you would contact my unit and procure for me my extra eyeglasses. I have 10% vision and mine are broken. There is one pair in my val-a-pac and another in my footlocker. Both are silver rimmed. I mention this because I also have in my footlocker a gold-rimmed pair which is not to my prescription.

"I will be very grateful for anything you may be able to do for me. Very truly yours, William J. Reynolds"

He folded the letter, put it in the hands of a nurse, and implored her with pleading eyes.

"Please get this to the Red Cross," he whispered.

From the look on her face, she seemed to understand. She smiled, took the letter, and slipped it into her skirt pocket.

Several days later, Hodges read the "Dear Sir" letter he had received from Dr. Reynolds. He reread the first and third paragraphs.

How in the world could this officer, injured and laid up in a German hospital, know about my negotiations with Lorient about a possible prisoner exchange?

FIFTEEN

THE CONDITIONS

Mid-November 1944

Oberleutnant Schmitt met with Andy Hodges on two more occasions in the small town of Le Magouer on the edge of the River Etel. Over several hours, the two men worked out the complicated details for the prisoners' exchange, now tentatively set for November 16.

When they stood to leave the corner table at the café, the Oberleutnant extended his right hand.

"Under different circumstances, Andy, I should like to hear more from you," Schmitt said.

Hodges nodded and smiled, taking the officer's hand.

"Thank you," he said.

Later Schmitt met with Reick and Oberst Otto Borst, the Commander of the German Atlantic Fortress at Lorient (or the Atlantikfestung Festungskommandant of Lorient), to discuss the details of a letter dated November 10, 1944, they had received from Bergquist.

Schmitt read the letter aloud to the others:

"1. This Headquarters concurs in the agreement to exchange prisoners of war in accordance with the terms discussed by your representative and Mr. Andrew Hodges of the American Red Cross.

"2. It is the understanding of this Headquarters that the terms of exchange will be as follows:

"a. That the rules for the exchange of prisoners of war as prescribed in the Geneva Convention will be strictly adhered to.

"b. That the exchange will take place at 0900, Thursday, 16 November 1944, in the vicinity of Etel and Le Magouer.

"c. That the exchange be conducted on a number for number, rank for rank, disability for disability, and condition for condition basis.

"d. That all prisoners included in this exchange will be volunteers.

"e. That prior to the actual exchange three (3) officer representatives of your command, one (1) to be a medical officer, will be met by Mr. Hodges and escorted to Etel to inspect the German prisoners of war. In turn you will conduct three (3) American officer representatives, one (1) a medical officer, to Le Magouer to inspect the American prisoners of war.

"f. Upon completion of the inspection ten (10) American prisoners of war will be transported to Etel and ten (10) German prisoners of war will be returned. This process to be repeated until the entire exchange is completed.

"g. That all firing in the area—Fort Louis, Nostang, and Carnac—be suspended for a period of six (6) hours beginning at 0900, 16 November 1944, and ending at 1500, 16 November 1944.

"3. It is requested that your concurrence to the above stated terms be indicated by endorsement hereon.

"From the Commanding General: Colonel Earl Bergquist."

Schmitt passed the letter to Borst.

"I have no problem taking this to General Fahrmbacher," Borst said. "But we shall insist that all German prisoners be volunteers—they must have no second thoughts about returning to combat, and a German doctor will examine and declare them physically fit and combat-ready. We won't be nursing sick soldiers. They must be returned to the front lines and be fit to fight for the Fatherland."

"I would also offer one more stipulation," Reick said. "At the beginning of the exchange, we insist that the Amis allow the German prisoners to be released and transported to our lines first."

"Agreed," Borst said. "I will contact Fahrmbacher."

Later that day, Schmitt, Reick, and Borst met again.

"The general concurs," Borst told them. "These arrangements will be made and the exchange will occur as planned on 16 November."

SIXTEEN

ON THE EVE OF THE EXCHANGE

Wednesday P.M., 15 November 1944

Andy Hodges couldn't sleep. He had too much on his mind, too many details swimming around in his head about the next day's exchange. Everything had to be perfect, flawless, and smooth. On his dresser, next to his ARC lapel pins, Red Cross flags, and medic's helmet, rested a pair of silver-rimmed eyeglasses for a nearsighted dentist. He hoped he was ready for the big day.

The ball was in his court. Not only was he accountable to chief of staff Colonel Bergquist, but also to Major General Malony.

"Andy, as the ARC senior field director for this division, this is your baby. Handle it," Malony had told him when he handed him Sarsfield's letter.

Hodges had delivered the food, clothes, and other supplies to the POWs imprisoned at Lorient and Île de Groix. And now he was responsible for their liberation! He took a deep breath and prayed everything would go right. Smoothly, with no embarrassments, no head-chopping.

Please! No surprises! Too much riding on this baby! Gotta make it work!

Hodges ran through his mind for the umpteenth time the host of possible screwups—the many things that could, and well might, go wrong.

And these are just the ones I've thought of!

The American and German officers. I will be introducing Bergquist to Borst and Schmitt. I don't know Borst from Adam. I'm sure he didn't get to be a colonel by being a nice guy. What if he's old school Prussian or a heel-clicking, nose-in-the-air Nazi snot? Time will tell. Well, at least I know it'll take a lot to rile Bergquist. He keeps his cool even when he's burning mad. And he wants to keep his head, too, as well as mine.

And what about the POWs? Will Borst allow all the prisoners to leave? Or will he be selective and hold some back for his own purposes? I'm sure Borst's no dummy. I trust Schmitt—as much as I can trust a German officer—but can I trust Borst? Who knows? Probably not. He might make big trouble.

Then there's our wounded POWs in the Lorient Hospital. How will the injured be transported, and in what shape will they arrive? Will the Germans have enough ambulances and medical staff to bring them to Le Magouer in one piece? Can we get them safely across the river? The French boat isn't exactly a hospital ship.

Hodges rolled over in bed and put the pillow over his head. His mind raced at the kaleidoscope of appalling and unpredictable possibilities.

A six-hour cease-fire. This show takes place in an active combat zone. Like the troopers say, "There's always that ten percent who don't get the word!" What if some guy drops his rifle and it goes off? Or some German gets his cease-fire dates mixed up, or an American with an itchy trigger finger fires at the first German he's ever seen with a weapon? What if a German or some GI lets off a round or two during the exchange? One side will think the other side tricked them, or that the cease-fire has fallen through. Then our quiet little exchange site will become a full-fledged battleground again!

Hodges sat up in bed.

"Stop it!" he said to himself aloud. "You've got enough to worry about without worrying about THAT!"

He stretched out on his bed, staring at the ceiling. But he couldn't turn off his racing mind.

The boat. What if . . .

Hodges had hired a twenty-foot-long boat from M. Francois Jaffré, a local French fisherman. Powered by an old, two-cylinder diesel engine, it could hold about fifteen people, including crew, at one time—if they were standing and packed like sardines. Not perfect, but the best he could do under the circumstances. He could find few French fishermen willing to take part in such a risky endeavor.

What if my boatman turns yellow and doesn't show? We'll have no way to transport the POWs. Or what if he's late, and we can't move all the prisoners before the cease-fire ends? Or what if the old engine won't start? Or it breaks down before we move all the POWs? Do we have enough diesel to make the number of trips? We've got some extra fuel. Maybe the Germans have some, too. No, can't bank on that.

Hodges made a mental note to take extra fuel.

Will a few extra gallons be enough? Maybe I should take more. Let's see—fifteen people to a boat, including the crew, American and German officers, medics, guards . . . and the wounded on stretchers—that'll take up more room . . . how many trips . . . we'll just have to see; too many variables.

Hodges rubbed his forehead. He was too dog-tired to do the math. He'd done the numbers a hundred times already.

He also worried about the German POWs in the prison camp at Rennes. They were fed decently and treated well.

What if they don't want to part with Uncle Sam's largesse? Why go fight for the Führer—the very one that caused them to be surrounded by the enemy in this forsaken and forgotten fortress? If we can't get enough German volunteers, will they go through with the swap? Or back out entirely?

The Germans demanded their POWs be exchanged on a volunteer basis only. Hodges knew the Kraut POWs could withdraw at the last minute if they saw fit. He also recalled that a German doctor would examine each volunteer to make sure he was healthy enough to return to combat—no matter what his rank.

What will be their medical criteria? For all I know they might decline a POW with a toothache or runny nose. And every German POW the doctors declare unfit and refuse means one of our boys will have to remain in Lorient. It's a man-for-man exchange. Who'll choose which American POWs to leave behind? That, thank goodness, clearly won't be my call!

Hodges realized he could do nothing about any of this now at the eleventh hour. He had made the best possible arrangements he could, considering the time constraints.

Well, whatever happens will happen.

Hodges had heard that George Tucker, a reporter with the Associated Press, as well as scores of military and civilian reporters and cameramen from Europe and the United States, would be there to record the details of the exchange and share it with the world.

Get ready, world, a gimpy halfback from Geneva County, and an "expert" on prisoner exchanges, will demonstrate how one should be performed flawlessly. I have done so many, no wonder they want me to do this one! Just wait till they find out that this exchange will be my first! What in the Sam Hill have I gotten myself into?!

Still in the hospital, and having no word about Le Barre and Spencer, Lieutenant Reynolds recalled Schmitt's visit to talk with him. He wondered about the negotiations with the Red Cross concerning a possible prisoner exchange that Schmitt had briefly mentioned.

"Go for it!" Reynolds had exclaimed to Schmitt in a voice louder than he realized. The other patients looked at him with expressions that seemed both curious and annoyed.

Days passed and Reynolds heard nothing more about the exchange. He decided the plan had fallen through. He'd also gotten no response to his November 5 letter. He figured it likely never reached the Red Cross. He knew it was a long shot anyway.

Reynolds's thoughts were interrupted by a nurse bringing him a bowl of cabbage soup and a piece of black bread smeared with lard—the same fare he had eaten at noon. But he was hungry, and it was food.

Later that night, he looked around at his fellow patients, some snoring loudly, others mumbling in their sleep. He tried to focus on an object he noticed on the dresser beside his bed. It looked like a straight razor.

How unusual.

. . .

For hours that night at the 94th headquarters, Major General Malony paced the floor in worry and frustration. He thought back over his long military career: the horrors of the Great War, the trenches, the dead and wounded hanging on the barbed wire fences. Then he brightened as he recalled the highlights: coming home, a surprise visit to the White House, and receiving the Army Distinguished Service Medal from President Woodrow Wilson. From the outhouse to the White House!

"To Lieutenant Colonel Harry James Malony . . . for exceptionally meritorious and distinguished services to the Government of the United States, in a duty of great responsibility during World War I."

He had memorized the words of his award, authorized by an Act of Congress on July 9, 1918, just six months after the award had been established.

"Lieutenant Colonel Malony successfully organized and administered the many complex and difficult operations connected with the arming and equipping of airplanes for service at the front, displaying sound judgment and acting with energy and initiative in times of emergency."

Those were exciting days to remember for Malony—the Great War. He never dreamed he'd be active again in his lifetime in yet another world war.

"He worked self-sacrificing and devotedly that there might be no delays, overcoming serious obstacles by the exercise of good judgment and through understanding of conditions in the American Expeditionary Forces."[1]

He had enjoyed the attention the medal brought him. It didn't hurt in those peacetime years either. Made him a national hero. But he knew if this prisoner exchange went badly, the public would remember the event as his failure, and all the rest—the medals and achievements—would be forgotten bygones.

I've put a heavy responsibility on the shoulders of that young, inexperienced American Red Cross officer. I hope I haven't made a huge mistake. And Bergquist sure better have all his i's dotted and his t's crossed, or . . . or . . .

Malony stopped pacing, pounded his fist hard on the nearby bed table, closed his eyes, and shook his head.

The American POW Camp, Rennes, France

"Sir, the German prisoners are packed and prepared to travel," the senior NCO reported to the camp's CO.

"How many Germans volunteered to be exchanged?" the CO asked.

"A lot less than we'd hoped, sir. Just about a hundred."

"Only a hundred out of five thousand?!" the commanding officer exclaimed.

"Yes, sir. Most don't want to leave," the NCO said. "When I told them of the prisoner exchange, that only volunteers could take part, and they must be willing to fight in the front lines, there were a few smiles, but most just sat there silently."

"But we do have a hundred, don't we?"

"Yes, sir. These are the ones still loyal to the Führer."

"Well, you know what they say—'you can lead a horse to water, but you can't make him drink.' I'm just glad we have a hundred volunteer horses— or maybe jackasses. Just get me enough Krauts to swap for our people! I don't want to leave any of our men behind at Lorient."

Île de Groix Prison Camp

Private First Class George Boyd smiled and said a quick "thank you" when the elderly German guard made his nightly rounds, grinning and wishing each Ami prisoner the same thing he said every night: *"Gut essen, gut schlafen, und gut stuhlgang."* ["Good eating, good sleeping, and good bowel movements."]

After the room became dark and quiet, Boyd leaned down and whispered to Glixon in the bunk below him.

"Glixon, are you asleep?" Boyd asked.

"Are you kidding, Boyd?!" Glixon whispered. "Can't sleep. With the exchange happening tomorrow, too much to think about."

"I know," Boyd said. "I'm as wide awake as a hoot owl."

"Do you really think the Krauts will let us go?" Glixon asked.

"Who knows? The whole thing might be a Kraut trick," Boyd said. "Wouldn't surprise me."

"Maybe it's just a rumor—all this exchange business," Glixon said, tossing on his side.

"Well, we'll know in a few hours," Boyd said.

"Get some sleep, you guys!" Connatser called from a nearby bunk. "Tomorrow's a big day. You'll need your energy."

"So you think the exchange is really going to come off?" Glixon asked Connatser.

"That's what I hear," Connatser said.

"Why on earth would the Krauts let us go?" Boyd asked.

"Don't know. Don't much care," Connatser said. "Maybe they're tired of us. Or tired of sharing their delicious chow. Maybe they want the rest of our Red Cross food and smokes. Doesn't matter. Stop beating your gums, and go to sleep!"

Boyd couldn't sleep. As much as he hated prison life on Île de Groix, he felt lucky to be alive. He'd survived the ambush of October 2, and he still had his lanky legs attached to the rest of his body. Others weren't so fortunate.

If this is a trick, the Krauts might kill us all tomorrow. They'll line us up and then throw a bunch of potato mashers at us. Why would they be willing to let us go? What's in it for them?

Boyd sat up and looked around the room. He noticed that no one was asleep—not Glixon or Connatser. Not Brady, Harden, Shulman, Harrington, Stewart, or the letter writer who had started the whole string of events, James Sarsfield. Or anyone else.

Are they as worried about tomorrow as I am?

American POW Sergeant Charles E. Hanson lay in the Lorient Naval Hospital recovering from a recent rifle wound to his left forearm. The native Kentuckian wondered why the German medical personnel were treating him with such a rare kindness that day—unlike all the days before.

When a hefty English-speaking nurse walked by his bed, he asked: "Hey! What's going on? Why are all the big wheels so nice to the American patients today?"

"Oh, haven't you heard?" the nurse said. "You and the other Amis are leaving us tomorrow."

"What do you mean?" Hanson asked. "Where are we going?"

"You're going to be swapped for our German prisoners. I guess you're going home . . . or to another hospital . . . or back into battle . . . or somewhere. All I know—this is your last night here," she said. She put her fingers to her lips and pretended to blow him a goodbye kiss.

Is she kidding me? Swapped with Germans? I've never heard of that happening.

"I'll be right back," she said, then turned around, and walked away.

Hanson called to a sleeping Trachtenberg and Rader in nearby beds.

"Trachtenberg! Rader! Wake up! Do you know anything about a POW exchange tomorrow?! That nurse broad . . ."

Before he could wake them, the nurse reappeared. She carried a tray of oysters on the half shell.

"Here, a surprise!" she said. "One oyster for each of you. A special occasion!"

Trachtenberg and Rader woke up, and the men slurped down the unexpected and slimy midnight meal. The nurse took a pen and signed the inside of each empty shell.

"Something to remember me by—a memento of our time together," she said, fluttered her eyelashes, and handed the shells back to them.

"What's that wacky woman talking about?" Trachtenberg asked Rader.

"I have no idea," Rader replied. "Why would we want to remember that nitwit anyway?"

"We're supposedly leaving this place tomorrow," Sergeant Hanson told the two men. "Some kind of prisoner exchange or something."

"Baloney!" Rader said. "Dream on, Hanson!"

Rader and Trachtenberg slipped the inscribed oyster shells under their pillows, pulled up the covers, and went to sleep.

Oberleutnant Schmitt had no intention of trying to sleep that night. Lighting a cigarette, he sat in a straight chair, smoked, and waited for the long night to end.

Hodges and I have worked together on every single detail of the exchange, yet it is Borst who will be supervising it tomorrow. I understand military protocol, but Borst? Of course, he has the ear of Fahrmbacher, so . . .

Schmitt pictured the haughty Oberst in his mind—the square head, the gray stubbled hair cut short, the square body, thick neck, pale face, bulbous nose, head held high, his chest thrust out displaying the Iron Cross First and Second Class, Infantry Assault Badge, plus several campaign ribbons.

With Borst's quick temper, he might unravel all the careful negotiations Andy Hodges and I have so carefully worked out. I know he's secretly proud he was born in London, but that doesn't mean he's comfortable speaking in English. He was in England only as a child. What if he makes a mistake, says the wrong thing, and perhaps insults Bergquist or Hodges?

The Oberleutnant tapped his fingers on the table.

Fahrmbacher will be closely monitoring the event. I hear that his photographer and Kriegsmarine Observer *reporter will be on hand. If all goes well, we shall give them a worthy, perhaps historic performance. If not? I can't bear to think about what will happen.*

He lit another cigarette and waited for daybreak.

SEVENTEEN

THE EXCHANGE, PART 1

Thursday, 16 November 1944, Lorient Sector

After a fitful night, Andy Hodges dressed, grabbed his gear and a can of diesel, as well as a number of other things he might need, and motored to Etel. Bergquist, two staff members, and Associated Press correspondent George Tucker, planned to follow behind him shortly.

By 0900, the cease-fire truce had gone into effect. American military police met Hodges at Etel with the German POWs who had volunteered to be exchanged for Allied prisoners. They were a mixed bag: some Luftwaffe, still wearing the blue-gray single-breasted, open-collared jackets and black leather boots, but mostly they were Landsers [*Landsknecht*], young, low-ranking infantry soldiers, some with overcoats, most without; some with garrison caps and/or field caps. The only things missing were the bucket helmets. Those were long gone.

"How many volunteers do we have?" Hodges asked one of the police officers.

"Not as many as we had hoped for, sir."

Hodges didn't like the sound of that, but he had no time to count the

Germans. They were placed inside a large, one-story school and guarded by helmeted American military police.

I hope we have enough to exchange! Otherwise we'll have some disappointed GIs!

Walking to the edge of the stone quay, Hodges looked across the river for the boat he had hired. Francois Jaffré was supposed to be there promptly at 0900. Hodges checked his watch. 0905.

Blasted! Can't be late! Too much at stake!

Hodges began to pace up and down the long quay. He again checked his watch. 0915.

Andy saw Bergquist and his companions pull up at the wharf. Hodges walked to the colonel's jeep, greeted him, and briefed him on the status of the operation.

While Hodges informed Bergquist of the morning's events, he again looked at his watch. 0920. He glanced across the water. Still no boat.

What if Jaffré doesn't show?! Or what if the boat's motor has a problem? Too late to find another boat and still ferry all the prisoners across the river before the cease-fire ends.

"Are our men to be exchanged assembled in Le Magouer?" Bergquist asked.

"They are supposed to be assembled and all ready for the exchange, sir. I'll cross over to Le Magouer, make sure everything is in order, and return with the German officers in charge of the exchange, Oberst Borst and Oberleutnant Schmitt. You can meet them and review the details before the exchange begins," Hodges explained.

"That sounds good to me, Andy," Bergquist said. "Where's the boat?"

Hodges swallowed hard and checked his watch. 0925. "It will be here any moment, sir," he said.

"Good work, Andy!" the colonel said. "I knew I could depend on you!"

0900, On the Edge of the River Etel

Francois Jaffré sat in his small fishing boat in a quiet spot at the river's edge about a mile from the Etel wharf. A black cap sat atop his weathered, wrinkled face. He turned off the motor. He needed to rethink the agreement he had made earlier with the American from the Red Cross.

Ma famille a besoin de l'argent. [Yes, my family needs the money.]

The fisherman wondered if he had made a mistake when he agreed to work with Hodges in this prisoner exchange.

Is the money worth maybe getting shot? They say they've called a cease-fire. No shooting during the exchange. But who trusts the Germans? I've seen what they're capable of.

For a full ten minutes the Frenchman argued with himself, trying to decide what to do.

Devrais-je aller? [Should I go?] Ou dois-je rester? [Or should I stay?] Surely my life is worth more than a few francs.

0927

Andy Hodges stood on the wharf at Etel and looked at the scene behind him. A line of helmeted military police wearing heavy overcoats guarded a schoolhouse full of German POW soldiers. Bergquist spoke to several reporters and posed for cameras. Flashbulbs popped all around him. Hodges knew that on the other side of the River Etel, Oberst Borst, Oberleutnant Schmitt, and seventy-nine American POWs, guarded by Germans, waited impatiently just beyond the dock in Le Magouer for the exchange to begin.

Where's the dang boat?! I could swim across the river faster!

Hodges took a deep breath and held it.

What if Jaffré has chickened out?! What will we do? Try explaining that to Bergquist! And how will Bergquist ever explain that to Malony? The reporters will splash the failed exchange story across the front pages of the world's newspapers.

Andy felt the knot twist tighter in his stomach.

If this is a disaster, by tomorrow the whole world will be laughing at the Red Cross, the U.S. Army's 94th Infantry Division, at Colonel Bergquist, Major General Malony, and that big-mouth redneck from South Alabama that started the whole thing in the first place!

0928. Just then, in the distance, Hodges heard the groaning thud-thud-thud of a diesel motor. A minute later, he watched the old fishing boat pull up to the quay's wide stone steps.

Thank goodness he came!

Hodges jumped from the steps into the boat.

"Let's go!" he shouted to Jaffré, who sat at the stern, his hand on the rudder. Hodges draped a Red Cross flag on each side of the boat and set the can of diesel in the stern. Jaffré pushed off from the dock with a long pole and turned the vessel toward Le Magouer.

And not a moment too soon.

EIGHTEEN

THE EXCHANGE, PART 2

Thursday, 16 November 1944, Lorient Sector

Andy Hodges sprang from the boat in Le Magouer as Jaffré turned off the motor and secured the vessel to the dock. The young German sentry at the guard station met Hodges. After so many visits to Le Magouer, Hodges noticed the sentry warming up to him, as if the lad looked forward to his visits.

Andy noticed that the boy held his rifle too tightly, and that his hands trembled.

Poor Klaus. He's nervous, too.

Schmitt and Borst came forward and greeted Hodges with the customary *Hitlergruß*. After formal introductions, the Oberleutnant introduced Hodges to the team of German doctors who planned to accompany them to Etel and physically examine each German volunteer. Each physician wore a white medical jacket and carried a large black bag.

"Are we ready to leave now?" Borst asked Hodges.

"Almost," Hodges said and smiled. "First I want to see our men."

"I don't see that that is necessary," the Oberst said impatiently.

"I must insist, Oberst Borst," Hodges said kindly, but firmly. "I, too, have my orders."

Borst clenched his jaw and replied coldly: "Certainly, Captain Hodges. If you must."

Schmitt stood behind Borst. Hodges saw the Oberleutnant lower his head and slightly smile.

I'm sure Schmitt knew I'd insist on seeing our men. He already knows me well.

"Bring the Americans!" Borst barked to the German guards.

Hodges smiled as he watched the large group of prisoners stream out of a nearby warehouse. They were dirty, their hair and beards bushy. He recognized the Red Cross–issued clothes they wore, new uniforms that hung like loose shrouds on their skinny frames. But they were all smiles.

They could use a bath and shave and better-fitting uniforms, but they're in good spirits. I'm glad to see that!

They whooped and cheered when they saw Andy Hodges in his dark Red Cross blouse with tan trousers. Hodges broke into a wide grin, but he didn't take time to mingle.

No time now. I'll do that later.

"Thanks for the food and clothes and smokes!" they cried out to him again and again.

Then they flipped questions at him with the speed of a machine gun firing rounds:

"Who won the World Series?!" they shouted.

"Who won the election?!" they called.

They yelled out more questions, and joyously slapped one another on the back.

"Is it true the American Army is halfway to Berlin?!" a POW asked.

Scores of beribboned German officers in baggy riding breeches and glistening high boots stood around and watched with some bewilderment as the Americans POWs shouted out cheers of gratitude.

Andy Hodges faced the group of Americans, raised his hands to quiet them, and said:

"President Franklin D. Roosevelt, by four hundred and thirty-two electoral votes!"

The men broke out in a loud, boisterous chant: "Roosevelt! Roosevelt! Roosevelt!"

Hodges again raised his hands, and the group calmed down.

"St. Louis Cardinals over the St. Louis Browns—four games to two!" he said.

Further cheering erupted, and at the same time, a deafening booing rose from the crowd. The confused guards, not understanding the sudden chaos, and fearing a riot, stepped forward and aimed their rifles at the prisoners.

Hodges quieted the crowd, decided not to answer their "Berlin question," and then explained briefly the plans for the day.

"Men," he said, "I ask for good behavior and an extra dose of patience today. This operation will take some time. We have one boat, and there are only so many we can squeeze in at a time. I promise I'll be back for you—all of you."

Then Hodges, along with Borst, Schmitt, and the team of German doctors, climbed into the boat. Hodges noted several Kriegsmarine [German naval] officers in their midnight-blue uniforms. Some had cameras. The word had definitely gotten around.

"Let's go," Hodges told the boatman.

Francois Jaffré attempted to crank the motor. Once. Twice.

"*Ancien moteur sans valeur!*" Hodges heard him mumble. On the third time, the two cylinders of the "old worthless motor" sprang to life, pouring out choking black smoke and the foul smell of diesel.

By 1030, the boat had crossed the river and reached the Etel wharf. Introductions were made among Bergquist, Schmitt, and Borst. American MPs led a small group of German POWs from the schoolhouse. The prisoners looked healthy and clean, with clipped hair and freshly shaven faces. They formed a line, standing side by side quietly so that German doctors could examine each one.

Hodges noticed that most of the Germans looked at the ground, did not smile, and asked no questions—a night-and-day contrast to the jubilant Americans waiting across the River Etel.

The doctors thoroughly checked each man—head to toe: eyes, teeth, gums, ears, arms, hands, legs, knees, feet.

"*Nein!*" one doctor shouted and rudely pushed a POW out of line.

Hodges glanced at Bergquist.

That German POW looked plenty healthy, yet the doctor rejected him. I sure hope we have enough Germans to pass the doctors' tests and swap evenly for our boys.

Andy kept his eyes on the colonel.

If the colonel's worried, he sure doesn't show it.

Looking at the teeth of another German POW, a doctor growled "*Nein! Nein!*" and motioned him to leave the line.

Hodges swallowed hard. Only ten men had passed the medical tests so far.

"Bring out the next group!" Borst ordered.

Bergquist nodded to the NCO in charge of the MPs.

Twenty-four German POWs lined up. Doctors repeated their routine. Hodges heard what sounded like a chorus of "*neins*" and saw more POWs exit the line. The prisoners did not appear to be unhappy at this turn of events. In fact, Andy thought most of them seemed relieved to be rejected by German doctors.

Hodges counted the accepted men so far.

Thirty-one men. We need forty-eight more volunteers.

He wondered how many POWs were still in the schoolhouse.

"Another group!" Borst snapped, turning to the American colonel.

"*Nein! Nein!*" the doctors said after more examinations. More Germans stepped to the side, unaccepted for some medical reason. None appeared downhearted at the news.

In his mind, Hodges quickly counted those that had passed the exams so far. *Fifty-one accepted. Twenty-eight to go.*

Hodges sidled discreetly to Bergquist's aide, a young captain.

"Any idea how many POWs are still left in the schoolhouse?" he whispered.

"Can't say for sure," the officer said. "But I think this next group is the last."

How will we tell our men in Le Magouer they must remain in the prison camp? How will we choose who gets exchanged and who stays behind? Of course, the wounded will get priority, but after that?

"Next group!" Borst called. He looked at his watch. "How much longer will this process take?" he asked one of the guards.

"We are almost finished, sir," an NCO responded from the schoolhouse door. "These are the last prisoners."

Hodges counted the final men as they marched out, stood in line, and waited to be examined.

Exactly twenty-eight men! If the German doctors reject even one of them, we'll have to leave at least one of our boys behind at Île de Groix.

Schmitt looked at Hodges, shook his head, and bit his lower lip.

Looks like Schmitt's feeling the pressure, too. He must want this exchange to succeed as much as I do. Those Kraut docs are really picky.

One by one, the doctors continued their exams of the prisoners. The first five POWs passed, then the next five. Hodges listened closely for the *"Neins!"* he half expected to hear from the German doctors. The next ten men passed the test.

Only eight more men to go. We might just make it!

The doctors examined each of the remaining POWs. The minutes seemed like hours. Hodges tapped his foot as he waited to hear the *"Nein!"* or the acceptance. The senior doctor—a major—conferred with the others, and shook his head. The men—all eight of them—had passed. They had their seventy-nine POWs, the exact number needed to exchange all the American prisoners.

Hodges exhaled, glanced at Schmitt, and smiled.

Thank goodness that's done! Now on with the exchange! No GI left behind!

Suddenly Hodges heard a murmuring among the prisoners, and then several POWs spoke in German all at once:

"I cannot do this!" a short, stocky Landser announced loudly. "Take me back to the American prison camp!"

At the far end, a lanky blond called out: "I also have changed my mind."

Then another shouted: "I, too, will not go! Return me also!"

By the end of the next two or three minutes, eight German prisoners had refused to be exchanged, and asked to be returned to the prison camp at Rennes. Borst, ashen-faced, touched with his finger the Iron Cross that adorned his barrel chest and addressed the men in German, using a low, slow, controlled voice.

The POWs looked down at the ground and seemed embarrassed, ashamed. But not one man changed his mind and volunteered for exchange.

Schmitt stood beside Borst—erect and still, eyes wide, seemingly not daring to move. Hodges understood nothing the men or Borst said, but the message was clear. Eight POWs had backed out, and Borst was not happy.

The MPs removed the withdrawing Germans and took them back inside the school.

"We are finished here!" the Oberst shouted to Bergquist. "We do not have the necessary number of volunteers. I am canceling the entire prisoner exchange."

Hodges felt his heart suddenly race, and he struggled to breathe.

What?! Cancel the exchange?! You can't do that! You just can't do that!

He thought about the seventy-nine men filled with hope and waiting in Etel, watching the distant shoreline for Hodges's boat to come and carry them back to American lines. Just as he had promised them.

How will I tell them that the exchange is canceled? Called off? Won't happen?!

Colonel Bergquist looked at Hodges, smiled, and winked.

Don't worry, young man. I've been at this business for a long time. I've got things under control.

Turning to Borst, Bergquist said: "Oberst Borst, a good commander always maintains adequate reserves."

Borst looked puzzled and said nothing.

Bergquist then turned to his MPs and commanded: "Bring me ten more German POWs!"

From a small building to the right of the schoolhouse, MPs escorted the additional prisoners to the colonel. The men looked clean, healthy, and battle-ready.

Bergquist turned to the German doctors and said: "Examine these men!"

Borst's face went blank. Expressionless. Pale.

Doctors checked each POW. They checked out with good reports and none withdrew.

Colonel Bergquist turned to Borst and looked him directly in the eye. "*Now* we are finished here," he said with a firm voice. "We have the necessary number of volunteers, and we are ready to begin the scheduled exchange."

Borst's nostrils flared, and without saying a word, he turned on his heel and walked away.

"Now, let's get this show on the road!" Bergquist said to Andy and smiled.

NINETEEN

THE EXCHANGE, PART 3

Thursday, 16 November 1944, Lorient Sector

Early that morning at the Lorient Naval Hospital, Lieutenant Reynolds had opened his sleep-filled eyes to see the blurred image of a nurse standing over his bed.

"It is time to wake up and dress," the nurse said in halting English.

She dipped a wooden-handled brush into a cup of soapy water and hastily spread suds on Reynolds's upper lip and chin. Then she took the razor from the nearby dresser and shaved his stubbled face.

"What's going on?" he asked.

"Today you are leaving us, Lieutenant Reynolds," she said.

What? Leaving? Maybe this exchange thing is happening after all!

The dentist dressed as quickly as his injured foot would allow him and ate breakfast. Before medics loaded Reynolds into an ambulance, he grabbed his old urine-stained boot.

I may need this.

He grinned, remembering how well the boot had served him—and the truckload of German soldiers—in the past. The white ambulance drove off, and he soon arrived in the small fishing village of Le Magouer.

Is this really happening? Or is this some kind of a trick?

Gray-clad German medics, wearing white Red Cross armbands, placed his stretcher on the ground and covered him with a black woolen blanket. He watched the ambulance drive away. A short time later it returned, and he saw the same medics unload another stretcher, cover the patient with a blanket, and again depart. The trips were repeated until a row of stretchers, filled with wounded POWs, lined the Le Magouer dock.

For a long time he waited with the other injured. No one said a word.

Somehow the pain seems more bearable now that I'm not alone. I wonder what will happen next.

On the Allied side of the river, Andy Hodges watched as German guards began leading German prisoners down the steep stone steps and into the boat. With the returning doctors, German and American officers, only about seven or eight POWs could fit in the small craft. Hodges slipped on his white medic's helmet, the red cross painted on both sides, and stepped into the boat. When they eventually reached the Le Magouer dock and disembarked, German medics immediately picked up the stretchers and began lowering each wounded American into the vessel.

From a list, Hodges read the names of the wounded: "Private First Class David Trachtenberg, Private First Class Bernard Rader . . ." The last name he called was Lieutenant William J. Reynolds. The dentist waved his right hand, his left hand still grasping his boot—just in case.

"Lieutenant Reynolds," Hodges said. "I have something for you."

Andy reached into his front pocket and pulled out a pair of silver-rimmed eyeglasses.

"I think you requested these," he said and slipped them into the dentist's hand.

Reynolds put them on immediately.

"Wonderful!" he exclaimed. "I can finally see! Thank you so much!"

The boat set out across the river.

So far, so good. The diesel motor started on the first crank, no shots fired from either side, no fight—not even an insult—has happened among officers or soldiers. Let's hope the peace and goodwill lasts the rest of the day.

Hodges and the small boat arrived in Etel, unloaded, then filled up with German prisoners, traveled across the river, and emptied its freed POWs in Le Magouer. Then it took a load of American prisoners and Hodges, traveled back across the river, and discharged those POWs in Etel. Back and forth the boat chugged as Hodges rode, nervously checking his watch. Hours had passed. The cease-fire was scheduled to last until 1500. Once the truce ended, the shooting would start again. He knew if they didn't finish transporting the POWs by 1500, they'd be right in the middle of a bloody war zone.

It'll be pushing it to get finished by 1500, but we can't move any faster, and we certainly can't rush with the wounded on board.

Hodges glanced at Schmitt. He, too, was checking his watch.

He's probably thinking the same thing.

The old fishing boat, weighed down with Krauts and Amis, Hodges and Schmitt, the French fisherman and others, poured black smoke from its two-cylinder motor and strained to haul its priceless cargo back and forth across the river.

On one trip to Etel, Hodges heard the old motor sputter.

No! Not the engine. I was afraid of that. Can't quit on us now!

The anxious look on Jaffré's face spoke volumes to Hodges.

He's worried, too. We're too close to the finish line for the old diesel to die on us!

Sputter. Sputter. Spit. The engine went dead. The boat sat still in the water, halfway between its two destinations.

Hodges heard Jaffré mumble: "*L'ancien moteur a mort!*"

Hodges turned to him. "What's wrong?" he asked.

"I do not know!" he answered. "Something in the motor. *Je vous ai dit que le moteur est vieux!*" ["I told you it is quite old!"]

"Can you fix it?!" Hodges asked.

"I hope so!" he replied. "*Je dois trouver le problème premier.* However I must discern the problem before I can fix it."

We'll never make the deadline now. It will take too long to find another boat, even if there is one available. Most of the fishermen in this area are still at sea. And there's no way we can swim the distance to Etel or back to Le Magouer. We're stuck.

Hodges remembered the can of extra diesel he had stored in the boat's stern that morning.

"Francois Jaffré?!" he asked. "Could we be out of fuel?"

A long shot, but worth a try.

"*Aucun!*" ["No!"] Jaffré answered. "*Je ne le crois pas!*" ["I think not."]

"Please check the tank, just for me, okay?" Hodges asked. "I brought extra fuel."

M. Jaffré, to his astonishment, discovered the tank was indeed empty. The boat was quickly refueled, and they continued the journey.

A few minutes before 1500, the exchange had been completed. Bergquist checked the American prisoner list when the last of the GIs finally reached Etel. After the final name had been checked off, he gave a warm welcome to the smiling soldiers.

Later that day, Bergquist talked with Hodges privately: "Andy, what divisions are most of these men from?"

"Most are members of the 301st patrol, captured on 2 October in the ambush. Some are from the 6th Armored Division, the 83rd Infantry Division, and a few other American units that took part in the sweep across Brittany," he replied.

"And how long have these men been imprisoned?"

"Some as long as ninety days, sir. Others fewer than forty-five days."

"Well, some of these men will be going home. Others will be returning to combat," Bergquist said.

That evening Bergquist settled into his office chair, poured a drink, and reflected over the day.

I wish I could give all these POWs a ticket home. They've been through so much. But rules are rules.

The colonel took a long, slow sip from the glass, smiled, and shook his head from side to side.

What an amazing guy Andy Hodges is! I'm recommending him for a Bronze Star. If it weren't for his bad shoulder, he'd have made a splendid officer. Heaven knows we can't get enough officers like him.

He finished his drink. As he dressed for bed, he pondered the daring young man from Alabama, the son of a poor, uneducated horse trader.

Andy Hodges may talk slow. But his brain sure thinks fast!

That night, as Hodges lay in bed and thought back over the day, he recalled an incident that happened that afternoon when the final boatload of American prisoners reached the wharf at Etel.

Andy had stood watching the men help each other climb the stairs leading up to the landing. One of the Americans was an unusually young guy. He later learned his name was Private First Class Louis Winn, from West Virginia. Hodges noticed that Winn carried a duffel bag in one hand and a large box of Oh Henry! candy bars in the other hand. When the soldier reached the top step, he bent over and, without embarrassment, kissed the stone landing.

Andy felt misty-eyed that evening as he remembered the heart-touching image and watching a photographer capture the kiss on film.

I guess that kid's kiss just about sums up the whole amazing day.

Late that evening, General Fahrmbacher received welcome news about the day's prisoner exchange. The general had spent a lifetime in Germany's army, joining at age nineteen, on July 18, 1907. He'd dedicated his life to the Fatherland, serving for decades in numerous capacities, becoming Hitler's highly decorated commanding general of the Army-Corps, Normandie and Brittany. He knew a well-planned, properly orchestrated military event when he heard about one.

He studied himself briefly in the mirror. Slowly he shook his head as he scanned the ribbons and medals: Deutsches Kreuz in Silber, Verwunde-tenabzeichen, Heeresbergführer-Abzeichen, Komturkreuz des Kgl. Ungar, and the coveted *Ritterkreuz*.

Two wars and so many missing comrades.

He adjusted the Knight's Cross of the Iron Cross he wore around his neck. It seemed so long ago when he received it, June 24, 1940, for action in France as Generalleutnant und Kommandeur der 5. Infanterie-Division. In a fast-moving campaign, he'd cut across miles of enemy countryside, and thus had become a hero.

A "courageous military hero"! Now here I am, only four years later, in a for-eign land, bottled up in one of Hitler's fortresses until the end of the war. What a waste!

Fahrmbacher, now fifty-six, a general der artillerie, reflected on the day's successful prisoner exchange, an event he helped bring to pass. He reached for a pen and began scribbling in his diary for others to one day read:

"Thus was accomplished, with much respect and a certain degree of solemnity, the exchange of three officers, two doctors, and seventy-four men at Etel. This exchange provided us with appreciable reinforcement since all the Germans who volunteered for the exchange were seasoned combat veterans."[1]

TWENTY

THE AFTERMATH

The month before, on October 26, 1944, Charles Hanson's family and friends back in the States read in the Washington County, Missouri, newspaper: "News came the last of the week that Charley Hanson, son of Fred Hanson, is missing in action. We hope it is not true. Charley graduated from Belgrade High School and is a boy loved by everyone."

On November 30, 1944, the same newspaper announced: "According to news reaching J. F. Hanson of St. Louis, his son Sgt. Charlie [*sic*] Hanson is back with his division in France after being a prisoner of the Germans for 47 days. Sgt. Hanson had been slightly wounded in the arm. On coming back to the American Army, Charlie said it was like a 'home coming,' after all a growing boy needs about five times as much to eat as he was given while a prisoner and that being a P.W. was 'a shade boring, confining and in general just no good.' "[1]

Sergeant Harrington felt exhilarated to be freed from the German prison camp.

Slapping a news reporter on the back, he shouted to his fellow soldiers: "We're going home, boys! We're free!"

"Sorry, GI," the reporter told him matter-of-factly. "You've been in the slammer only forty-five days. Only a sixty-day confinement entitles you to return to the States."

"What?! Are you sure about that?" Harrington asked.

"Quite sure, soldier," the reporter said. "Pack your bags. You're probably heading for the battle in Germany."

Martial music blared over loudspeakers greeting Private Frank Keenan and the other POWs when they arrived at the 94th's headquarters. After a routine interrogation, they ate, showered, dressed in new uniforms, and bunked down in comfortable tents.

"War's not so bad after all!" Keenan joked with his patrol as the company cook served up three hot square meals for three days, and on time!

"Don't get too used to it, Keenan," the cook said. "Tomorrow you guys are going back to the front line—and back to your foxholes."

Private Harry Glixon received an official greeting from Captain Simmers when he stepped off the bus at division headquarters. Swamped by fellow soldiers, he fielded a number of questions about the October 2 ambush and his life in prison.

"What happened out there?!" someone shouted. "Why did you surrender to the Krauts?!" another asked. "What men were killed?!" "Who was wounded?!" they hollered as Glixon tried to shout answers over the din of yells and blaring music.

"We heard the Krauts held a funeral for our guys," they exclaimed. "Is that really true?" one asked.

"How did the Krauts treat you in the prison camp?" "Did they interrogate you?" "Did they torture you?!" "What did they feed you?!" they asked, their voices growing louder as each tried to drown out the other ones' questions.

"He'll answer your questions later," Simmers called out to the crowds. "Come with me, Private Glixon," he said.

Simmers ushered Glixon into a small room where they were alone and away from the mobs. The young private then noticed a sudden change in Simmers's mood.

"First of all, Private Glixon, you won't be going home to the States," Simmers said. "And second," Simmers laughed, "you'd better not get captured again. If you do, the Krauts will most likely shoot you as a spy! You know too much about them now!"

Why are you laughing? Do you really think that's funny?

"Yes, sir," Glixon said softly.

"You know, Private, after the 2 October ambush, I had put your name in for a Silver Star," Simmers told him.

"Thank you, sir. That's quite an honor," Glixon answered with respect.

"But," Simmers said and sneered, "my request was rejected when they found out you were still alive. Had you been dead, you would have received one of them."

Small price to pay.

"Yes, sir," Glixon responded.

Glixon was given two weeks off, along with Sergeant Connatser and some other men, to battalion reserve, for a period of rest and relaxation.

"Roy," Glixon told Connatser, "I think that you and I are to be recognized for our 'valor' at a divisional parade. Might just be a rumor. "

"You're kidding!" Connatser responded. "If so, I wonder who will make the presentation."

"Don't know. But I hope it's not Hagerty," Glixon said.

"Why not?" Connatser asked.

"Hagerty was the regimental commander that I argued with on 2 October during the ambush. We had a . . . ah . . . 'communication problem.' He refused to let us surrender, and I guess I said some things that I shouldn't have. It's a good thing the radio went dead when it did, or I might be in big trouble."

"We had no choice but to surrender," Connatser said.

"I know, but I don't think Hagerty knew how bad it was," Glixon said.

Several days later, the rumor proved true, and Glixon and Connatser stood straight and tall at the divisional parade, ready to receive the distinguished Purple Heart.

Glixon felt his body tremble and his heart race when the dreaded Colonel Hagerty stepped forward on the field to make the award presentations. A lieutenant followed, carrying a velvet-covered tray that held the awards.

Oh no! I knew it! Why does it have to be Hagerty?! Maybe he won't remember me!

Picking up a Purple Heart, the colonel leaned over and pinned the medal on Connatser. He then moved to Glixon. With the second Purple Heart in his hand, the colonel leaned over to the young soldier and paused, staring at him quizzically.

Why are you taking so long? And why are you smiling? Let's get this over with!

The seconds dragged. Finally the colonel whispered: "Aren't you the radio operator with the Lorient combat patrol?"

Beads of sweat popped out on Glixon's forehead.

He recognizes me. My goose is cooked.

"Yes, sir," Glixon responded, swallowing hard.

Then the young private dared to speak:

"Sir, we had five men dead, more than twenty wounded, and we were out of ammunition. We had no choice but to surrender," he said as he stared the colonel in the eye.

"Is that right?" Hagerty asked, raising his eyebrows. "Well, that's too bad, soldier. Captain Simmers put you in for a Distinguished Service Cross."

"Yes sir, I know," Glixon responded.

"Oh, so you already know this?" the colonel asked. "Do you also know that when your radio went dead, we thought you'd been shot doing your duty? That medal would have been good for the division."

"Yes, sir."

The colonel looked up and smiled for the applauding audience, and then pinned the medal on Glixon's blouse.

"Well, Private, I'll give your company another chance to show its guts," Hagerty whispered into Glixon's ear. "I've returned you to active duty. I'm sure you'll do well in combat now."

The young soldier tried hard to stand straight and at attention. But he felt like he'd been hit in the face with a baseball bat.

Back into combat? How can I stand it?!

His shoulders sagged, and he felt a painful lump lodge in his throat. No matter how hard he swallowed, the mass wouldn't move. His body, mind, and soul felt whipped and bone-tired.

The colonel picked up another item, leaned over, and pinned the Combat Infantry Badge on the startled Glixon.

I didn't expect this one. At least now I feel validated. But more combat? I just hope that one day I make it home alive.

22 November 1944, Thanksgiving Eve, New York, USA

"Philip!" Mrs. Glixon called to her husband. "We have received another telegram from the War Department. It's about Harry!"

Private Harry Glixon's father, Philip, grabbed the telegram from his wife's hand. Just five weeks before, Glixon's parents had received a telegram from the War Department claiming their son was missing in action in France. Mrs. Glixon didn't even know Harry was in France, but had thought he was still in England.

Philip read the telegram and said: "Now the War Department is telling us that Harry is one of seventy-nine soldiers that have been exchanged for the same number of German captives in the Nazi-held Lorient section of France on November 16!"

"That makes me happier than if I had just received a free two-hundred-pound turkey for Thanksgiving Day!" she shouted.

"What in the world made you think of a two-hundred-pound turkey?" Philip asked, somewhat surprised by his wife's choice of analogies.

"Because that's how much our Harry weighs!" she said.

1 December 1944, 94th Infantry Division Headquarters, Châteaubriant

Private First Class Bernie Rader felt thrilled to be out of the Lorient Naval Hospital and back with his buddies at the 94th Division. He wiped his eyes as he read three letters sent to him by his mother, dad, and sister, Gloria. Then he sat down and penned the letter he had wanted to write them since his capture and imprisonment on October 2, 1944.

"Friday, 1 December 1944: Dear Mother, Dad and Gloria:

"I received three letters from you not over a half hour ago, and I've never been so affected by letters before—honest, I almost cried. I knew, of course, that you'd have terrible anxiety and worry because of the 'missing' report—in fact while I was in [the hospital] my greatest sorrow was the grief that would be caused to you by the report. Many were the hours that I lay looking up at the white ceiling thinking to myself, 'Do they know I'm a prisoner? Do my letters get through and let them know I'm safe? Has the army reported me a POW?'"

Bernie then thought back over the ambush on October 2 and tried to remember all the confusing and chaotic details of battle.

"Mom, I'm going to tell you the whole story (or as much of it as I can put down on paper). I'm glad you took the news like a good soldier because it helps me feel you're with me no matter where I am and what I'm doing. It may sound silly to you but more than once, around two or three a.m., before going to sleep in [the] hospital, I'd think of you home and try to transmit my thoughts to you and let you know I'm well. I've read about it being done, and to get you to know how things were, I'd have tried anything. It might be superstition but it was worth a try—did you ever, around eight or nine o'clock New York time, feel suddenly reassured about me? It's so easy to believe in that kind of thing over here.

"I was going to tell you the story or a part of it anyway. On 2 Oct., my company sent out a combat patrol to the German lines. It started out like almost any patrol I'd been out on—everybody laughing and joking till we left our outposts and then, stealing along searching with our eyes and ears every bit of ground around. We had no trouble until about eleven o'clock, we'd just passed a French farm village and had been told by a Frenchman (I'd like to see him stood against a wall) that there were no Boche in the valley we were entering, when we were hit in the front. I can't tell you exactly what happened afterward, but I'll give you the general idea. We were pinned down by automatic weapon fire—I bandaged the leg of an F.F.I. Lieutenant that had been hit and then, as we were being driven back, I managed to drag him some five hundred yards to a road bounded by two high hedgerows where they finally stopped the whole patrol by weapons they'd planted in our rear—it was terribly hard going and we were under fire the whole time.

"We were stopped at this place and never were able to smash out. We fought for six hours . . . they gave us everything they had—88s, mortars, at least five machine guns, grenades, rifles, added to that, we called our own artillery so close that shrapnel from them came into our defensive area. We didn't have a chance. We found out later that we were up against three companies—outnumbered some twelve to one. They couldn't understand how we were able to hold them off even half as long as we did.

"I'm going to tell you this, Mom, because I'm completely better and it shouldn't worry you. About three p.m. they laid three concussion mortar shells right down the center of the section of road we were holding. I was hit by shrapnel from the last one—some in both legs, both hands, and some in my right upper arm. They weren't serious but the force of the concussion and the pain took all the fight I had out of me and I spent the remaining two hours of the battle laying on the side of the road.

"At 5 p.m., we saw we couldn't get out and that the patrols sent to rescue us couldn't break through, and almost everybody being down, we threw in the towel. And that's the story. It doesn't matter much but we caused the enemy nearly four times our number of casualties and even counting the number of men they captured, we put twice as many of them out of action. The Germans themselves respected us to the extent of not searching us for weapons (taking our words for it) and not forcing us to hold our hands up, telling us we were too good a bunch of fighters to be shamed in such a way. I don't know for sure if I killed, and I don't want to.

It's hard to write because I hate to remember, but I know you want to know just what happened.

"I spent most of my time inactive in [the] hospital recovering from wounds, and the Germans gave me the best medical care. I'll leave how it was to be a prisoner for when I get home. Well, I've written it.

"When I read about how everybody brought you hope and trust in my safety, well, you know how I felt, you're right—a good friend is a wonderful thing. I couldn't very well express my gratitude to everybody that took such an interest in us, but I know they'll understand. The most wonderful thing they could have done for me was to make my burden on you a little easier and that's what they did. I won't forget. The part about Mr. Powell's factory and the people there who didn't even know me—well, it gives you a faith in people and a love for them—I just don't know how to write this— the words just won't come—you understand what I feel.

"I guess that's about the story—today is a happy one for me. I'll write again tomorrow. Take care of yourselves, give my love to all and be happy.

"Your loving son and brother, Bernie."[2]

PART TWO

THE SECOND EXCHANGE

That monster is still butchering our people and killing members of the Resistance. And all I've done is allow myself to get caught and end up in this dreadful place.

—CAPTAIN MICHAEL R. D. FOOT,
MEMBER OF THE ELITE BRITISH SPECIAL AIR SERVICE (SAS),
REFERRING TO HITLER'S SICHERHEITSDIENST, OBERLEUTNANT
BONNER

TWENTY-ONE

THE "TIGER OF THE CHANNEL"

18–19 September 1944, The North Sea Near Ostend, Belgium

Lieutenant John Humphreys, the senior British naval officer of the frigate HMS *Stayner* and two heavily armed motor torpedo boats [MTBs], patrolled the turbulent North Sea waters near Ostend, a small fishing village off the Belgian coast and one of several major English ports. The British flotilla searched for German *Schnellboots* [S-boats], the fast and deadly boats that ran the Allied blockade bringing needed supplies to Fortress Dunkirk. The S-boats proved a powerful, unstoppable force. Their famous *Schnellbootflottille* had taken a heavy toll on Allied frigates, destroyers, and MTBs.

Around midnight, Humphreys, the flotilla commander aboard MTB 724, spotted four German S-boats. Creeping up on the formation in the total darkness, he unleashed torpedoes at the port S-boat. A flash shattered the night sky.

"Direct hit, sir!" his crew shouted. "Target disabled, stationary, and burning."

Humphreys radioed Lieutenant Francis Thomson aboard nearby MTB 728: "Thomson, we've disabled an enemy S-boat. Stay here and finish it off. We're going after the other three fleeing contacts."

Thomson and his crew radioed to Humphreys that they had destroyed the damaged S-boat. They described how flames reached high into the dark sky, leaving the vessel, officers, and crew a mass of scattered remnants upon the rolling sea's surface.

Humphreys's MTB raced toward the second S-boat and destroyed it, too. Now he spotted a third S-boat stopped dead in the water. He saw no movement aboard.

"The Germans have jumped ship!" he told his crew and laughed. "They won't last long in the cold water. Nowhere to run. They're as good as dead already!"

Humphreys ordered the S-boat destroyed.

"Sink the fourth one!" Humphreys shouted to his men.

Speeding away at forty knots, the men watched as the powerful fourth S-boat tried to outrun the slower MTB. Trailing behind, Humphreys stalked the German vessel in the darkness, but couldn't muster the speed to catch it.

"Thomson!" Humphreys radioed MTB 728's officer. "Circle around and hit the enemy vessel from the side!"

Thomson kept radio contact with Humphreys as he altered his course.

"Sir, we are in contact with the vessel. We have fired, and the S-boat is now returning fire!" Thomson said. "We are battling a blaze onboard. The enemy vessel is right beside us."

Lieutenant Humphreys's MTB finally caught up to the skirmish.

"Fire on the S-boat!" Humphreys ordered his crew. But in the darkness of the night, and with the dense smoke pouring from Thomson's MTB, visibility proved zero. Humphreys became confused.

"Fire!" he ordered again and again as shots rang out from Humphreys's MTB and made direct hits on the vessel.

Humphreys continued to fire and to receive returned fire.

"Keep giving that S-boat everything we've got!" Humphreys ordered his crew. The sky blackened between the two vessels as both struggled to stay afloat during the battle.

When the smoke cleared, Humphreys realized that his MTB and Thomson's MTB were firing on each other. He shouted into the radio: "Stop firing! We're firing on each other! The S-boat has already been destroyed! Pick up the survivors!"

In the early hours of the morning, Humphreys, red-faced and apologetic, summarized the results of the battle: The English had killed three of its own crew members, had destroyed four German S-boats, and had scooped up sixty-seven enemy prisoners from the clutches of the sea.

About 0900, Humphreys radioed the MTB 728.

"Lieutenant Thomson, have you found any more survivors this morning?"

"No, sir," Thomson replied. "I can't imagine that anyone would last more than nine hours in the open water."

"I agree," Humphreys said. "I recommend, however, that we remain in this area awhile longer and collect any bodies we may have missed."

"Yes, sir," Thomson replied.[1]

Kapitanleutnant Karl W. Müller, commander of the third destroyed S-boat, struggled mightily in the darkness to keep his face above the sea's surface. He had jumped into the water's open arms—his only salvation—only seconds before the English MTB demolished his vessel. He'd had no choice but to abandon ship and jump overboard. He felt thankful for the rubber inflatable life vest tied about his neck and waist keeping him afloat.

It had to happen to me one day. I could not be victorious forever.

The cold, violent waves lashed him, threatening to take him under. He looked up into the midnight sky and saw nothing but darkness—black sky, black water, and little hope for survival.

He had grabbed his life vest, hit the water with a hard splash, and then taken off swimming as fast and as far as he could, not looking back, a sudden burst of energy driving him into the darkness.

My boat? Gone. My crew? Probably gone, too.

His finger grazed his neck and chest.

Well, at least my medals are still here. What to do? I must stay alive. I must survive. For the Fatherland.

His arms and legs shivered uncontrollably.

Hypothermia.

He tried to recall what he had learned about water survival and the symptoms of hypothermia: shivering, drowsiness, disorientation, and at the end, irrational behavior.

Just shivering now. But the other symptoms can't be far off.

He kicked the water to improve circulation in his legs and to keep his head above the high waves. His feet and lower legs had already gone numb.

No gray whales out here anymore.

His limbs churned the water beneath him.

Two hundred years ago, the whales might have presented a problem to me. But not now. Gone. I must keep my mind active. Think of anything, but keep swimming.

He made a quick mental survey of the marine life in that part of the water, dangerous sea creatures—other than the extinct gray whales—that might be attracted to his moving body.

Nothing that can hurt me. Just a bunch of harmless fish. At least one thing is in my favor.

Two hours passed. Müller felt nothing below his waist. He struggled to keep moving, to suck in gasps of air as his nose bobbed up to the surface between breaking waves. He closed his eyes. They seemed so heavy, and he felt so tired.

I could just go to sleep, and . . .

He jerked open his eyes.

Hypothermia! Drowsiness! Stay awake, Müller! You must not go to sleep!

The Kapitanleutnant thought back over his life, his proud military career. Images appeared in his mind, one by one.

He remembered the hot summer day—July 8, 1943—when he was awarded the coveted, prestigious *Ritterkreuz* [the Knight's Cross]—one of the highest awards made by Nazi Germany. It was Hitler's way to recognize extreme battlefield bravery and outstanding military leadership. He had felt the envy of his fellow officers and men when the German official draped the ribbon and heavy cross around his neck. The newspapers hailed him the "Tiger of the Channel."

He pulled his hand from the water to his throat, and touched the Knight's Cross once more.

It is my treasure. I will die wearing it. What an honor it is! Only Hitler's best receive the Ritterkreuz.

Then he felt suddenly sorrowful.

I had so hoped to give it to a son one day.

He remembered the other medals and badges presented to him: the Iron Cross, the Sudetenland Medal, the Destroyer War Badge, the Minesweeper War Badge, the Fast Attack Craft War Badge, and so many others during the brief war years.

Kapitänleutnant and commander of Schnellboot *S-52 in the* 5. *Schnellbootflottille, and mentioned in the* Wehrmachtbericht *[German armed forces report]. Such honors for so young an officer.*

As he bounced upon the waves, he dreamed about the slim, fast crafts that had made him the much-vaunted "Tiger"! He knew the S-boats had proved powerful and dependable vessels, and that the Germans had used them to their full advantage. They could cruise forty or fifty knots, and were well suited to the open sea. They were far superior to the American PT boat and the British motor torpedo boat. The S-boats' wooden hulls gave them the ability to cross magnetic minefields unharmed. They had served the Kriegsmarine well during the war. Fast! Reliable! Unstoppable! He smiled when he remembered that the Britishers called them E-boats—the "E" for "Enemy."

Müller felt an unexpected and heavy sense of shame.

That is, until now. All four S-boats destroyed. On my watch, and under my command.

He recalled the spring of 1943, April 14, when as commander of *Schnellboot* S-52 he helped sink the British destroyer HMS *Eskdale* off Lizard Head, Cornwall.

Now, that was a day!

He and his crew had made numerous successful forays against Allied shipping in the English Channel, sinking a number of warships, freighters, and tankers. Constantly engaged in Channel action, he had personally participated in every sortie of his command.

But now the enemy has become smarter, more astute at locating and intercepting our flotillas. Unlike the old days—the "Happy Times"!

Kapitanleutnant Müller endured the long night and greeted the morning sun, riding the waves for three more hours. Then he relaxed his exhausted body and allowed it to float freely on the surface of the water. He could no longer remember where he was, or who he was, or what had happened to him. He just felt cold and tired, and could fight the sea no longer. The waves rolled him from side to side, and up and down in a steady, sickening motion. He turned his head to the side and vomited.

If the sea wins, so be it. I will die a hero. I have honored my Fatherland.

Then he closed his eyes and went to sleep. He wanted only to dream of a little village in northwest Germany, Essen-Borbeck-Mitte, where twenty-eight years and seventeen days before, he was born.

Lieutenant John Humphreys scanned the distant water one last time that morning.

"No more survivors," he told his crewman. "No one could have remained alive in the sea for"—he looked at his wristwatch—"for nine-and-a-half hours. Let's go."

"Yes, sir," the crewman said.

But before Humphreys returned his binoculars to their case, he thought he spied something bobbing on the surface of the water to starboard. He looked closer.

"I see something!" he shouted. "It looks like . . . a body perhaps. Let's pick it up," he told his crewman.

The body was pulled from the water and laid on the deck.

"A German, sir," the crewman said. "I think he's alive. Still breathing. Slightly."

"Wrap him in a blanket, take him below," Humphreys ordered. "Have a medic check him out."

Later that afternoon, Humphreys went belowdecks and examined the survivor pulled from the water that morning. Now awake and conscious, the German folded his arms across his chest and stared at the ceiling. Still wrapped in heavy woolen blankets, he had refused to allow the medic, or anyone else, to remove his clothes, boots, or precious medals.

"Name, rank, and serial number?" Humphreys demanded as he looked at the dark-haired, broad-shouldered young survivor-prisoner in the damp navy-blue uniform and the *Ritterkreuz* around his neck.

The survivor didn't stir; he made no movement and gave no response.

Humphreys smiled. "You don't need to tell me," he said. "I know who you are, Kapitanleutnant Karl W. Müller. You are . . . ah . . . were . . . the infamous 'Tiger of the Channel.'"

"Even though you are the enemy, Kapitanleutnant Müller," Humphreys said, "we will treat you with respect and take care of your needs while you are on board. Please let us know what you require."

"Zank you, sir," Müller said. "Zank you much."

TWENTY-TWO

THE "GOONEY BIRD" CREW

30 October 1944, St. Nazaire Sector, France

Pilot First Lieutenant Leonard Keller, USAAF, didn't expect the thick, unexpected haze that enveloped "Little Elle" after the cavernous Douglas C-47 took off from Denain, Belgium. Loaded with much-needed supplies, the aircraft headed toward Cambrai in northern France. Dubbed the "Gooney Bird," the plane was the last of the formation to leave the airfield. Bad weather suddenly closed in, causing Keller to lose sight of the rest of his flight.

"Corporal," Keller called to his radio operator above the noise of the engines. "Contact the formation for a heading."

"Yes, sir," Corporal Bush responded. He radioed the formation leader, and reported back to Keller. "Sir, we are advised to stay on our current heading."

Two hours passed. Keller watched the weather worsen, the clouds thicken, and the skies blacken. Visibility became more limited by the minute.

"This heading can't be correct," Keller told Flight Officer Jack Norelius. "I see no sign of the formation, and we are long overdue at Cambrai. I think we're lost."

"And we're running low on fuel," Norelius said.

"Watch for a possible landing site," Keller said. "I'll try to break out of this overcast so we can tell where we are."

Keller brought the plane as low as he dared, beneath the clouds and haze, made a sharp turn to the right, and headed north.

"There's the coastline," he said. "Let's see where this takes us."

"I see a town ahead of us, sir," Norelius said, "at the mouth of a river."

"Yes," Keller said. "I see it, too. It's fairly large—"

Before he could finish, the sound of anti-aircraft rounds cut him short. He could see tracers riddling Little Elle's front and side. Like showers of hail striking a tin roof, the sound of ack-ack-ack grew more intense, and trails of smoke issued from the right engine. The propellers turned more slowly, then stopped. Flames billowed from the plane's right side.

"The right engine's on fire!" Keller shouted, struggling to lower the Gooney Bird's landing gear.

At that moment, Keller saw a large chunk of flak burst through the cockpit's side window, striking Tech Sergeant Louis Milke, who stood behind him. Milke groaned and sank to the floor, dazed and clutching his bleeding stomach. Ground fire continued pelting the plane, ripping foot-long holes in the cockpit and fuselage. Small fires started in the aircraft's interior, spreading quickly to the cargo compartment.

"We'll crash-land on the first field we see!" Keller shouted as he watched flames licking at the boxes of precious supplies. He pulled up the gear and made a right turn inland, diving to treetop level over the town. They passed directly over a large POW camp. He could make out the fence and guard tower, and he saw men waving.

"Hold on!" he shouted. "We're going down!"

Keller made a wheels-up landing, bouncing hard across a grassy meadow just beyond the town. Once stopped, Keller shouted to his crew: "Milke! Clark! Bush! Exit! Quickly! Go! Go!"

He and Norelius helped the men out of Little Elle through the escape hatches. After Keller and the men stood safely on the ground, Keller noted how badly some of his crew were wounded.

"I'm going back for the first aid kit!" he shouted.

Turning around, he started running toward the burning plane. He didn't get far. A German patrol quickly surrounded him and the men.

"Welcome, Amis, to St. Nazaire," a grinning German said to him in passable English. "You are now prisoners. For you the war is over."

"Clark, Bush, and Milke are seriously wounded," Norelius whispered to Keller when the German guard turned his head.

Norelius watched a German medic and other Landsers place the injured Americans on litters, pick up the stretchers, and walk away.

"Wonder where they're taking them," Keller said.

"I don't know," Norelius replied. "But I hope they receive some good medical care—and quickly."

"I hope so, too, but I'm not counting on it," Keller said.

Tech Sergeant Milke screamed in pain as the stretcher bearers took him to a makeshift first aid station. A fragment from the plane was deeply embedded in his side, the sharp metal end visible through the wound. Blood soaked his trousers.

Milke glanced at Corporal Bush lying beside him. Blood flowed from a deep gash on the corporal's wrist.

"Corporal?" Milke asked. "Are you okay?"

"I'll live, Sergeant," he replied. "How 'bout you?"

"Not so sure," Milke said. "I brought part of Little Elle with me!"

Milke watched a German medic bandage Bush's wrist. He then felt faint, and . . .

When Milke awoke, he was on a bed in a room by himself.

Where am I? Am I still alive?

He stared at his gut, and the metal shard protruding from his belly. Feeling dizzy, weak, and nauseated, he closed his eyes. Moments later, a tall German doctor entered the room.

"We will give you a shot in your arm and another in your leg," the doctor said. "Hopefully, it will help reduce the pain of surgery. Then we will try to remove the flak fragment lodged in your abdomen."

The surgeon patted his arm.

"Unfortunately," he said, "we have no blood or plasma to give you in case of an emergency."

Closing his eyes, Milke prayed the shots would be strong enough to block the pain.

They were not. Somehow he survived the surgery, but post-op proved a long, intensely painful nightmare. After four days of stabbing discomfort, someone brought him a bowl of tasteless soup and a piece of bread, and a surprise—several books in English. He was treated kindly by the German staff, something he didn't expect. Then he was interrogated about his specific duties on the plane, and asked why his C-47 was flying over St. Nazaire.

"I was the fourth member of the crew, the flight engineer," Milke said. "We were delivering supplies. That's all. The weather turned bad, and we got lost. We didn't know we were flying over St. Nazaire."

His interrogator listened and then paused, furrowed his brow, and stared at Milke for several seconds. Then, without a word, the German got up and left the room.

I know you don't believe me. But that's the honest truth.

Two hours after the crash and capture, Norelius, along with Keller, was taken by car to a small building in St. Nazaire. An English-speaking German officer questioned them, but neither American officer said anything.

"Relinquish all your personal possessions," a guard ordered.

Norelius, then Keller, emptied his pockets of billfolds, knives, lighters, and letters. Guards led the two men to a small boat and motored them across a river. When the boat docked, they were marched down to a building where they spent several uncomfortable nights.

After more lengthy interrogations—totally unproductive for the Germans—Norelius and Keller were issued blankets, straw sacks for mattresses, two more for pillows, and, after some hours, a light dinner. Then they were locked in a room with a group of Allied prisoners.

That night, as they tried to settle into their straw sacks, the POWs in nearby bunks introduced themselves: an American pilot, Second Lieutenant Jim Silva; a Frenchman, Lieutenant Léon Spanin; Sapper George H. Tegg; an English officer, Captain Michael R. D. Foot; and several others.

"It's nice to meet you guys," Norelius said. "But I wish it could be under better circumstances."

"We'd love to hang around and get to know you better," Keller said. "But we won't be here that long."

Captain Foot smiled, glancing at Spanin and the others. "Neither will we, mate," Foot said in a crisp, clipped English accent. "Neither will we."

TWENTY-THREE

CAMP FRANCO

2400, 3 September 1944, Camp Franco

Captain Michael Foot lay awake that night dreaming of escaping from Camp Franco. His restless mind was filled with thoughts of the Sicherheitsdienst's Oberleutnant Bonner, whom the SAS had sent Foot to capture or kill.

No doubt, that bloody monster is still butchering our people and killing members of the Resistance. And all I've done is allow myself to get caught and end up in this sodding place.

He bristled as he recalled his capture on August 24. After seizing him, two Germans had marched him a mile and a half to their platoon head-quarters, where an officer of the Luftwaffe barked questions at him.

I gave him only my name, rank, and serial number.

The German officer had then become quite affable, even offering Foot a glass of cognac—which Foot flatly refused.

Cognac with the enemy?! Never! How disgusting!

After the officer interrogated him, the German guard marched Foot a half mile up the road. A truck filled with German soldiers met them, and Foot was placed between two guards in the back and ordered to remove his shoes.

How absurd! All these guards—armed to the teeth, and the driver, assistant driver, and two soldiers standing on the rear bumper of the truck! How could I possibly run away—barefooted?!

He remembered how more interrogations followed, the last one conducted by Hauptmann Heinz-Roland Schmuck, a slim officer with a long neck, hawk-like nose, and a sneer he tried to pass off as a smile.

Ugliest Jerry I've ever seen! Not even a mum could love that face!

Foot recalled Schmuck's questions: "Who are you? What are you doing in this area?"

Schmuck certainly isn't the smartest Jerry on the block.

"How do I know you are a soldier and not a terrorist?" Schmuck had asked Foot.

Admit I'm an assassin and he'll shoot me on the spot. Does he take me for a fool? What is the Jerry thinking? "Das ist ganz einfach, wenn er Terrorist ist, ist er sofort erschossen." *["That is quite simple, if he is a terrorist he is shot at once."]*[1]

"I was going from Nantes to Redon," Foot explained in phrases, nodding his head for emphasis. "I am not prepared to state the object of my trip. A stupid peasant gave me the wrong directions. Practically drove me headlong into your machine gun emplacements."

Fortunately, upon Foot's capture, Lieutenant Bernstein had snipped the SAS insignia from the captain's shoulder. Cursing himself, Foot remembered he still had one item on his body that could link him to the SAS—his cheque book.

"Empty your pockets," Schmuck had ordered.

Captain Foot dutifully deposited his watch, handkerchief, a pocket copy of Shakespeare's *Antony and Cleopatra*, keys, and the SAS cheque book on a small table. The Hauptmann failed to order guards to check Foot's uniform for other hidden objects.

That's wizard! I'm surprised they didn't search me. I still have my compass and my MI 9 hacksaw! Must hide it somewhere quickly after I leave.

Schmuck returned his watch and handkerchief. "You may keep these," he told him. "But not the keys. They could be made into a file, and used for escape."

Escape?! Do you actually think I would try to escape? If only you knew I was SAS, then you would know that I must escape! It is my duty to escape!

Schmuck opened Foot's copy of *Antony and Cleopatra.*

"Your address is written in the front of the book," he said. "Oxford?"

"Yes," Foot replied. "I studied at Oxford before the war."

Captain Foot froze when the Hauptmann picked up the cheque book.

If he opens it, he'll see "P.M.C.H.W. Mess, SAS Troops" printed on each check. He swallowed hard, silently chastising himself for not destroying it earlier.

"And what is this?" Schmuck asked, holding out the cheque book.

"Just my cheque book, sir," Foot replied, holding his breath and hoping Schmuck wouldn't open it.

Schmuck's eyebrows rose. "Your cheque book?!" he laughed. Without opening it, he tossed the cheque book to Foot. "You won't be needing this where you're going!" he said. "Tear it up! Now! In front of me."

I will be delighted to destroy my cheque book. Very quickly and into little pieces!

Once Schmuck finished questioning the British officer, he ordered Foot locked in a concrete block cell with two other prisoners—both of them Royal Engineers: Second Lieutenant G. Goss and Sapper Tegg.

After brief introductions, Foot asked them: "What's the gen on escape possibilities?"

"Very tough," Goss said. "The bars on the windows are iron; the same for the bar on the door."

"And the thick concrete paving beneath the floor rules out tunneling," the small-statured Tegg added.

"But," Goss said, "most of the POWs are quite close by, at Camp Franco. They live in small huts in an enclosed area that are much more comfortable than this place. And I hear that the bars on the window were rather amateurishly installed."

"The guys there tell me the bars are thick," Tegg said, "but the metal frame holding the bars to the window is only nailed to the building. They used ordinary household nails, so cutting through the nails that hold the frame, and pushing out the set of bars should be a piece of cake. That is, if we had a hacksaw, getting out of Franco shouldn't be a problem."

"I have the hacksaw," Foot said and smiled. "Are you two planning on escaping?"

"Of course," Goss told him. "We will certainly plan an escape if we are moved to Franco and have the opportunity."

"No," Tegg said. "Not me. I'll help you get away, but I'm staying put. I owe it to my missus not to take the risk."

The days and nights dragged that first week as Foot checked window and door bars and concrete pavings, arriving at the same conclusion as Goss and Tegg: escape was impossible.

On the morning of September 1, the trio was awakened by a German guard, told to pack their few belongings, and unexpectedly moved to Camp Franco.

A marvelous piece of luck.

Each night at Camp Franco, Foot lay on his straw sack and thought about his parents, the dreaded telegram they had likely received, their heartache and worry about his MIA status. The quiet night was broken only by the soft tenor voice of Sapper Tegg singing the Irish song "Danny Boy."

Foot had heard the tune many times, but had never really pondered the words. Now, locked behind the walls of Camp Franco, he heard the heart-grabbing words in a new way, sharp and clear.

They tell of a father missing his son who is far away in a foreign land. He calls to him, expressing his deep love for the young man, and his yearning to see him again, in either summer or winter, in either sunshine or snow.

Foot saw some of the men in their bunks blinking back tears as the sapper's mellow voice sang long into the night. It was as if Foot could hear his own father's voice calling him through the words.

Oh, if by some stroke of luck, I could be home before the valley filled with snow, before my father—like the summer flowers—died and rested forever beneath the winter's soil. At least I hope my father might feel a bit that way. Maybe just for a moment, he can forget he is the stiff-upper-lip Brit military commander and experience some deep human feelings.

Night after long night, Tegg's lone voice carried the heart-grabbing strains of a yearning father's dream of seeing his boy one last time. The melody floated throughout the prison huts of Camp Franco, and the tender words touched Foot's very soul. It was as if, in his own way, Tegg tried to offer Foot and the other men a little note of hope during the dark, dismal nights.

During the early morning hours, as Foot lay shivering under a thin, dirty blanket, only one thought consumed him: *It's time to go home to my father. . . .*

TWENTY-FOUR

THE ESCAPE

6 September 1944, Camp Franco

That afternoon Foot waited until the elderly guards, Bachmann and Kling, walked away, and then he whispered to Goss.

"We'll make a break tonight!" Foot said. "Have you cut through all the nails holding the window bars' metal frames in place?"

"Yes, it's done," Goss said. "We can simply push out the whole set of bars—as quietly as possible I hope."

"Do you have the compass I gave you?" Foot asked.

"Yes," Goss replied.

"Once we're past the guards," Foot said, "we'll bash on and work our way northeast across the mud flats, and try to find an empty farmhouse to lay up in, hide, and rest for a while."

"Do you think Bachmann and Kling will give us any problems?" Goss asked.

"Not likely," Foot said. "I don't think they care much either way. They hate it here, and they're stuck in this camp for the length of the war."

Foot had learned much about the two German guards during his short time at Camp Franco. Unteroffizier August Bachmann, a forty-four-year-old schoolmaster from the Stuttgart area, had joined the Nazi Party in the thirties, but had admitted to Foot he'd become disgusted with the party and the war. He treated the POWs with kindness. And, unlike most of the German guards, Josef Kling had also endeared himself to Foot and the camp's prisoners. A brawny, heavyset South German, Kling routinely sneaked supplies from the storerooms and shared the spoils, mostly food, with the hungry POWs.

By 2300, Foot, Goss, and the rest of the men had bunked down. In minutes, with lights off, most everyone was asleep. Foot listened to the guards as they sat outside the huts, supposedly securing the doors, but sleeping and snoring loudly. Foot and Goss slipped from their beds, crawled across the floor, and began pushing hard against the window bars.

"They're tighter than I thought," Goss said. "Let's push harder."

The two men struggled to move the iron bars and metal frame, ever mindful of the noise they made, however slight. As both applied more pressure to the bars and frame, one of the nails snapped and made a loud pop. The pair scurried back to their beds, pretending to be asleep when the hut door flew open and the lights came on.

"What is that?!" a guard exclaimed. "What made that noise?!"

The watchman called for a roving patrol, and for the next two hours, Foot and Goss heard guards methodically and noisily comb the entire compound: huts, buildings, wash rooms, and latrines. But, of course, they found nothing unusual.

By 0200 the excitement was over. The men were asleep in their bunks, and the guards once again snored outside the hut's door.

"Let's have another go," Foot said. The two crept back to the window, and quietly wrestled with the bars and frame. Moments later, they had pushed out the bars and frame with scarcely a sound.

The men slipped out the window and squatted on the ground beneath the wooden hut.

"We'll pass the ammunitions structure, then the officers' quarters," Foot whispered.

Bending low, they scrambled, unseen and unheard, until they reached the long, narrow slit trench used by German officers for protection against sudden air raids. Both men jumped in and caught their breath.

"We've made it, Foot!" Goss whispered.

"Not yet, Goss," Foot said. "We still must get under the wire."

A thick, outer barbed wire fence encircled the entire prison compound. Both men knew that beyond the sharp strands to the northeast, lay a large mud flat called La Brière.

"Ready for La Brière?" Goss asked, recalling an earlier discussion of the area.

"I've heard it can be very tricky," Foot replied. "It's big and swampy in some spots, with few dry trails. But I'm quite prepared to have a go at it, especially since we have so few options."

Goss found a bottom section of barbed wire over pooled muddy water, and both men began to dig the ground with their fingers. Soon they had dug a large hole, and were able to crawl through the mud and under the wire without getting sliced. Once out, they darted under the black night and into the swampy flat.

The wet, spongy marsh tugged at their legs as they struggled to take one step after another. They quickly discovered that La Brière had justly earned its fearsome reputation. It proved a hungry morass, sometimes pulling the men waist-deep in black sludge as they inched forward. Fighting to escape the marsh took an immediate toll on their energy. Every movement proved painful, exhausting, and incredibly slow. Sometimes they slipped into deep pockets of water, their heads momentarily disappearing into the deep bog. Other times the earth seemed to be swallowing them whole. But they always managed to find a way to the surface, kicking and thrashing, gasping for breath, and wondering what horrors their next steps would bring.

For two agonizing hours, they wrestled with the grueling swamps of La Brière. Every step produced a challenge, until at last the feat exhausted not only their strength but their resolve as well.

"We must turn back!" Foot finally shouted. "If we don't, this will become our burial grounds!"

"I agree!" Goss answered. "I've had it. We can't cross this bog. Let's find dry ground."

With some effort, the men fought their way out of the swamp's grasp.

Eventually they found a dirt path coming north of St. Nazaire, and for the next few hours, they continued their journey on dry earth.

"We must stop and rest, mate," Foot said as the two men slipped to the shoulder of the path. "We still have a very long way to go."

Wet and covered in mud, they collapsed beside the brush, partially hidden in thickets, and planned the next stage of their escape.

"Michael," Goss asked while the two men rested. "I wonder how we will be remembered in history."

Foot gave a wry smile.

"More properly put, mate," he said, getting to his feet, "I wonder if we'll be remembered at all."

"We should separate, Goss," Foot said. "If we stay together, we'll be easier to catch. If we bash on our separate ways, perhaps at least one of us will make it."

"Makes sense," Goss said. "Let's move out."

As the two men parted ways, they shook hands.

"Good luck!" Foot said.

"You, too, Michael!" Goss replied, and turned to leave.

"Wait!" Foot called, turning back. "Let me give you my father's address. Memorize it. If you make it, please contact him. Tell him I am alive and well, and will do my best to return to him."

"Wonderful idea. I'll do the same," Goss said.

The men quickly exchanged and memorized each other's information, then moved off in different directions into the dark night.

Around 0400, a dog-tired Foot stumbled upon a sleepy German sentry guarding a small bridge.

"*Halt! Hände hoch!*" the guard shouted, and pointed his rifle at the Englishman.

Another daft Jerry! I guess the party's over.

Foot promptly stopped and raised his hands. The sentry marched Foot back to Camp Franco at gunpoint.

Two weeks later, a guard told him: "Foot, we have decided to give you ten days in solitary confinement as a punishment for your escape attempt."

Foot served nine of the ten days, using the quiet solitude to plan his next breakout. When released and returned to his hut, he noted that the old guards, Bachmann and Kling, had been replaced by Kriegsmarine Kapitänleutnant Menger, a fifty-five-year-old commander of a sunken minesweeper. Foot cared little for his new minder.

A slow, stupid type. A man almost sure to say "no" to anything asked of him.

Late that night, as he lay wrapped in his blanket on his straw bed, Foot's thoughts turned to Goss.

I wonder if Goss is making it. Or has he also been captured? Or shot?

In the deep silence of the night, Foot heard the familiar voice of Sapper Tegg softly crooning of a father's missed son named Danny.

If Goss gets through, will he remember to contact my father?

But, ever the realist, Foot knew that crossing German-occupied territory could take weeks and would be difficult, if not impossible and quite deadly.

I'm glad he has my compass. At least he'll have some direction for his long, dangerous journey.

Foot realized that if Goss survived and contacted his father, Brigadier Richard Foot would have no idea his son had been recaptured and returned to Camp Franco. Nor would the brigadier even know his son was still alive.

Long after Tegg's smooth tenor voice fell silent, and the last stanza of "Danny Boy" ended, the young English captain could still hear the calling pipes, the softly treading feet upon the meadows, and the haunting words "I love you" as they echoed from glen to glen, in sunshine and shadow, and down the mountain's side.

"I hope Goss makes it!" Foot whispered, clenching his fist. "He must make it!"

TWENTY-FIVE

THE COURT-MARTIAL

September 1944, St. Nazaire Sector

Second Lieutenant G. Goss snaked beneath hedgerows, crawled through thick mud, swam through water-filled trenches, and tiptoed around German minefields until, some three weeks later, he reached the Loire, the river that flowed past Camp Franco to the sea and marked the boundary between Axis and Allied troops. Further upstream, on the banks of the Loire, he met some local French Resistance fighters. He explained his situation, and they offered to help, ferrying him across the river to the Allied side in a small boat. He made his way to British headquarters, where he related his story to several officers. Eventually he faced the commanding officer, who announced he was referring him to a court-martial.

Goss couldn't believe his ears.

A court-martial?! I've traveled all this way to get court-martialed?!

"Lieutenant Goss, do you understand why we are taking this action?" the CO asked.

"Yes, sir," Goss responded, recalling the ill-fated and unauthorized attempt he had made before his capture to visit his French girlfriend.

"And where is your driver, George H. Tegg?" the CO asked.

"He is in the German POW camp in St. Nazaire, sir," Goss said.

"Dismissed!" the CO ordered. Two red-capped MPs promptly escorted Goss from the room and to a nearby brig.

In his cell, Goss had plenty of time to think about the reason for his court-martial.

If only . . . What was I thinking?! What an idiot I was! If only I had used better judgment that night. No girl is worth a court-martial . . . where was my brain?!

Goss remembered the impulsive decision he had made on August 4, 1944—it seemed like months ago—when he wanted to visit his French girlfriend several miles away and had no way to get there.

What a pretty auburn-haired lass. Just a stupid wartime fling! Why didn't I just stay away?

He had ordered the gentle Tegg to drive him in the middle of the night—just for a few hours—so he could visit his sweetheart.

And surely the officer wouldn't mind if we borrowed his jeep. We'd have it back before morning—before he even knew it was gone.

Sapper Tegg did as he was told, helped Goss "borrow" the jeep and drove him toward what Goss hoped to be a fun-filled night with the girl he had met in South Brittany. Tegg and Goss had driven only a few miles when they came upon an unexpected roadblock. To their dismay, the guards at the roadblock were not British.

"*Halt! Hände hoch! Halt! Hände hoch!*" the German guards shouted, and pointed their weapons at the two wayward Brits.

Goss and Tegg were promptly dispatched to the German prison camp in St. Nazaire. Later Goss noticed that the stolen jeep was transporting German officers.

1 October 1944, England

Brigadier Richard Foot paced the floor of his English manse for hours, as he had done nightly since August 24, 1944, the day he learned Michael was missing in action. He'd had no word of his son since that time.

Is he dead? Is he alive? Is he well? Wounded? Imprisoned? If so, where? Will I ever know what has happened to him?

In the early predawn hours, Brigadier Foot finally went to bed, his eyes staring at the ceiling. Under his breath, he cursed the dark and sleepless night that stretched so miserably before him.

My son. Winchester, Oxford, artillery officer, SAS . . . such a promising young fellow . . . Oh God, please keep him safe and bring him home. . . .

Not a religious man, the brigadier surprised himself when he heard simple childlike prayers pour effortlessly from his heart and lips for his missing son. He did not stop praying until he saw the first light of dawn.

TWENTY-SIX

THE SECOND ESCAPE

28 October 1944, Camp Franco

French Lieutenant Léon Spanin invited Captain Foot to walk with him in the compound at Camp Franco on the afternoon of October 28.

"Any word about Goss?" Spanin asked.

"Nothing," Foot said. "He may be lying at the bottom of a bog or put out of his misery by a German bullet."

"You don't believe he made it to Allied lines?" Spanin asked.

"Hard to tell. A long way and unfamiliar territory," Foot replied. "If he did, I hope he remembers to contact my father. The odds are against it, though. Horrible terrain. No food. No papers. His French is only passable." Foot shook his head. "Not a word for seven weeks. No, it doesn't look good."

"We must, as you say, 'have another go' at it, Michael," Spanin said. "If we plan carefully, together we might just make it."

"Yes, we certainly have better odds with you, since you are a native of France," Foot said, smiling. "At least, as a Frenchman, you know the countryside and the language. Goss and I knew little about the local landscape. The marsh was a bad show—almost did us in."

"You believed my lie," Spanin said. "I am very convincing, Michael, but I am not originally from France."

"Are you not a lieutenant with the French Resistance?" Michael asked. "That is what you led me to understand. And you speak French impeccably."

"I am a Russian," Léon said. "I emigrated from Russia to France with my parents."

"A Russian?!" Foot exclaimed. "That's wizard! I would have never imagined."

"Nor would anyone else. The French Army drafted me while I was in medical school in France, just eight days before the Germans took Paris in 1940. My regiment retreated to Bordeaux and then Toulouse. When the army discovered my Russian origin, I was interned. I ended up cooking in one of the quarries in the Pyrenees."

"From which you escaped?" Foot asked.

"*Oui!*" Spanin answered. "I ran away and joined the French Resistance— a brutal, but highly effective, bunch of rogues. They despise the Germans, of course, and attack and kill them at every opportunity. The Resistance has grown by tens of thousands since I joined them."

Spanin continued: "After the invasion in Normandy, we liberated Rodez and the South West, and afterwards we fought on the Atlantic front."

"And where were you captured?" Foot asked.

"Near Vannes on the edge of the St. Nazaire pocket," Léon said. "And, by the way, Michael," he whispered, "my name is Léon Spanin. Léon Rollin is my Resistance name."

Spanin suddenly straightened and glanced toward the gate. A large supply truck pulled up just outside the barbed wire fence and headed for the kitchen.

"Wait!" Spanin whispered to Michael. "Here comes the lorry. If we sneak inside the kitchen and hide, when the supplies are brought in we may have a chance to nick some food."

They slipped inside, hid, and watched the German sentry open the outside gate as well as the kitchen door. Deliverymen shouldered large sacks and boxes, placing them inside the building, and then they left. The sentry, busy checking the supplies against a long list, neglected to close both doors.

"Forget the food!" Foot whispered. "The daft sentry has left the door and gate wide open! Let's make a run for it!"

The pair crawled through the kitchen undetected, and passed unnoticed through the open door and gate. They could scarcely believe their luck. They ran a good hundred yards before they heard a shout.

"Halt! Halt!" a loud voice demanded.

Stopping quickly, they raised their hands. In front of them stood the camp commandant, his pistol drawn and aimed at their chests.

"What are you doing, Foot, Spanin?!" the German commandant snarled. "And where do you think you are going?"

The escapees put their hands behind their heads and, without a word, turned and headed back inside the compound.

"Surely this must be the shortest escape in history!" Spanin told Foot as the guards led them back to the hut. "We should have known escaping from Camp Franco would not be this easy."

"We made a dog's breakfast out of this escape, but not to worry, Léon Spanin . . . I mean . . . Rollin . . . ah . . . whatever your name is," Foot whispered. "We will most definitely try again."

29 October 1944, Camp Franco

The following morning, Foot and the other prisoners noticed something different about the prison compound. Extra barbed wire had been strung around its perimeter, the guard details had been doubled, and a definite change in attitude had occurred throughout the whole enemy garrison.

"Captain Foot," Lieutenant Keller said after noting the changes, "I heard about your attempted escape. In doing so, you and Spanin have made it much tougher for any escape attempt now. Let's put our heads together, carefully plan our next breakout, and do it right this time."

All nodded in agreement.

Later that evening, Foot, Spanin, Keller, Norelius, Silva, and RAF warrant officer John Hill gathered in a corner of the hut and spoke in low tones for several hours. At last, after considerable back-and-forth conversation, often quite heated, they came up with a viable escape plan. They decided to aim for November 20, and hoped for a moonless night with a good chance of bad weather. They were sure this escape plan would work.

Bored, restless, and hungry, Jack Norelius began keeping a diary to help pass the time.

1 November 1944: "Was very restless all night long trying to think of a way to escape. Finding no way, finally slept for four hours. Woke up at 0800 hours and started off on another day."

3 November 1944: "The food wasn't bad today. About the same as before. Not much food value in it, and most of us feel hungry all the time. We get soup at noon and bread at supper. Sometimes we are able to save enough bread to last till breakfast. We don't drink the water, but the coffee keeps the thirst away. The coffee is terrible, and wouldn't be fit to drink under any other circumstances."

4 November 1944: "Today we had a little excitement when we saw an aircraft being shot at. The A.A. guns seemed to be out of his range, and I don't think they came close to him. He seemed to drop something and then made for the clouds.

"The food took a slight decrease in the last two days. We don't get potatoes, and the bread is now divided four to a loaf instead of three. It doesn't show any signs yet, but we are hoping for the best. The men in solitary confinement were given a little bit of freedom today. They will be out tomorrow."

5 November 1944: "We are now learning to pass our afternoons away by playing bridge, which isn't too bad. We are still looking for a way out. Writing a letter home. Hope it gets there."

6 November 1944: "Still waiting for a good way to get out, but I guess it is hopeless so far, but we never give up hope. The food isn't very good. The soup sure wrecks one's kidneys. Have plenty of coffee, but it isn't good. Keller and I have been wondering what our outfit has heard about us. We are also wondering just what the chances are of getting freed before Christmas. We got a shower which was very nice."

TWENTY-SEVEN

THE MESSAGE

3 October 1944, England

Brigadier Richard Foot took the unopened letter from his wife's hand.

"Do you know anyone by the name of Goss?" she asked her husband.

"No," he replied. "Put it on my desk. I'll look at it later."

Heading up London's anti-aircraft defenses, the brigadier received lots of mail, quite a bit from people he didn't know. He had a hectic morning, and it wasn't until that evening he remembered the unopened letter. Before turning in, he picked up the envelope, studying the return address.

Second Lieutenant G. Goss, British Headquarters.

No doubt some British serviceman wanting a favor.

He opened the letter and his jaw dropped. He sank into his chair, the letter in his hand, his mouth still agape. Then he called for his wife. When she entered the room, Foot read it to her aloud.

"Dear sir," he read. "Your son, Michael, and I were fellow prisoners—with a large group of American, British, and French POWs—at Camp Franco, in the German St. Nazaire POW camp. Conditions are very bad there. The men are cold and hungry, and many of them are sick. Michael and I tried to escape on 6 September. We got as far as the main road, and then we separated. We exchanged home addresses and promised to contact each other's family if one of us made it. I made it to safety across Allied lines. I don't know if Michael made it or not. I have not heard. But when we escaped, he was alive and well. I'm sorry I can't be of more help. This is all I know. G. Goss."

Mrs. Foot collapsed in the chair next to her husband, and covered her mouth with her hand.

"Michael was alive on 6 September, and imprisoned at Camp Franco at St. Nazaire," she said. "He tried to escape with this man, Goss. Did Michael make it to the Allied lines? If he had, surely we would have heard from him by now."

The brigadier poured himself and his wife a whiskey each. For the next few minutes, they took long sips and sat still, facing their thoughts. Finally Richard Foot spoke.

"Since we haven't heard from him, it could mean only two things," he reasoned. "Michael was shot and killed as he tried to escape, and he did not make it through St. Nazaire and to Allied lines. Or the Germans captured him, and took him back to Camp Franco at the St. Nazaire POW camp."

"I hope it is the latter," Mrs. Foot cried, wiped her eyes, and left the room.

Foot lifted the glass to his lips and emptied it of its calming golden liquid. He knew his wife hated for him to see her cry.

So we still have some hope. If Michael has been recaptured, he might still be alive and in the St. Nazaire German POW camp. I will work on that assumption.

The next morning, Foot rose early. He made phone calls and wrote dozens of letters to authorities across England and Europe. He called in every favor he was ever owed in an attempt to find Michael.

Several days later, Brigadier Foot received a copy of a letter written by his friend, John Bankes from London, to Lt. Col. J. M. Langley, G-2 S.H.A.E.F.

"Would it be possible for one of your officers to reconnoiter the position [at the St. Nazaire POW camp] with a view of freeing Captain Foot, and possibly infiltrating some Frenchman into St. Nazaire to help them to escape?" one English officer wrote another, trying to find a way to rescue Brigadier Foot's son.

When the reply to Bankes's letter came from Lieutenant Colonel Langley, John Bankes sent a copy to Brigadier Foot. "I am rather dubious as to the possibilities of success," Langley responded. "And also whether we are justified in making special efforts to rescue one officer."

The SAS leaders told Brigadier Foot they were very anxious to recover Michael, and that he was valuable to them. But it all proved a dead end. It seemed that neither wealth, power, rank, nor the "old boy network" could save one lone English officer.

On November 17, Brigadier Foot opened *The Times* to find an article about an unprecedented prisoner exchange that took place the day before in the Lorient sector of France. The reporter wrote that Andrew G. Hodges, a Red Cross senior field director for the U.S. Army's 94th Infantry Division, negotiated a swap involving seventy-nine Germans for an equal number of American prisoners.

"Why, I've never heard of such a thing!" Foot exclaimed to his wife. "If that could be done at Lorient, maybe this Hodges fellow can do the same thing for Michael at St. Nazaire—if that is, indeed, where the lad is!"

Brigadier Foot telephoned Major General Malony of the 94th Division, and shared with him the details of Goss's letter.

"Brigadier Foot, we are not aware Allied prisoners are being held at St. Nazaire," Malony said. "But I'll speak with Mr. Hodges. I suggest you make arrangements to come to France and talk with him personally. I can make no promises, but if it involves our POWs, Hodges is our go-to man. We'll give it our best shot based on his advice."

TWENTY-EIGHT

AN ARMISTICE DAY TO REMEMBER

11 November 1944, Camp Franco

Before dawn Captain Foot lay awake on his straw mattress, thinking about Britain, the war, and Armistice Day.

We thought the Great War would be the "war to end all wars." Now here we are again—fighting yet another bloody war with the Jerries. When will it end?

Michael had been a mere toddler on that first Armistice Day in 1918 when the war ended between the Allies and Germany on the Western Front. Ever since, Foot's military family had always observed Armistice Day with a special celebration to mark the truce and suspension of hostilities. When Michael was growing up, the Great War seemed to dominate dinner table conversation, and heeding Armistice Day had become a sacred family tradition.

The eleventh hour of the eleventh day of the eleventh month.

He wondered how many of his own family members, some decorated military heroes of World War I, had attended the very first Armistice Day remembrance at Buckingham Palace, in 1919, an event hosted by King George V.

After the prisoners returned from breakfast that morning, Foot broached the idea of a brief Armistice Day remembrance.

"The Krauts won't allow it," Sergeant Thompson remarked. "But if we decide to risk it, we should do it secretly and quietly."

"I think we should definitely do it!" Foot said.

"If we get into trouble," Jim Silva warned, "as senior Allied officer, you'll be the one, Michael, to catch the flak."

"First they must catch us," Foot said and winked. "Let's be very discreet."

"Yeah, mum's the word," Silva said.

"We should meet in the prison yard a few minutes before eleven," Foot suggested. "We can line up in formation, observe a moment of remembrance, and then, when I turn to leave, you can all disperse."

"Sounds like a good plan," Silva said. "But first, let's mark this day with our signatures."

The young pilot pulled from his pocket the French one-hundred-franc bill he had hidden and saved since his capture.

"Sign your name, address, phone number—anything you want to include on this bill," he said. "If we make it out of here, I plan to keep it forever—to remember this day and all of you."

The men passed the paper bill around, penned their names, and gave it back to Silva.

That morning, a few minutes before the eleventh hour, Foot ambled into the large open area on the south side of the compound. One by one, the POWs joined him. At 1100, for a full minute, the men stood still and quiet, some with bowed heads. Then Michael turned around and headed to his quarters. On his way, he looked back and saw the others quietly dispersing, just as they had planned.

Michael smiled. *Armistice Day has been officially observed. And the daft Jerries didn't even notice.*

At that moment, Michael saw camp commander Kapitänleutnant Menger storm from the officers' building.

"Captain Foot!" Menger shouted. "Do not think you have fooled me! Don't pretend you don't know such observances are verboten, verboten— strictly prohibited!"

His face flushed, Menger called the guards: "Arrest Captain Foot!" he ordered. "Place him in solitary confinement!"

As the guards led the young captain away, Foot overheard Menger growl to an interpreter in German: "Does he not see what a fool he has made out of me?! Observing their Armistice Day in the middle of a German prison camp!"

The guards released Captain Foot after three days of solitary confinement.

"I'm sorry you got punished," Silva told Foot when the captain rejoined the POWs.

"Not a problem, mate," Foot said and grinned. "A one-minute Armistice Day observance was well worth three days of solitary confinement!"

TWENTY-NINE

THE FINAL ESCAPE

2300, Monday, 20 November 1944, Camp Franco

"It's time!" Lieutenant Léon Spanin whispered to Captain Foot. "Keller just came in from the latrine with the keys to our hut. After room check, the guard forgot and left the keys in the door. Keller was doing his necessary business in the latrine, and he spotted the forgotten keys in the door. What luck!"

"If Keller was in the latrine, how did he pass roll call?" Foot asked.

"Norelius answered for him," Spanin said. "This may be the best chance we have of ever escaping. Get the word to Silva and Hill. We'll leave the hut in pairs and meet at midnight in the southeast corner of the compound—just like we planned."

"I'll tell them straightaway," Foot replied.

"And remind Norelius to bring the wire cutters," Spanin added.

At midnight, Spanin and Foot quietly opened the hut's door with the keys and sneaked undetected to the southeast corner of the prison yard. Minutes later, Keller and Norelius joined them.

Norelius, the strongest of the four, cut the strands of barbed wire while they waited for Silva and Hill.

"Where are they?!" Spanin whispered. "They should have been here long before now!"

"I don't know, but when I finish cutting these wires," Norelius said, "we're leaving—with or without them."

As Norelius snapped the last sharp strand of wire, the men heard a loud clanking sound at the back of the hut, followed by shouting German guards.

"Let's go!" Spanin whispered, pointing them to the newly cut opening.

The four POWs squeezed through the fence's ragged slit and ran helter-skelter northwest toward the compound's main fourteen-foot wall.

"We'll have to scale it!" Spanin said. "Did anyone bring rope?"

"No! But look!" Foot said, and pointed to a ladder resting against the barrier. "Some stupid guard forgot his ladder! What a stroke of luck!"

The men scrambled up the ladder and jumped to the ground on the other side.

"We should split up," Spanin said. "That will give us a better chance for escape."

The men divided into two parties. Keller and Norelius ran in one direction, and Spanin and Foot headed due north, the other direction.

"I wish I had the blasted compass I gave to Goss," Foot told his companion.

"We won't need it. No direction is a good one out here," Spanin said. "We have a deadly swamp to the east, the Loire River to the south, and wasteland everywhere else. I suggest we simply follow the North Star and hope for the best."

"That sounds like a good plan," Foot said. "We'll just follow the North Star."

The Russian and the Englishman darted across the French countryside, keeping their eyes on the star and watching for possible Germans hiding behind every bush. Amazingly, they met no one. They continued north, crossing country roads unseen and enjoying the exhilaration of freedom that swept over them. Their spirits soared with the realization of having outwitted the enemy and escaped the camp.

What a wonderful break—raining and overcast. Marvelous weather for escaping!

Clouds formed in the black sky, temporarily hiding their North Star and pelting them with heavy rain. But it didn't slow them down. They turned slightly eastward and soon came to a main intersection on their way to the village of Trignac.

"Just a short time now," Spanin said, "And we'll be . . ."

A German sentry stood directly in their path. They stopped, frozen in place. But it was too late. They had been seen.

"*Halt! Hände hoch!*" The sentry aimed his weapon at them and again shouted: "*Halt! Hände hoch!*"

Spanin saw the German squint, as if straining to make out the identity of the pair. But the driving rain and cloudy, dark skies seemed to obscure his vision.

"Who are you?!" the sentry shouted in German. "Identify yourselves!"

In a loud voice, and in impeccable German, full of authority, Spanin snarled: "How dare you speak to a German officer in that tone! Stand aside at once!"

The sentry immediately lowered his weapon.

"I am truly sorry, sir," he stammered, fully convinced he had stopped German officers on their way to important business. He quickly snapped to attention, allowing the two to pass.

The two POWs walked away calmly, and when they were out of the German's earshot, Foot exclaimed: "You continue to amaze me, Léon! Where did you learn such perfect German?!"

"After my parents left Russia," Spanin explained, "I spent five years of my adolescence in Berlin."

Spanin and Foot hiked along the wooded backroads and soon reached a narrow river.

"Are you up for a swim, Foot?" Spanin asked. "We must cross this river to reach Trignac."

"Why, of course, mate!" Foot replied with enthusiasm. "This adventure wouldn't be complete without a blazing river to swim!"

The men dove into the freezing water, thrashed about, fought the surprisingly strong current, and eventually reached the opposite bank. Soaking wet and shivering, they entered the village of Trignac.

"We must find a place to stay the night," Foot said, his teeth chattering. "We'll freeze out here."

"We must not stop yet," Spanin said. "But I promise we will find a place very soon."

Michael Foot had never met a man quite as talented and resourceful as Lieutenant Léon Spanin.

This Russian émigré never ceases to surprise me!

When they came upon the edge of a large marsh that stretched deep and long into the distance, Foot recalled only too vividly his miserable experience on September 6, when he and Lieutenant Goss had tried unsuccessfully to traverse the brutal La Brière.

"We avoided crossing La Brière. But now another marsh! Must we cross it?" Foot asked.

"Yes," Spanin said. "We must."

Once bit twice shy. No other choice but to cross it.

Cautiously and with great reluctance, Foot stepped down into the thick mud. He sank deeper with each step he took, until the icy slush hugged his waist. He struggled, groaning as he tried to move his legs through the heavy sludge. The young captain grabbed a small bush and bits of stray vegetation trying to propel his body forward.

He watched Spanin progressing more quickly through the muck, making far more headway than he could. Soon he could scarcely make out his companion's form in the far distance.

That squirmy, skinny little man! He should not be able to outdistance me! Where does he get that huge reservoir of strength and endurance?!

"Spanin!" Foot yelled. "Spanin! Wait for me!"

But by now, Foot had been left far behind, up to his middle enmeshed in mud. And the Russian was nowhere to be seen.

THIRTY

THE PIT OF DESPAIR

Before Dawn, Tuesday, 21 November 1944, the Marsh

When Michael Foot stepped into the large opaque puddle, he instantly regretted it. He sunk slowly into the liquid mix of mud, sand, and slime, deeper and deeper, his body not stopping until the gunk settled around his shoulders.

Don't panic! You survived La Brière. You'll get out of this mess, too. Blast it! Where in the world is Spanin?!

He kicked both legs hard, trying to find something solid to rest his feet on, to hoist his body up from the sucking bog. But the more he struggled, the deeper he descended. He turned his head, searching in the darkness for a vine or twig—for something he could grab onto before it was too late. The murky water now reached his chin.

"Spanin!" Foot screamed. "Spanin! Come help me!"

Even the movements of his vocal cords, and the motions made by his struggled breathing, seemed to pull him deeper into the abyss.

Shan't make it. Foot held his breath. He tried not to move lest he sink completely under and drown.

Struggling will not only exhaust me, but it will pull me under. Quicksand? Didn't I hear that somewhere? Sod it! I must be trapped in quicksand.

The rain, now gentle and steady, sprinkled the captain's face as he prepared himself for death.

Foot, like his father, wasn't a religious man, but for some reason quotes from *The Book of Common Prayer*—a leftover from some of his childhood's mandatory Church of England services—filled his thoughts.

Almighty and most merciful Father; we have erred, and strayed from thy ways like lost sheep.

The words poured from his heart.

We have followed too much the devices and desires of our own hearts. We have offended against thy holy laws. . . .

He forgot the rest of the prayer, but could remember five more words, and he said them to himself, over and over and over as he continued to sink. . . .

"Lord, have mercy upon me. . . ."[1]

He envisioned his father at home, sitting in his favorite chair, agonizing about him, wondering what had happened to his son, the promising English SAS captain.

I hope Father knows I did my military duty. I tried to live up to his expectations and make him proud. He will soon recover from my death because that's what old English military families do. They put their dead son-soldiers behind them and move on.

Michael thought about the burial service he would receive.

Hard for Father to have a burial service without a body. Maybe he will arrange a brief memorial service and put a brass plaque somewhere with my name on it.

He pondered his death.

It will be a quick death. Suffocation. A gift of mercy perhaps. Less painful than a bullet.

Michael envisioned the young soldiers he had seen fall across many battlefields during the years of the war.

Why did I ever think I was anyone special? I'm just another Tommy sacrificed on the battlefield, buried beneath a nameless grave, lost to family, lost to history. Why should my death be any different from another soldier's death? Surely, they, too, were some father's son.

Slowly Foot stretched out an arm, one last attempt to grasp something to help stop his final underwater descent. His arm swept cautiously in a wide arc. He touched something. His fingers wrapped around the object. But the movement of his arm caused his head to slide briefly under the watery mud. He was barely able to lift his nose and mouth above the muck and take a breath, sputtering and spitting. Still grasping the object, he began to pull himself toward it.

A root. And it is holding!

Now, inch-by-inch, he grasped and pulled, forward and upward. The root held, and after considerable time and effort, he extracted himself from the bog and onto a small patch of grassy soil. He wiped the mud from his face, cleared it from his eyes, nose, and ears.

"Michael! Michael!" he heard Spanin's distant shout. He soon saw the faint but familiar form of his friend emerge from the darkness, as the Russian fought through the marsh and moved toward him.

"Michael! I thought you were right behind me! I turned around and you had vanished! I came back and have been looking everywhere for you!"

"Thank you for coming back!" Michael gasped. "I thought . . . Oh, never mind, mate."

"*Mon dieu! C'est un endroit affreux!* Certainly a dreadful place!" Spanin said. "We will be lucky if we survive it!"

The pair struggled through the rest of the marsh and eventually reached solid dry land. After some time, they approached the hamlet of Crossac-en-Brière, and spied an old farmhouse.

"It looks abandoned," Michael said. "No dogs about. No motor vehicle anywhere. Reminds me of a picture on the page of the escape and evasion course book. A perfect place to hide. Let's hole up here and get a bit of rest."

"Good idea," Spanin said. "I have no strength left."

THIRTY-ONE

THE EMPTY FARMHOUSE

Before Dawn, Tuesday, 21 November 1944

Michael crawled beneath the window of the old farmhouse, stood slowly, and peeked inside. Spanin squatted on the ground beside him.

"What do you see?" Spanin whispered.

"Nothing. No one," Michael replied. "No lights. No movement. It's empty."

They opened the window and crawled inside a large, empty bedroom.

"Maybe we can find something to eat," Michael said.

They walked through the darkened rooms and began to search for the kitchen.

Michael stopped abruptly when he heard muffled footsteps. He turned around. In the doorway facing him stood an elderly gray-haired man clad in a nightshirt. Spotting the intruders, the old man put his hands to his face and began screaming in a loud terrified voice:

"Au secours! Aidez-moi ! Au secours!"

Spanin smiled reassuringly and, in French, tried to explain that they had escaped from a German POW camp, meant him no harm, and only sought a safe place to hide and rest till morning.

"Nous voulons dire aucun mal à vous sir!" ["We mean no harm to you, sir!"] Spanin said again and again.

The old man stopped. His hands still holding his head, as if trying to gather his senses, he stared, bug-eyed, at the disheveled, soaking wet, and caked with mud duo standing before him. He blinked his eyes, as if trying to decide whether his life was in danger or if he could trust these bizarre strangers who had broken into his house and disrupted his sleep. He gently nodded his head, put his arms down to his side, but he never took his eyes off the outsiders.

Foot and Spanin exhaled a breath of relief.

"He seems to understand," Spanin whispered. "I think he'll help us."

At that second, the frail old man jerked his head toward the back of the house and bellowed: *"Voleurs! Assassins! Sauve-moi! Voleurs! Assassins! Sauve-moi!"*

Spanin tried again to tell the man that he and Captain Foot were certainly *not* robbers or assassins, but it did no good.

Two muscular, underwear-clad young men burst into the room, each bearing a pitchfork. One man gently moved the old man behind him, as if to protect him from the intruders. Then the men began inching closer to Foot and Spanin, all the while pointing and jabbing their pitchforks toward them in a threatening motion. One man rammed his pitchfork's wooden handle against Spanin's forehead, deeply gashing his brow above his eye. Blood poured down his face and neck as he tried to fight off the attacker's next assault.

Foot had little strength left from his ordeal in the marsh. He struggled to protect his companion and disarm the assaulters. But the pitchfork-bearing men proved too strong.

After a few seconds of hand-to-hand fighting, Spanin screamed to Foot: "Let's get out of here!"

They turned and ran to the bedroom window where they had first entered the farmhouse. The attackers followed, stabbing hard at the air with their pitchforks, aiming at the prisoners' backs.

Just before Foot and Spanin reached the large open window, Spanin saw one of the men run in front of Michael, turn around, and thrust the pitchfork at his face. The prongs sunk deep into the captain's forehead, and he collapsed in a heap. His attacker stood over him as Michael's blood pooled on the floor at his feet. Then he raised the pitchfork high in the air, positioning it to plunge into Michael's chest. Spanin sprang at him, both feet leaving the floor, and knocked the weapon out of his hands. The pitchfork bounced across the bedroom floor. But before Spanin could help Michael, the attacker regained his balance, lunged toward the young captain, and kicked Michael's neck with considerable force. Foot's head jerked back and then lay limp in an awkward and physically unnatural position.

They have killed him, broken his skull and neck.

With his last ounce of strength, Spanin screamed wildly and dove headfirst at the two men, knocking them both to the floor. While they shook their heads, tried to recover from the unexpected foray, and gathered themselves for another charge, Spanin picked up Foot, limp and heavy, and somehow managed to escape through the window.

With Foot's deadweight hanging over his shoulder, Spanin ran as far from the farmhouse as his legs would take him. The attackers followed for a short distance, then stopped and returned to the farmhouse.

Exhausted and gasping for air, Spanin came to a large haystack, and gently laid Foot at its base. He checked for a pulse and felt nothing. He placed his ear on Foot's chest and listened. He thought he heard a faint heartbeat, but he couldn't be sure.

What now? If Foot is still alive, he's just barely alive. He may be dead in minutes. I cannot carry him any farther. What do I do? Leave him here and let him die? And save myself?

Spanin had only a few hours until dawn. He knew if he didn't cover more miles before daylight, he'd be easy prey for the German search parties.

Foot needs immediate medical help. It may already be too late. He may die before I can find help. If I leave him here, I can make a successful escape. If I wait and try to help him, I'll be captured and killed.

Lieutenant Spanin looked at the open road that lay before him, a clear route of escape into the predawn darkness.

I could make it. Foot is so badly butchered, he will die anyway. Better one of us is saved than both of us die.

Spanin pulled some straw over Foot's body to hide him from enemies and wild animals. Then the Russian stood up and ran as fast as he could down the open road before him.

THIRTY-TWO

THE DECISION

Tuesday, 21 November 1944

Lieutenant Léon Spanin journeyed south on his path to freedom. He felt a new burst of energy as he ran unhindered across the countryside on his way toward Allied lines. But the voice inside his head tormented him.

How could you save yourself and allow your friend to die alone?

Again and again the chastiser within him tore at his heart, convicted his conscience, and criticized his choice.

Michael might have survived if you had helped him! Turn around and go back to him! Quickly, before he dies!

Spanin stopped. He brooded over the brave young Englishman, his companion POW in the harsh German camp, the soldier that had become his friend and confidant.

I cannot save myself and let Michael die. I simply cannot.

Spanin changed his direction and headed back toward the nearest village in the German-occupied territory.

Surely I will find someone there who can help Michael—a German no doubt. I'll be captured, but I have no other choice.

As he ran down the road toward the village, he encountered a group of soldiers clad in *Feldgrau* German uniforms. He recognized them as Eastern Troops—Russian prisoners that had probably chosen to serve in the *Heer*—the German Army—to escape the horrible conditions of the German POW camps.

Hiwis! A stroke of good luck!

Approaching them, and addressing them in his native Russian language, Spanin said: "I, too, am Russian. I escaped from the St. Nazaire POW camp. How long have you been stationed here?"

"Too long," one answered. The others nodded in agreement. "Do you have news of our homeland? Have Russian troops reached Germany yet?"

"I do not know," Spanin answered. "However, I desperately need your help. I have a badly wounded friend—an Englishman—who needs medical attention."

"Why have you stopped?" one asked. "Keep running. You can escape. The Landsers will only return you to the camp—or shoot you for trying to escape."

"My friend will die if I desert him," Spanin said.

"It's no problem," a soldier replied. "We will be glad to help you and your friend."

The Hiwis escorted Spanin into the village, where they encountered German soldiers and explained their desperate need.

"Return Lieutenant Spanin to the prison camp at once!" a German soldier ordered the guards.

"Wait!" Spanin said in German. "I have hidden my friend in a haystack on a nearby farm. He needs immediate medical attention. I will go back with your guards to the camp, but you must find Captain Foot and help him. I will draw you a map to the place where I left him."

Spanin pulled a scrap of paper from his pocket and drew a crude map to the location of the haystack where Foot lay dying or already dead.

"Please," Spanin implored the Germans. "Find my friend and take him to a hospital. Otherwise he will die."

"We make no promises to prisoners," the German Unteroffizier told Spanin. He snatched the paper from his hand and ordered the guards to take him back to the prison camp.

The Pornic exchange. The fifty-four German prisoners to be exchanged are escorted by American military police from the 470th MP&G CO. Pornic, France, November 29, 1944. J. B. SCALES COLLECTION

Andrew Gerow Hodges in France, summer 1944.
ANDREW GEROW HODGES FAMILY COLLECTION

On Right: Andrew Gerow Hodges played football at Howard College (now Samford University) in Birmingham, Alabama. Photo taken before his shoulder injury in 1942.
COURTESY OF SAMFORD UNIVERSITY

Below: Hodges's father's horse- and mule-trading storefront business in Hartford, Alabama, 1930s.
ANDREW GEROW HODGES FAMILY COLLECTION

Mary Louise and Andrew Gerow Hodges holding his son, Gerry. Birmingham, Alabama, March 1944.
ANDREW GEROW HODGES FAMILY COLLECTION

Second Lieutenant James L. Silva.
160th Tactical Recon Squadron, 9th Air Force, 1944.
HOBART GROOMS COLLECTION

Private First Class Bernie Rader, 1944.
HOBART GROOMS COLLECTION

Kerentrech Cemetery at Lanester, France (Lorient Sector), October 5, 1944. The German funeral was held for five American soldiers killed by German troops on October 2, 1944. NATIONAL ARCHIVES

U.S. prisoners of war at the funeral for members of K Company patrol. Lorient Sector, October 5, 1944. NATIONAL ARCHIVES

U.S. prisoners of war at the funeral, saluting fallen comrades. Lorient Sector, October 5, 1944. NATIONAL ARCHIVES

Oberleutnant Schmitt, Oberst Borst, and Andrew Hodges meet in Le Magouer on the day of the POW exchange, November 16, 1944. This photo
made the cover of American magazine *Newsreel*. NATIONAL ARCHIVES

Andrew Gerow Hodges brings back Schmitt and Borst, as well as German
medical officers from Le Magouer to Etel to examine German POWs from
Rennes, November 16, 1944. The French fisherman at the bow of the boat is
Mr. Francois Jaffre. Notice the Red Cross flags on the boat. NATIONAL
ARCHIVES

Oberleutnant Schmitt, Colonel Bergquist, and Oberst Borst discuss the exchange—taking place that day—on the wharf of Etel. November 16, 1944. NATIONAL ARCHIVES

The American delegation is transported by boat to Le Magouer to inspect American prisoners, November 16, 1944. NATIONAL ARCHIVES

Transporting wounded American POWs, the first group of Americans to be exchanged. Le Magouer, November 16, 1944. NATIONAL ARCHIVES

Dr. William Reynolds, transported from the hospital in Lorient, November 16, 1944. Notice the eyeglasses. NATIONAL ARCHIVES

From Le Magouer, the Americans are transported by boat to Etel. Three wounded former POWs are in the boat, including Bernard Rader (left) and William Reynolds (covered with a black blanket on right). Andrew Hodges is wearing the medic's helmet with the Red Cross. November 16, 1944. NATIONAL ARCHIVES

American POWs arrive at the Etel wharf, November 16, 1944. NATIONAL ARCHIVES

At Etel, German POWs ready for the ferry alongside Colonel Bergquist, Oberleutnant Schmitt, and Oberst Borst. November 16, 1944.   NATIONAL ARCHIVES

Colonel Bergquist verifies that all American prisoners to be exchanged are present, November 16, 1944.   NATIONAL ARCHIVES

Former American POW, Private Louis Winn, seventeen, kisses the dock at Etel, holding on tightly to his Red Cross box of Oh Henry! candy bars.   **NATIONAL ARCHIVES**

Photocopy of the original 1939 Michelin map Captain Schmuck gave to Andrew Hodges on November 23, 1944. Hauptmann Schmuck's message and signature are on front of the map.   **ANDREW GEROW HODGES FAMILY COLLECTION**

The Pornic exchange: Bergquist, Hodges, and German officers. Pornic, France, November 29, 1944. NATIONAL ARCHIVES

German officers are introduced to American officials, Lieutenant Colonel William H. Patterson and Lieutenant Colonel Clarence Brown from 94th Division Headquarters. On the left is German naval doctor Pinski. NATIONAL ARCHIVES

The Pornic exchange: Allies and Germans talk; two French officers are present at the exchange to welcome the 32 FFI to be exchanged. Andy Hodges, second from right. Pornic, France, November 29, 1944.   PHOTO TAKEN BY JOHN B. SCALES PFC, 470TH MP&G CO, COURTESY OF THE J. B. SCALES COLLECTION

The Pornic exchange in Pornic, France, November 29, 1944.   PHOTO TAKEN BY JOHN B. SCALES PFC, 470TH MP&G CO, COURTESY OF THE J. B. SCALES COLLECTION

The Pornic exchange: A German doctor examines the teeth of German POWs. Pornic, France, November 29, 1944.   PHOTO TAKEN BY JOHN B. SCALES PFC, 470TH MP&G CO, COURTESY OF THE J. B. SCALES COLLECTION

The Pornic exchange: A German officer addresses his ex-POWs while German prisoners are photographed by an American reporter. Pornic, France, November 29, 1944.   PHOTO TAKEN BY JOHN B. SCALES PFC, 470TH MP&G CO, COURTESY OF THE J. B. SCALES COLLECTION

The Pornic exchange in Pornic, France, November 29, 1944.   PHOTO TAKEN BY JOHN B. SCALES PFC, 470TH MP&G CO, COURTESY OF THE J. B. SCALES COLLECTION

The Pornic exchange: A German officer and his ex-POWs. Pornic, France, November 29, 1944.   PHOTO TAKEN BY JOHN B. SCALES PFC, 470TH MP&G CO, COURTESY OF THE J. B. SCALES COLLECTION

ON RIGHT: The Pornic exchange: British Private Sapper George Tegg has his possessions examined by a German guard. Pornic, France, November 29, 1944. NATIONAL ARCHIVES

BELOW: The Pornic exchange: The American POWs are released. As they pass through the barbed wire and realize they are free, the former prisoners smile. Leading them is British officer John Hill. Pornic, France, November 29, 1944. This photo would appear on the front page of the American newspaper *Stars and Stripes*. NATIONAL ARCHIVES

The Pornic Exchange: Andrew Hodges negotiating with Oberst Harry Pinski. Pornic, France, November 29, 1944. NATIONAL ARCHIVES

The second POW exchange. The German officers arrive and salute the American delegation. Ever since the failed attempt by several German Army generals to kill Hitler on July 20, 1944, the official military salute—hand to the cap—had been ordered changed to the straight-arm salute. From left to right: Major Karl-Heinz Kerrl, adjutant to Generalleutnant Hans Junck (Festungskommandant St-Nazaire), Oberst Harry Pinski, Hauptmann Heinz-Roland Schmuck, Andrew Hodges (dark uniform, middle of photo), Colonel Earl Bergquist, Oberleutnant-zur-See Joachim-Hans von Reibnitz (public relations officer) with his camera, and Captain Hochstetter (translator from the 94th Infantry Division). Pornic, France, November 29, 1944. NATIONAL ARCHIVES

> ISLE DE GRO[]
> DEC 17, 1944
>
> DEAR SIR,
>   THERE ARE 12 AMERICAN SOLDER[]
> BEING HELD PRISONERS OF WAR HERE.
> FOOD IS VERY SCARCE HERE AND WE
> WOULD GREATLY APRECIATE IT IF YOU
> COULD SEND US SOME RATIONS. WE ARE
> VERY HUNGRY.
>
>   GREATFULLY YOURS,
>   "THE AMERICANS"

The December 17, 1944, letter written to the American Red Cross from American POWs held at Île de Groix, Lorient Sector. ANDREW GEROW HODGES FAMILY COLLECTION

The POW Reunion on January 25, 2002 at Samford University in Birmingham, Alabama, given in honor of Andrew Gerow Hodges (fifth from left, back row). Back row from left: James Silva, Harold Thompson, David Trachtenberg, Wayne Stewart, Andrew Gerow Hodges, Morris Shulman, Roy Connatser, George Boyd, Kermit Harden, Jr. Front row from left: Dr. William J. Reynolds, Bernard I. Rader, Harry Glixon (in wheelchair).   USED BY PERMISSION: 2002. AL.COM/LANDOV
PHOTOGRAPHERS/SOURCE: STEVE BARNETTE/AL.COM/LANDOV

Harlan Hobart Grooms, Jr. (LEFT) with Andrew Gerow Hodges (RIGHT), Birmingham, Alabama, 2002.
COURTESY OF SAMFORD UNIVERSITY

Andrew Gerow Hodges standing in front of the Andrew Gerow Hodges Chapel, Beeson Divinity School, Samford University. The chapel is named in his honor.
COURTESY OF SAMFORD UNIVERSITY

German guards at Camp Franco threw Spanin into a solitary cell after they beat him to a bloody mess. Alone in confinement and suffering deep internal pain, he looked over his bruised and broken body. He knew that healing from such a brutal battering would take a long time. He thought about Michael Foot, lying unconscious or dead at the base of the haystack, his head visibly damaged and his neck probably broken.

I hope the Germans followed my map and found Michael in the haystack. And I hope my friend is still alive.

Before Dawn, Tuesday, 21 November 1944

When the escaped POWs Flight Officer Jack Norelius and First Lieutenant Leonard Keller parted ways with Foot and Spanin, they headed northeast and struggled through the deadly bogs of La Brière. After several days of difficult journey with little water and scant food, they reached the edge of Saint Joachim, a small town in a group of islands located within the marshes of La Brière.

"When we enter Saint Joachim," Norelius said, "Goss said to contact a Monsieur Alexis Bocéno. He is with the FTPF [Francs-Tireurs et Partisans Français]. Goss planned to contact Mr. Bocéno before he escaped in September. Here are his directions," Norelius said, pulling a sheet of paper from his jacket and handing it to Keller.

The two followed the map and soon found M. Bocéno. On the evening of November 22, he led them to the home of Monsieur Pierre Philippe, who fed them, gave them a comfortable place to sleep, and hid them for the night.

The next morning, M. Bocéno rushed in through M. Philippe's front door.

"Norelius! Keller!" he shouted. "You must leave now! The Germans have placed posters all over town asking for information about you. They're offering a reward of ten thousand francs to anyone that helps in your capture!"

The airmen quickly dressed, gathered their few belongings, and headed north toward La-Chapelle-des-Marais, where members of the FTPF led them to a new safe house. They spent the night at the home of M. Gautier Généreux. At daybreak they continued their journey.

During the evening of November 27, beneath a full moon and cloudless sky, with the help of a French policeman and a friendly ferryman, the pair boarded a small boat and inched across the Loire River, pushing through reeds and muddy rivulets seemingly for hours, carefully avoiding German gunboats. They eventually reached Saint-Etienne-de-Montluc, the location of an Allied headquarters.

When Norelius and Keller stepped ashore, at 0400 on Tuesday, November 28, they were surprised to be greeted by high-ranking American officers. The Americans stood on the Loire's banks, shaking their hands, slapping their backs, and welcoming them home.

1300, Tuesday, 21 November 1944

Hauptmann Heinz-Roland Schmuck, the staff intelligence officer at Festung St. Nazaire, stood at the base of a lone haystack on the isolated French countryside, staring at the unconscious, blood-covered form of the escapee Englishman Captain Foot. He ordered the detail to place him on a stretcher and take the wounded officer to a nearby ambulance, already waiting with its engine running. Turning to a medic, Schmuck said:

"Take him to the military hospital in Hotel Hermitage in La Baule. If he is still alive when you arrive, see that he gets medical attention."

Over the next few days the Hauptmann visited Foot, checking on his condition and listening to the doctor's grim prognosis.

"He has been badly wounded," a German doctor told Schmuck. "His neck is broken; his skull is badly damaged. He likely will not live. We are not equipped to offer him the high level of care he must have in order to survive."

The Hauptmann stared at the smooth, boyish face of the dying Brit, his aristocratic features partially hidden by thick bandages. Foot lay perfectly still, save for the scarcely noticeable moving of his chest when he took a labored breath.

Why should I even care about this injured Tommy? He'll die anyway. It is a waste of our limited medical supplies. We have our own men to care for.

While Schmuck watched the prisoner sleep, he caught the flickering of Foot's eyebrows. Once the injured Englishman opened his eyes, blinked, and looked straight at the Hauptmann. For brief seconds, their eyes met but no words came. Then the officer turned on his heel and left the room.

"The prisoner is conscious," he told the German doctor as he left the hospital.

THIRTY-THREE

THE REQUEST

17 November 1944, 94th Infantry Division Headquarters, Châteaubriant

Major General Malony called Colonel Bergquist and Andy Hodges into his office at headquarters.

"Bergquist, Hodges," he said. "I just heard from a British Brigadier Richard C. Foot, head of London's air defenses. He claims the Germans are holding a large group of American, British, and French POWs in a prison camp in St. Nazaire. He thinks his son, Michael, might be one of the prisoners. If this information is correct, I'd like to see if we can negotiate an exchange at St. Nazaire like the one at Lorient. And Hodges," Malony said, "I want you to handle this one, too."

"Yes, sir," both men said, before saluting and leaving the office.

"Andy," Bergquist said as the two men walked down the hallway from the major general's office. "That was the 'word from on high.' It seems you must pull the rabbit out of the hat again. You just tell me what you need, and I'll make sure you get it. See if the Germans will talk with you. If so, turn on your Southern charm, and see if we can get a deal."

"Yes, sir, Colonel," Hodges said. "I'll do my best."

"Do more than your best, Andy," Bergquist said. "The general's aware of the publicity generated by the Lorient exchange, and he doesn't want to disappoint our Allies. And, for crying out loud, he doesn't want some senator asking why some mother's son is still behind bars when we've got the German pocket completely surrounded by our troops. Let's get our people out of there."

18 November 1944, 94th Infantry Division Headquarters, Châteaubriant

Andy Hodges worked late that evening. As Bergquist was leaving the building, he saw Hodges's office light on and stuck his head in the door.

"Is it tonight you meet with Brigadier General Richard Foot?" he asked.

"Yes, sir," Hodges responded, rising to his feet.

"Let's move the ball downfield quickly," Bergquist said. "This war may be over by Christmas. We need those men freed ASAP."

Minutes later Hodges answered the knock at his office door and welcomed inside a tall, pink-faced Englishman, Brigadier General Foot.

"Good evening sir," Hodges said.

"Thank you, Mr. Hodges, for meeting with me so late in the day," Foot said. "I have been traveling since early morning. The traffic is horrendous."

"You are most welcome, Brigadier Foot," Hodges said, and then added: "Please call me Andy." He motioned the brigadier to a straight-back wooden chair.

"Let me get right to the point," Foot said. "I have word that my son, Captain Michael R. D. Foot, with our Special Air Service, was captured by Germans on 24 August 1944, in the St. Nazaire sector. I have reason to believe he is a prisoner there."

"So I understand," Hodges said.

"I read about the prisoner exchange you so magnificently negotiated at Lorient," Foot said. "I was hoping you might bring off some similar results at St. Nazaire."

"General Malony has spoken to me today, sir," Hodges said, "and I am authorized to contact the German commander about such a possibility."

"Then can I depend on you to secure my son's release?"

"General, my orders are to negotiate the release of all the Allied POWs held in the St. Nazaire POW camp, not just one prisoner," Hodges said.

"I understand. When will you make contact? How soon can you leave?"

"General, I can tell you're tired from a long day's travel. Please take my chair; it's a bit more comfortable. Let me brew us some coffee. I'll be right back."

Foot couldn't relax. His muscles grew tenser with each moment he waited for Hodges to return with the coffee.

How could that man think about coffee at a time like this?! I rarely drink the foul-tasting stuff! I don't want coffee! I want action! Now!

Foot drew his hands into fists and pounded them on the arms of the chair. He tapped his right foot hard on the floor, feeling quite angry that Andrew Hodges was wasting his time brewing coffee.

When Andy returned, he placed a tray on a nearby table, poured black coffee into a cup, and handed it to Foot.

"Do you take sugar or cream in your coffee?"

No! Forget the horrid coffee! Tell me how you plan to rescue my son!

"Ah . . . yes, thank you," he said politely, hoping Hodges would once again leave the room to fetch the cream and sugar.

"I'll be right back," Andy said and left.

Foot slipped the sterling silver flask from his inside jacket pocket and poured a hefty amount of whiskey into his cup of coffee.

Perhaps this will make this dreadful brown liquid somewhat bearable! I'd rather have a cuppa, not coffee!

When Hodges returned, and Foot had sugared and creamed his coffee, Andy started to talk.

"Tell me a little about yourself, sir," Hodges said. "Where do you hail from?"

Foot looked at Hodges, his eyes wide.

Can this American be serious?! Where do I hail from? What does that matter?!

"England, of course," he said stiffly and took a gulp of coffee.

"Have you lived there all your life?" Hodges asked.

Is he quite mad?! I don't know what you're up to, my good man, but I'll play your game if it helps get my son.

"Yes," he replied and drank the rest of the liquored brew.

"I had never been to England before this summer," Hodges continued. "I came over with eighteen thousand troops on the *Queen Elizabeth II*—that ship was only prepared to hold three thousand passengers, so it was pretty crowded. We arrived in Scotland last 6 August, and then I spent three weeks in training in Chippenham, Wiltshire, before heading for Southampton and France. I wish my visit to England had been under better circumstances. Maybe I'll come back after the war and bring my family."

"I hope you do," Foot said in a formal tone, his chin held high, his nostrils visibly flaring with each breath.

"Besides your son, Michael, do you have other family members, sir?" Hodges asked.

What the devil is he after?!

"Yes," Foot responded, as a proper British gentleman was taught to since childhood. "I have a large family. We are a military family, going back many centuries."

"Have you always been in the military?" Hodges asked.

For the first time that evening, Foot took a deep breath, exhaling slowly. He had finished a full cup of whiskied coffee, and he felt his muscles starting to relax.

"No," he said, then dropped his head and closed his eyes. "Would you believe for ten years before the war I was in the baking business? At this time of year—for your American Thanksgiving holidays—I baked hundreds of pies. My goodness!" he exclaimed, his eyes lighting up, "pumpkin pies! Our biggest overseas customer was R. H. Macy's Department Store in New York City! Over the years, I sold them thousands of pumpkin pies!"

"That's incredible!" Hodges exclaimed. "My mother always baked pumpkin pies at Thanksgiving back home in Geneva County, Alabama. I bet she'd love to have your recipe!"

"I have it memorized." Foot beamed, becoming more relaxed. "We made so many, I will never forget it. We made other kinds, too. But how those Yanks loved our pumpkin pies!"

Hodges handed Foot paper and pencil. The brigadier patiently wrote down the recipe and, with a certain flair, signed his name at the bottom of the sheet.

"Tell your mother the secret is in the crust, and that she must follow this recipe precisely!" Foot quipped, and for the first time that evening, he smiled.

"Thank you. I'll certainly do that, sir!" Hodges said, folding the paper and placing it in his pocket.

For the next hour or so, the elderly Englishman enjoyed quietly reminiscing with the genial Southerner about families, careers, sports, Churchill, Roosevelt, and the war.

"My family has always been split between the Royal Navy and the Army," Foot said and laughed. "Surely there is no warfare quite as venomous as inter-service warfare!

"My great uncle First Sea Lord Jackie Fisher sent his favorite niece a ten-pound note for her wedding," he said, "accompanied by a terse message. He promised he would never speak to her again because she was marrying an army officer. He kept his word."[1]

"I'd like to have met Jackie Fisher," Hodges said and laughed. "Sounds like he'd fit right into Geneva County, Alabama!"

Hodges poured the last drops from the coffeepot and dispensed with the small talk. A serious look came over his face.

"Sir, I know how worried you are about your boy. I'll do my best to negotiate his release, along with every Allied prisoner in that POW camp. I can't promise anything; I hope you understand that. The Germans may not be willing to even talk with me."

"I understand, Mr. Hodges . . . er, pardon, Andy," Foot said as he stood and warmly grasped the young captain's hand. "I want you to know how much I appreciate your efforts. Godspeed, Andy."

"Thanks, sir," Hodges said.

Andy Hodges shook Richard Foot's hand and said goodbye. After the brigadier left his office, Hodges dropped into his chair, laid his head on its back, and looked at the ceiling.

Don't these people know I'm just a poor horse trader's son from South Alabama with a little Red Cross flag? Oh well, here we go, sports fans, it's kickoff time! Again!

THIRTY-FOUR

DEAD ENDS

Monday, 21 November 1944, 94th Infantry Division Headquarters, Châteaubriant

Andy Hodges sat at his desk, rubbing his chin and slowly shaking his head. He had telephoned, written, and buttonholed all his known sources trying in vain to inform himself about the enemy situation inside Fortress St. Nazaire. And he had come up with precious little to show for all his efforts. Even the identity of the fortress commander still remained a mystery.

They keep their information as hidden as they do their U-boats. How can I get our prisoners released if I don't even know who to contact?

At noon he sought out Colonel Bergquist.

"Sir," Hodges told him, "I'm making no progress with our POW situation at St. Nazaire. I can't identify the German commanding general, any of his staff, or the division CO. I should probably just go there, but I don't relish driving up to the German front line without an invitation."

"Quite right," Bergquist replied. "That's a pure suicide mission! Drive anywhere too close to the enemy lines and someone's sure to take a crack at you."

"Not many options, sir," Hodges said.

The colonel stood quietly for a moment, as if in deep thought.

"I must trust your judgment on this decision, Andy," Bergquist told him. "And I'll support you whatever you decide. But I wouldn't advise going to St. Nazaire uninvited and unannounced."

"Thank you, sir," Hodges said.

"And Andy, one more thing," Bergquist said. "If you do hear from the Germans, you don't know when it will be. Just in case you're out of pocket, it may be wise to get a Red Cross rep backup."

"Good idea," Hodges said. "I'll contact Ralph Chase, and get him to stand by in case we need him."

"Stay with it, Andy," Bergquist added. "There's got to be a way. And, by the way, I don't want to lose you!" he said with a grin, putting his hand on the young Alabamian's shoulder.

That afternoon, Hodges contacted Ralph Chase and received his consent to be a standby Red Cross representative. Then he worked on several drafts of a letter to the German CG. When at last he was satisfied, he made his way to the G-2's office.

"General Malony wants this letter typed and sent to the German commander at St. Nazaire. He doesn't care how you get it there, just get it done," Hodges said. "Lives are depending on it."

Hodges knew that mention of the general's name would silence any queries. Soon Andy had his letter. He polished it further and gave it to another soldier, who turned out the German version. Once both letters were typed on Red Cross letterhead, Hodges gave them a final review.

"21 November 1944. *An den Deutschen Kommandanten*, St. Nazaire," the letter began.

"In Betreff der amerikanischen Kriegsgefangenen die sich jetzt in St. Nazaire befinden, wird ersucht, dass Herr Andrew G. Hodges, Feld-Direktor . . ."

"Could you read the letter back to me," Hodges asked the typist, "in English?"

"Certainly, Mr. Hodges," he responded. "The letter asks the German commander at St. Nazaire for his permission for you and possibly a Mr. Ralph E. Chase, as representatives of the American Red Cross, to enter into their lines to discuss the possibility of an Allied and German prisoner exchange. You also ask for safe passage to and from the Axis-held territory."

Andy thanked him, folded his copies of the letter, placed them in an envelope, and put them in the pocket of his blouse. Turning to the officer in charge, he said: "As you can see, sir, it is crucial that this goes out today."

"Yes, sir," the officer said. "I'll see if a recon team is going out. If not, we have some reliable French people who have dependable line crossers. You may assure the general it has top priority."

Wednesday, 22 November 1944, Hospital at La Baule

Hauptmann Schmuck again visited young Captain Foot the day after he was taken to the German hospital at La Baule. The Englishman, looking paler than the white sheets, lay still and quiet, making no movements, his eyes closed, his breathing labored.

"Will he live?" Schmuck asked the German doctor.

"He is in a coma. The prognosis is not good," the doctor said. "We have neither the skills nor the facilities to give him the treatment he requires."

"No matter," the Hauptmann said. "I can't prove it, but I strongly suspect he may be a spy."

The doctor nodded, knowingly.

Schmuck smirked. "Spy or not, he will likely die either way."

Thursday, 23 November 1944

Before dawn, as a cold rain spattered the still sleeping French countryside, Andy Hodges stuck the white flag with red crosses on the front of his jeep, climbed under the canvas roof, and started the engine. With a copy of the letter in his blouse pocket, he began his trek toward Nazi lines and into St. Nazaire.

It was Thanksgiving Day back home in Geneva, South Alabama. The night before, he had posted a brief note to his wife.

"Sweetheart, it would be so wonderful if you were here with me tonight, or if we were anywhere together. Honey, it has been so long and I miss you more than you could ever imagine. I keep telling myself that it won't be much longer, but that still doesn't ease that constant longing I have for you."

In case he didn't make it back to headquarters alive, Andy needed his wife to know again how much he dearly loved her.

THIRTY-FIVE

JOURNEY INTO DARKNESS

23 November 1944, Thanksgiving Day, Chauve, France

Alone in the foggy, wet darkness, the twenty-six-year-old Alabamian continued his journey toward enemy lines. As he inched toward St. Père-en-Retz, he moved farther from Allied territory, and closer to the barbed wire blockade that announced his crossing into German borders.

It can't be much farther.

He stopped and shined his flashlight on the old French map he'd borrowed from the Intel Section. Andy's heart beat faster.

How will a German sentry react to a lone American clad in a strange uniform with Red Cross insignia, driving a jeep sporting a large white flag and appearing out of the morning mist, unexpected?

He'd never felt so lonely and so vulnerable.

I sure hope the German commander—whoever he is—got my letter.

Before he realized it, he was at the barricade.

If not, I'm in big trouble.

He paused a few yards from the wire and killed the motor.

Let's hope these red crosses and white flag will protect me from getting shot on sight.

Andy saw no soldiers. No one guarded the wire barrier or the road that ran beyond it, ribboning through a thick, dark woods. A crow cawed above him. The Atlantic wind swept through bare tree limbs. They rattled and clanged together like dry bones. Sitting still and searching the darkness, he began to mumble softly:

"Our Father who art in heaven, hallowed be—"

A helmeted sentry suddenly sprang from the woods, waving and pointing his automatic weapon at him, and screaming: *"Achtung! Halt! Achtung!"*

Andy's fingers tightened around the steering wheel. With one hand, he pulled a copy of the German-language letter from his blouse pocket.

Here it comes! This ball game may be over before it even starts!

Hodges raised his arms high above his head, the letter grasped in his right hand, and shouted the only two correct French words he knew: *"Croix Rouge! Croix Rouge!"* ["Red Cross! Red Cross!"]

Seconds passed. Eyes locked. Neither man moved.

Is he going to shoot me or let me in?

Several more seconds passed. Nothing happened.

Okay, buddy, the ball's in your court.

Andy broke into a friendly grin.

The sentry did not.

Without lowering his weapon, he motioned Hodges out of the jeep. After Hodges exited slowly, his hands still in the air, the sentry patted him down and found no weapon. Andy slightly waved the letter in his hand, and then pointed to the ARC pin on his collar and the American Red Cross patch on his left shoulder.

"Croix Rouge! Croix Rouge!" Hodges said again.

The sentry took the letter, read it, and lowered his weapon. He then disappeared into the brush, leaving Hodges standing in the rain, his hands still raised high.

Sometime later, a black civilian car pulled up to the guard hut. A driver stepped out and opened the back door for a German officer. The sentry presented the officer with the letter. After reading it, the German officer walked to Hodges.

"Andrew G. Hodges? American Red Cross?" he asked in reasonably good English.

"Yes," Hodges said, then smiled and lowered his arms.

"I am Hauptmann Heinz-Roland Schmuck, chief of intelligence," he said, giving the *Hitlergruß*. "We received this letter of 21 November. We prepared for your visit, although we were uncertain of the day you would arrive, or if you would arrive at all."

Hodges took a deep breath and exhaled in slow relief.

They received the letter, so they know why I'm here. Now if they'll just listen to me. They don't know me from Adam, but maybe—just maybe—they'll hear me out.

"Your reputation has preceded you, Herr Hodges," Schmuck continued, raising his chin high and attempting a smile that came off as a comical sneer.

Schmuck stuck out his narrow chest and clasped his arms behind his back. "Oberst Pinski, the headquarters commander of the Festung St. Nazaire, and I have been informed of you by Hauptmann Reick and Oberleutnant Schmitt in Lorient. They described the prisoner exchange of 16 November, and assured us that you can be trusted, that though you are a Yan . . . ah . . . an American, you are a person of integrity."

"Well, thank you, sir," Hodges said and grinned. "I am honored and humbled."

"Hauptmann Reick expressed his pleasure that the negotiations brought our Fatherland seventy-nine volunteers to increase our troop strength," Schmuck said.

"I would hope, sir," Hodges said, "we can repeat the process here at St. Nazaire."

"Yes," Schmuck said. "Once we received your letter, we began preparations for your visit. You will come with me, Herr Hodges. But first . . ."

The Hauptmann pulled a large handkerchief from his pocket.

"I must blindfold you before we make our journey to St. Nazaire headquarters," he said.

Without another word, he tied the handkerchief tightly around Andy's eyes, and then led him by the arm to the open door of the car.

Andy sat blindfolded in the car's backseat. The trip took several hours. He felt the car swerve around curves in the road, start and stop. The Hauptmann said nothing during the entire trip, save for an occasional word in German to the driver.

I have no idea where I am or where I'm going. I sure hope I can trust this bird. Not that I have much choice, sitting here blindfolded and without a weapon.

Hodges felt the car slow to a stop. Schmuck said something to the driver. Someone assisted Andy from the car and led him down a path. He could hear water lapping against a dock and the sounds of distant boats. He caught the smell of washed up, rotting fish.

Smells and sounds like we're at a river. Maybe the Loire?

"We must now travel by boat," Schmuck announced.

Someone led Andy by the arm and helped the blindfolded American step aboard some sort of vessel. For what seemed a long time, Andy felt the strong water's current rock the boat up and down, until, at last, it docked. A man helped Hodges step onto a wharf, climb stone steps, and walk into a building. When Andy sat down, Schmuck removed the blindfold.

THIRTY-SIX

THE TERMS

23 November 1944, Thanksgiving Day, German Headquarters, Festung St. Nazaire

After the blindfold came off, Andy Hodges blinked his eyes several times, trying to adjust them to the light, and then looked around. He was seated at a large table with four German officers, resplendent with brass, braids, medals, and ribbons, and clad in breeches and high, polished boots. He tried swallowing, but his mouth felt too dry. He hoped his unsmiling hosts couldn't hear his heart thumping with anxiety.

Hauptmann Schmuck addressed the group in German, read aloud the Red Cross letter, presented Hodges to the officers, and then introduced the officers to Herr Hodges, *feld-direktor des Amerikanischen Roten Kreuzes.*

Hodges's head was swirling. He forgot all the names except for that of Pinski, the short, burr-headed Oberst sitting opposite him. Hodges noticed how his oversized ears protruded so prominently from his small, pale face.

He doesn't look important, but he's got the elite red stripe on his britches, so obviously he's the top dog. If he doesn't buy what we're offering, we're done.

Schmuck motioned for Hodges to speak.

"Gentlemen," Hodges said. "I come as a representative of the American

Red Cross, in hopes we might negotiate the release of the Allied prisoners being held here at St. Nazaire."

Andy cleared his throat and took a deep breath. He noticed the officers staring at him with matching scowls.

"As you know, on 16 November, the German commander at Lorient, and the U.S. Army 94th Division under Major General Malony and Colonel Bergquist, carried out a large POW exchange at Lorient. Seventy-nine prisoners were exchanged—one-for-one and rank-for-rank—during a six-hour cease-fire. The exchange was completed successfully. On behalf of the Red Cross and the 94th, we trust we might negotiate and conclude a similar agreement here."

"We are prepared to hear what you have to propose," Pinski said, his chin held unnaturally high as if to demonstrate his superior authority. "Know that whatever is agreed to, of course, must be approved by our commandant, Generalleutnant Hans Junck. His adjutant, Major Karl-Heinz Kerrl, is here with us, and will represent this committee to Generalleutnant Junck."

"We must also agree to the terms of the exchange," Hodges said, becoming visibly more relaxed. "For instance, we must all agree to abide strictly by the rules of the Geneva Convention, the time and place of the exchange, the details of a cease-fire, etc."

"I see no problem in this," Pinski stated in a loud, impatient voice. "I think our general will agree as well." He crossed his arms on his slight chest.

"The prisoners must volunteer to be exchanged," Andy continued, "and the exchange must be conducted on a man-for-man, rank-for-rank, and branch-for-branch basis."

Schmuck added: "We wish to add a further condition, Herr Hodges. That prior to the actual exchange, three officer representatives of your command—at least one to be an officer of field grade and one to be a medical doctor—will be met by you and escorted to the Allied lines, where an inspection of German prisoners will be made."

"That should be no problem," Hodges replied.

"You understand, Herr Hodges, that we want no sick or wounded

German soldiers," Schmuck said, pointing his index finger at the American. "We want only those Germans who are healthy and fit for combat—those able to fight for the Fatherland."

"Naturally, and we would ask the same conditions," Hodges said. "Three American field officers—one to be a medical doctor—and a French field grade officer will be escorted through your lines to inspect our prisoners."

"And, likewise, you also want no sick or wounded soldiers returned to you?" Schmuck asked.

"To the contrary, Hauptmann," Hodges said. "We desire all our prisoners returned—wounded or fit. After the exchange is completed, the representatives of both forces will inspect the prisoners and match the names with their respective lists, and confirm the exchange has been successfully completed to everyone's satisfaction."

Schmuck and Pinski whispered briefly to each other.

"We agree to these conditions," Schmuck said, "pending the approval of Generalleutnant Junck."

"Likewise," Hodges said. "I must secure the concurrence of General Malony, the American Red Cross, and the International Red Cross. And we all realize there will be a strict enforcement of the cease-fire. No military advantage will be taken by either side during the suspension of firepower."

The officers around the table nodded in agreement. By the time they had ironed out most points at length, the discussions had lasted more than one hour. Pinski stated that, if approved, the exchange would take place on 29 November 1944, at Pornic, France, on the Atlantic coast.

"All firing on the Pornic Peninsula will be suspended between the hours of 0900 and 1800 on that day," Pinski announced.

"If we are agreed on the conditions," Hodges said, "I will return to St. Nazaire on 27 November and bring all the necessary papers, executed by our chief of staff, Colonel Bergquist."

"At that time, we will review them, and if we find them in order, and if these conditions are approved by Generalleutnant Junck, Oberst Pinski will sign them and we will proceed with the exchange on 29 November," Schmuck said.

. . .

Oberst Harry Pinski stood up, straightened his narrow shoulders, and strutted toward Hodges. In his hand, he held two sheets of paper.

"When we received your letter of 21 November," he stated, "our Intelligence Section prepared a list of all Allied prisoners."

He handed the lists to Hodges. Pinski held his head high and watched without expression as Hodges closely studied each POW's name on the first list.

"You will see that this list contains the names of the French prisoners," Pinski said, "some of whom are hospitalized, as noted."

He watched as Hodges counted the number of French prisoners.

"I count thirty-one French prisoners," Hodges said. "Is this the total number of French POWs?"

"Yes," Schmuck intervened. "It includes *Offiziers*, *Unteroffiziers*, and *Mannschaften*," he said. Schmuck picked up a pen and signed his name at the bottom of the list.

"This next list contains the American and British prisoners," Pinski said, pointing to the other sheet.

"I see you have only one American officer, a Lieutenant James L. Silva? Is that correct?" Hodges asked.

"Yes, Herr Hodges," Pinski replied. "The rest of the Americans are *Unteroffiziers* and *Mannschaften* . . . ah, as you say, under-officers and servicemen."

Again Pinski watched as Hodges studied each American's name and counted up the total.

"You are holding nineteen Americans as POWs at St. Nazaire," Hodges said. "And I see several prisoners are injured and in the hospital at La Baule."

"That is correct," Pinski said. "We had two other American airmen held here: Lieutenants Keller and Norelius. They escaped on 20 November. We have had no further word of them."

Then Hodges checked the British names on the list. He knitted his brows, hesitated, and then looked up at Pinski.

"Oberst Pinski," Hodges said. "I see only two British prisoners' names on this list: W/O John B. Hill and Private George Tegg."

"That is correct," Pinski replied. "A Brit . . . ah . . . Second Lieutenant G. Goss, escaped from Camp Franco on 6 September."

Hodges said nothing for the next few seconds.

"Oberst Pinski," Hodges said, breaking the intentional and uncomfortable silence. "Are you telling me these are the only British prisoners you are holding at St. Nazaire?"

Pinki's eyes started to narrow into thin snake-like slits and locked onto Hodges's eyes.

"I am telling you, Herr Hodges," Pinski said slowly and firmly, "that these are the only British POWs we are willing to exchange."

THIRTY-SEVEN

"FOR ONE ENGLISH OFFICER?"

23 November 1944, Thanksgiving Day, German Headquarters, Festung St. Nazaire

Andy Hodges stood up from his chair and faced Oberst Pinski, towering over the small man with the pale face and large protruding ears. For a long moment, Hodges just looked at him. Finally he spoke.

"Oberst Pinski. Let me be frank. I know you have a British prisoner here by the name of Captain Michael R. D. Foot. Is that not so?"

Pinski's face hardened. "Yes. That is so."

"Then why is his name not on this list?" Hodges asked.

"Foot will not be exchanged," Pinski said.

"Why not?" Hodges asked.

"Captain Foot has tried to escape several times," Pinski blurted out. "He has given us a large amount of trouble. He must and will remain here. That is my final word."

Now I understand. Foot's the best horse on the lot—smarter than the Germans. He's learned too many Kraut secrets in all his escape attempts, and he just knows too much about the Germans' operations here. Pinski's afraid to trade him.

"I want to speak with Captain Foot," Hodges said in a calm but firm tone.

Pinski's pale face started to pinken. "That is not possible," Pinski stated. "Captain Foot was wounded during his last escape attempt. He is now in hospital at La Baule."

"What is his medical condition?"

"It is not good. He is beyond medical repair. He is dying. At present, he is unconscious and suffering from severe head injuries and a broken neck," Pinski said. "So you see, Herr Hodges, Foot cannot be exchanged, even if we agreed to his release. It is not possible—it is dangerous in his condition. We will not agree to his exchange."

The Oberst pulled back a chair and sat down hard. He crossed his arms, raised his chin high in the air, and peered at Andy's face.

Reminds me of one of Dad's stubborn old mules. Similar ears. Small as a pack mule. But not nearly as smart or good-looking.

Andy Hodges also pulled back a chair and sat down. He returned Pinski's stare and, for a few seconds, said nothing.

"Never pull on a stubborn mule, son," Dad used to tell me, "'cause the jackass'll just push back hard against you. Just step back a bit and give 'im a choice. Be patient. Let 'im make up his own mind. He'll come round soon 'nuff."

"Oberst Pinski," Hodges said in a slow drawl, his eyes fixed on the officer. "If Captain Foot's not included with the rest of the Allied prisoners, there will be no exchange. It's your choice."

Pinski clenched his jaws and flared his nostrils. His face turned from pink to blood-red. He glared unblinking through eye slits at the Red Cross representative who had just threatened to destroy everything they'd agreed on. He jumped to his feet, knocking his chair to the floor with a loud crash, and pointed an accusing finger at Hodges.

Andy stayed seated, unfazed, and watched the drama unfold. He almost expected Pinski to kick, bite, stomp, and spit like the hinnies on his father's horse lot.

Pinski shouted, his finger pointing inches from Andy's face: "You would dare sacrifice the freedom of all the prisoners for the sake of just one English officer?!"

"Yes," Andy said calmly: "For just one English officer, or for one French private. I will not consider leaving any Allied prisoner behind. It's all or none."

Hodges put away his pen and slowly, but deliberately, folded his papers and tucked them inside his blouse pocket. He stood up and prepared to leave.

Oberst Pinski motioned abruptly to the other officers, and together they stormed out of the room and slammed the door, leaving Hodges alone inside.

"We cannot allow Captain Foot to leave St. Nazaire," Schmuck explained. "He knows too much about the camp and our security."

"But unless he is bluffing, the American will cancel the exchange if we don't allow Captain Foot to go," Pinski said. "We stand to lose fifty-three healthy, combat-ready Landsers if the exchange fails. This will make us look very bad to our superiors. And we must still feed fifty-three useless allied POWs who are rapidly draining our limited resources."

"When the time comes, perhaps Captain Foot will not be well enough to survive the transport," Major Kerrl said. "Offer to exchange him, and then, at the last minute, our doctors can declare him too ill to travel. Perhaps we can trick this American into the exchange and also keep Captain Foot here."

"A sensible alternative," Schmuck said. "We must not lose so many healthy, able-bodied German replacements because of a wounded, dying Englishman."

"Yes," Pinski said. "It is a good idea. We will work this plan. We might even make the pot a little sweeter for the Fatherland."

"What do you mean?" Schmuck asked.

Pinski smiled. "Just watch 'the Master' at work," he said, "and you will see shortly."

Andy Hodges sat alone in the room waiting patiently for the German officers to return. He imagined the Thanksgiving dinner he would miss that evening, both the one at home with his family in Geneva County and the expected feast that would be served up at division headquarters.

Oh well. Maybe the guys will save me a plate of government-issued canned turkey and dressing.

His musings were interrupted as the German brass, led by Pinski, filed back into the room and sat down.

Pinski, his face now returned to its original colorless tone, was the first to speak.

"Herr Hodges," he said. "We have made a decision. We will allow Captain Foot to be exchanged on 29 November."

Andy smiled and remembered his father's advice. *"Let the jackass make up his own mind. He'll come round soon 'nuff."*

Pinski continued: "But for Captain Foot, we must ask a higher price than for the other Allied prisoners."

I knew there was a catch! The stubborn old mule made up his mind much too quickly. Something's up.

"And what is your price, Oberst?" Hodges asked.

Andy saw Schmuck grin.

"Herr Hodges," Pinski said. "We must have five German majors, each holding the *Ritterkreuz*, in exchange for Captain Foot. Do you know this decoration?"

"Yes," Hodges said. "It's the Knight's Cross—the 'Iron Cross of the Neck,' one of your highest military awards."

"Yes. It is Hitler's way to recognize extreme battlefield bravery and outstanding military leadership," Pinski said. "That is our price. Five German majors—all with the 'Iron Cross of the Neck.' Each must be a *Ritterkreuz* recipient. Do we have an agreement?"

Andy grinned and shook his head from side and side. "Why, that is absurd," the Southerner said slowly and deliberately. "You know as well as I do, the American military will never agree to those ridiculous demands. Like I said earlier, the exchange must be on a man-for-man basis."

"I'm sure this Captain Foot is very valuable to the British," Pinski said, his face growing pink again, his patience seeming to wear thinner.

If you only knew! This Brit is SAS. "Valuable" doesn't even come close to describing his worth to the British! Captain Michael R. D. Foot is Hitler's worst nightmare!

Pinski continued: "So, Herr Hodges, if the British want him returned, this is what we must have. Captain Foot will not be released on any other basis. Five officers, each a recipient of the *Ritterkreuz*."

Andy Hodges rubbed his chin, shook his head, and then grinned again. He sat silent for several seconds before he spoke.

"Gentlemen," he said. "I've always heard that you Germans think you are a superior race, and better educated than the rest of the world—that you have developed geniuses and intellectuals who far surpass all other nations."

"Yes, Herr Hodges," Pinski said and smiled. "That is true."

Hodges, still grinning, continued: "Now you tell me that one wounded, dying British captain is equal to five German majors holding your highest *Ritterkreuz* military decoration?!"

Pinski sprang to his feet; his face glowed a brilliant red, and his eyes widened and blazed like fire. He slammed his fist on the table three times. "*Nein! Nein! Nein!*" he screamed out. "A German captain with the *Ritterkreuz* is far superior to your Captain Foot!"

"Okay," Hodges said. "Then it's one for one?"

Pinski held his chin high and frowned. "Let him have his English captain. We will exchange the Brit for one German captain with the *Ritterkreuz*!" he shouted between clinched teeth to the other Germans.

"Then we have an agreement, Oberst Pinski," Hodges said, rising to his feet.

"Agreed," Pinski snapped. Turning to Schmuck, he again snarled: "Give him his English captain!"

Andy Hodges took a pen from his pocket and handed it to Pinski. "Will you please add Captain Foot's name to the list of British prisoners?" Hodges asked.

Pinski snatched the pen from Hodges's hand, and in tiny print, he wrote "Michael R. D. Foot" between the names of John B. Hill and George H. Tegg.

"Have we completed our business here?" Schmuck asked Hodges.

"Almost," Hodges replied. "But not quite."

THIRTY-EIGHT

THE 1938 MICHELIN MAP

Late Afternoon, 23 November 1944, Thanksgiving Day, St. Nazaire Sector

"We still have two matters to attend to before I leave St. Nazaire," Andy Hodges told Pinski, Schmuck, and Kerrl.

"Before we attend to those matters," Kerrl said, in an effort to restore a measure of calm and dignity to the proceedings after Pinski's embarrassing outburst, "may I suggest that this agreement be sealed with a toast of brandy?" Kerrl gave Pinski a long, hard glare.

"Certainly, Major Kerrl," Hodges said and smiled.

Kerrl, ever the diplomat. Not that I would ever trust him, but he seems to work hard at trying to appear a gentleman.

Hodges watched the major pour the golden liquid into tiny glasses and pass to the others. After everyone had toasted, emptied his glass, and returned it to the table, Pinski spoke, now somewhat more civilized.

"And what might those two matters be, Herr Hodges?" he asked stiffly. His patience had noticeably reached its limit with the Yank that couldn't take "*nein*" for an answer.

"I wish to return on 27 November with written confirmation of the exchange. I will, of course, come to Pornic on 29 November to participate in the actual prisoner exchange," Hodges said. "And I want to do so safely, without getting shot by one of your soldiers. Crossing the lines without a cease-fire in effect can be dangerous to one's health."

"Yes," Schmuck said. "I understand your concern."

Schmuck walked to a nearby desk and began to rummage through its drawers. He finally returned with an old black-and-orange-covered Michelin map and a sheet of tissue paper.

"This will provide you safe passage," Schmuck said. "It will also show where we shall meet you on the 29th for the exchange."

He took a pen and scribbled something in German on the front of the French map, and then signed his name.

"This states: 'In confirmation of our agreement, made on 23 November 1944. Hauptmann Schmuck.' Show this to anyone that challenges you."

Unfolding the map, he marked the coordinates for the 29 November meeting place. He then positioned the tissue paper over the map coordinates and marked several places with a large "X."

"Thank you, Hauptmann Schmuck," Hodges said as he took the map and overlay, folded them, and tucked them inside his pocket.

"You said you had two matters to attend to before you left us," Schmuck said. "What is the second one, Herr Hodges?"

"I want to go to the hospital and speak with Captain Foot," Hodges said.

"But he is unconscious!" Pinski piped in, loudly protesting. "He is far too ill to be disturbed."

"Then I must see that he is alive," Hodges said. "I shall not leave without seeing him."

"We cannot allow this!" Pinski shouted and stomped his foot hard on the floor.

There's the stomp! Now I'm waiting for Pinski to kick, bite, or spit.

"Take Herr Hodges to see Captain Foot," Kerrl ordered, then rolled his eyes to the ceiling and poured himself another strong drink.

THIRTY-NINE

THE DYING PATIENT

23 November 1944, Thanksgiving Day,
German Headquarters, Festung St. Nazaire

Andy Hodges agreed to be blindfolded once again for the trip to the hospital, several miles up the beach from the German headquarters. Riding alone in the backseat, he thought about the young English patient whose freedom he'd negotiated, assuming he lived that long.

I hope he's still alive and able to travel on the 29th. A head wound and broken neck sound plenty bad. I hate to break this news to his father. Michael could die before I can get him home.

Hodges also thought about the difficulty of locating a German replacement to exchange for Foot.

How in the world will I find a German captain with a Ritterkreuz *who will volunteer and willingly return and fight on the front lines for Germany? And how do I get him to Pornic by 29 November, just six days from now? Thank goodness Malony offered to help. Surely, it will take someone with stars to rattle some cages to pull this off in time! Otherwise it'll be impossible.*

When the car stopped at the La Baule hospital, Schmuck removed the handkerchief from Hodges's eyes, and the men walked inside. With its spacious, well-appointed lobby, the facility looked more like a luxury hotel than a military hospital.

Clearly this is no ordinary medical facility!

"A beautiful place," Andy said.

"Yes," Schmuck replied. "Before the German occupation, La Baule had been a hotel for the very wealthy. Makes a good hospital for us."

A white-coated German doctor met them at the door of Captain Foot's room.

"Surprisingly, the patient is conscious and awake," he said. "But I'm not sure he will understand what you say to him. With his head injury, I do not know his level of awareness."

Hodges walked over to Michael's hospital bed. Michael lay between several blankets, neatly spread under him and on top of him. His thin face looked gaunt and yellow.

"Jaundice," the doctor told Andy before he could ask. "The yellow skin is caused by jaundice."

A slight tuft of curly brown hair escaped from the white bandages wrapped around Michael's head.

Andy leaned over and looked into the Englishman's half-opened eyes.

He looks so weak. But he's awake. Maybe he'll understand me. I've got to try to get through to him.

"Michael," Andy whispered and placed his left hand gently on the Englishman's shoulder. "My name is Andy Hodges. I am with the American Red Cross. We're going to get you out of here and to a British hospital."

Michael blinked his eyes several times.

Good. He seems to understand what I said.

Suddenly Michael's eyes widened and his eyebrows furrowed deeply as he glared at the stranger hovering over him.

"Michael," Andy said. "I'm here to help you. Don't be afraid."

Michael's expression showed obvious terror. He opened his mouth and tried to scream. But no sound came out.

"You must leave now, Herr Hodges," the doctor said. "Your presence is obviously upsetting the patient."

• • •

Michael Foot lay flat on his back in his bed. His body felt cold, even with all the blankets covering him. His head throbbed; his neck hurt. As hard as he tried, he could move no part of his body. It just wouldn't respond to his mental commands.

Where am I? What happened to me? I hurt so bloody badly! Why can't I move?

He watched the door open and the two men walk into the room. He seemed to recognize the German captain, and the sight of him made him shudder.

The enemy. His uniform is not Gestapo. Intelligence type for certain. Must be here to interrogate me. I can't hold up to much in this condition.

The other man wore a different, darker uniform—no ribbons or medals—certainly not German. Then Foot noticed the patch on his left shoulder.

American Red Cross—unless I'm mistaken. It's a trick. He's pretending to be from the Red Cross. But if he were, he wouldn't be here with this Jerry. He can't get me to talk. So he's brought a bloody ringer in hopes I will give him information. I will say nothing. They shall never discover I'm SAS.

Michael saw the man in the darker uniform approach him. He immediately stiffened as a hand touched his shoulder.

This man in the Red Cross costume doesn't fool me. I may be helpless, but I'm not stupid. Let him rave on.

He glared at the man, wide-eyed, and wondered what his next move might be.

Andy was determined he wouldn't leave the room until the young Brit knew he had come to help him. He stood back against the wall and waited for Michael to settle down, all the while noticing how Michael's eyes stayed frightfully fixed on him, closely watching his every move.

After several minutes, Hodges decided to try something else. He walked slowly toward Michael's bed. Remembering his recent conversation with Michael's father, he leaned down to whisper in his ear.

"Michael," he said. "I once knew a man by the name of Foot who sold pumpkin pies to Macy's department store in New York City."

Andy looked into the young man's face and smiled.

Michael raised his eyebrows and sharply focused his eyes on Andy's face. For a few seconds, he simply stared at him, as if seeking to digest the words he'd just heard. Then Michael's expression and demeanor changed completely. The scowl of anger and distrust and the look of fear left his face. A certain calmness seemed to settle upon him.

I think I see a flicker of understanding. Michael looks as if he believes me. Maybe he'll listen to me now.

Hodges continued to whisper.

"Michael," he said. "Your father has asked me to bring you home. I will come back in a few days and get you."

Michael cracked his swollen lips and tried to speak. Andy put his ear down to Michael's mouth, straining to catch his words.

"Do . . . you . . . think . . . I . . . can . . . make . . . it?" he said softly and with noticeable great effort. He was clearly in pain.

"Sure you can!" Hodges said with a broad smile. "I'll make sure you get the best medical care on the whole dang continent!"

The patient appeared to relax. He closed his eyes and said no more.

FORTY

ERNTEDANKFEST

**Late Evening, 23 November 1944, Thanksgiving Day,
St. Nazaire Sector**

That evening, Andy was again blindfolded, put into the backseat of a car, and driven to German headquarters.

Andy felt relieved to have found Michael not only alive, but conscious and able to grasp the fact that he would soon be freed. But he felt quite concerned about the medical care, or lack of, that Michael would receive at the La Baule hospital.

No doubt, the Germans are doing their best, but not much can be done with such limited personnel and supplies. He's in bad shape, and he might not live until the exchange date.

Hodges wondered if Michael's condition might deteriorate so much that he could no longer be transported by November 29.

I sure would hate to tell Brigadier Foot that I found his son and arranged an exchange, and then report that it would kill his son to move him. Or, worse, that he had died while being transported.

When the car arrived at the German headquarters building, Schmuck removed Andy's blindfold and the two men walked inside. Andy looked at his wristwatch.

"Hauptmann Schmuck," he said and smiled. "I had no idea this meeting would last all day. I've missed Thanksgiving dinner with my division."

Schmuck looked at the young Yank, and for the first time that day, the thin, neat officer smiled.

"Thanksgiving?" Schmuck asked. "What is that?"

"It's a traditional holiday in the United States. A national day to give thanks to God for what we have, and for the courage of our forefathers who came to America. Back in Alabama, we celebrate with family and friends, and eat turkey and dressing and sweet potatoes. I get hungry just thinking about it. My mouth is already watering."

"Ah, yes!" Schmuck said and thrust his sharp chin in the air. "We, too, in Germany, have a day of 'thanks-giving.' We call it: *Erntedankfest*—our 'harvest festival of thanks.' We celebrate Erntedankfest in October. But it sounds much different than your American Thanksgiving."

Schmuck then added, much to Hodges's surprise: "Herr Hodges, since we have delayed you and caused you to miss your Thanksgiving feast, perhaps you would allow our cook to prepare for you the food we eat on Erntedankfest."

"Why, that's very kind of you," Hodges said. "I'd be delighted."

Two hours later, Andy Hodges, Major Kerrl, Hauptmann Schmuck, a disbelieving and somewhat irritated Oberst Pinski, and an assortment of bemedaled officers sat down at a table covered with plates of steak, fried potatoes, and vegetables.

During the meal, one of the German officers remarked: "You can see for yourself, Herr Hodges, that we are eating excellently here at St. Nazaire."

"Yes, I can," Hodges replied with a nod and grin. "But I believe this may just be a show for my benefit. I doubt whether you eat this well very often."

Hodges heard a few coughs and muffled chuckles. He noticed a few of the Germans sitting around the table glancing and grinning at one another. Even Major Kerrl put his hand to his mouth and tried to hide a smile.

Just like I thought.

After supper, Hodges thanked his German hosts for the unexpected Erntedankfest.

"*Danke schön*," he said with a drawn out Alabama accent.

"You are most welcome, Herr Hodges," Kerrl said.

"Please, sir, call me Andy," Hodges said.

Hodges returned safely to division headquarters sometime before midnight. The next morning, he briefed Bergquist on the discussions and agreements that had taken place the day before with the officers at St. Nazaire.

"Good work, Andy!" the colonel said. "I knew you'd pull it off!"

"Hauptmann Schmuck asked me to return to St. Nazaire headquarters on 27 November, to iron out the final draft of the exchange agreement," Hodges said. "But I'm concerned, sir, about locating a German officer with a *Ritterkreuz* to swap for Captain Foot."

"That will be a tough one," Bergquist said. "Those fellows are few and far between. And if we find such an animal, he may be reluctant to volunteer himself to be exchanged. Only a lunatic or an ego-driven idiot would purposely make himself available for front lines battle when his side is losing the war."

"This officer must be a volunteer. He must come freely and of his own accord," Hodges said. "Any coercion or funny business, and they'll call the deal off."

"I understand. Like I said, we'll be lucky if any highly decorated German officer freely volunteers, especially one with the *Ritterkreuz*. I'll contact our people in the UK, and ask them to help us try to find someone in their POW camps," Bergquist said, and slowly shook his head.

"Thanks, Colonel."

"Andy," Bergquist said, and placed his ample hand on Hodges's shoulder. "No one said this would be easy."

FORTY-ONE

THE *RITTERKREUZ* SEARCH

Friday, 24 November 1944, Officers' POW Camp, Scotland

Kapitanleutnant Karl W. Müller woke, shaved, dressed in his midnight-blue uniform with shiny brass buttons, and ate breakfast with the other prisoner-of-war officers. He had been held in the officers' prison camp in Scotland since his capture on the morning of September 19, 1944, after a British flotilla destroyed his *Schnellboot* in the North Sea near Ostend, Belgium.

The infamous "Tiger of the Channel" wore proudly the *Ritterkreuz* around his neck that day, positioned high at his throat, as he had every day since he had received it on July 8, 1943. Among the other German prisoners at the camp, the prestigious medal gave him a distinction and status that fed his needy ego.

Friday, 24 November 1944, 94th Infantry Division Headquarters, Châteaubriant

Colonel Bergquist had contacted every POW camp in the UK and Europe. But so far in his search for a POW replacement for Michael Foot, he had discovered only six German prisoners of war in Allied camps who had received the *Ritterkreuz*. When approached with the offer of exchange, five of the officers had outright and vehemently declined.

"Andy," he told Hodges later that day. "We've found six German POWs with the *Ritterkreuz* in our camps. I've received immediate answers from five of them. Not one of the five will volunteer for the exchange!"

"I was afraid of that, sir," Hodges said.

"The Germans aren't fools," Bergquist said. "In our POW camps, they get humane treatment, three square meals a day, and no one's shooting at them. They know they won't get that on the German front lines."

"What about the sixth one, sir?"

"I'm still waiting to hear from him, but I don't have much hope for an affirmative answer. He's a recipient of the *Ritterkreuz* and is interned in Scotland. His name is Kapitanleutnant Karl W. Müller and he's a well-known *Schnellboot* commander. I hear the Germans are quite proud of him. Call him the 'Tiger of the Channel'—or some such animal. He's a real terror from what I'm told. I suspect he'll turn us down, too, like the others."

"It's a shame to put a bird like that back out on the sea," Hodges said. "But I hope for Captain Foot's sake, Müller will agree to the exchange."

"Well, the 'Tiger' can't hurt us much in St. Nazaire," Bergquist said. "We've sunk just about everything the Krauts have put in the water over the last few months. I should hear back from the prison commander today and get Müller's answer. I'll let you know the minute I hear."

"Thank you, sir," Andy said. "He seems our only hope."

Friday, 24 November 1944, Officers' POW Camp, Scotland

Kapitanleutnant Müller listened quietly as the Allied camp commander explained plans for the exchange scheduled for November 29 somewhere in France.

"You understand, Kapitanleutnant," the commander said, "that the prisoner swap is for volunteers only? If you don't wish to go, you don't have to."

"Zank you, sir, zank you that I have been given a choice. Am I the only candidate for this exchange?" Müller asked. "Have other German officers also been approached and offered this deal?"

"You are one of six men chosen. The other five have declined the offer," the commander said. "They have refused to go to the front lines—maybe they are afraid of getting shot. You can think about this, but I must have your decision by 1500 hours today."

"Whom will I be exchanged for?" Müller asked.

"He's an Englishman. Captain Michael Foot. I'm told he is of great significance to the British military and government. Your comrades in St. Nazaire refused to release him unless they received in return a German officer of considerable importance—they distinctly specified that he must be a recipient of the distinguished and prestigious *Ritterkreuz*."

Müller raised his cleanly shaven face up to the ceiling light, showing off the deep cleft in his chin. At twenty-eight years old, he had proved himself a naval hero. He reached to his neck and touched the *Ritterkreuz*. He focused his small, dark eyes on the camp commander and simply said: "I will consider this offer. Again, I zank you, sir. Zank you much."

Müller walked back to his barracks, paced the floor for hours, and pondered his decision.

I am safe here, well fed, and have my basic needs met. If I agree to the exchange, I will be expected to take command of a Schnellboot and return to the battle at sea. If Germany wins the war, and I survive the battles, I will become a war hero. If Germany loses the war, I will be killed in combat or taken prisoner.

Müller sat down on his bunk and put his head in his hands.

Five German officers, also holding the Ritterkreuz, *have already turned down the exchange offer. I cannot believe they are afraid! Do they know something I don't know? Or are they, like I, tired of combat and wish not to fight further battles?*

He remembered the dark night on September 18–19, 1944, when his S-boat took fire from the British MTB and he had to abandon his ship. The freezing deep waters had engulfed him, causing his legs to go numb, and had threatened to drive him to the bottom of the sea. Yet he fought for his life. He fought so that he could continue to serve the Fatherland. He faced the terror, the exhaustion, the heavy eyelids, and the grasping cold hands of his approaching death. For nine hours in the icy water, he struggled to gulp one breath of air after another, to stay alive—for the Fatherland.

He recalled his last thought before he finally closed his eyes, submitted himself to the powerful sea, and felt himself float helplessly on its surface: *If the sea wins, so be it. I will die a hero. I have honored my Fatherland.*

The Fatherland. My Fatherland.

Müller rose from his bunk. He had made his decision.

I have no choice. I must go. I must honor the Fatherland while I still have life and breath to do so.

FORTY-TWO

GOOD NEWS TRAVELS FAST

27 November 1944, Camp Franco

At thirty-five years of age, American Corporal Onald Nelson was the oldest POW in Camp Franco. He recorded in his diary bits and pieces of everyday prison life.

14 September: "The water is undrinkable, so we only drink coffee."

26 September: "Still no water."

29 October: "Excitement last night! Two lieutenants found that the guards had left the door open. . . . They tried to get away, but the guards were nearby. They heard them and fired two shots. The lieutenants are in solitary confinement."

6 November: "Coyne tried to escape yesterday during the headcount, but he was caught and given five days in solitary."

7 November: "Today is Election Day at home. We took a vote amongst ourselves. Roosevelt won."

8 November: "Five German deserters were shot."

20 November: "Fantastic! Mass escape! Four officers have gotten away!"

21 November: "We were locked in all day. The Germans are furious. Two of the officers who tried to escape have been recaptured and brought back. They are seriously beaten."

24 November: "The best news in the whole wide world! The [German] general called us together and told us there will be a big prisoner exchange one day next week!"

26 November: "Another difficult day for the nerves; exchange could be tomorrow."

Second Lieutenant James Silva picked up the forsaken diary of Jack Norelius on the day Norelius escaped from Camp Franco—November 20, 1944. Silva read the earlier entry scratchings and then began writing his own diary on the day and page where Norelius stopped. Silva wrote:

20 November: "The highlight of the day was that four men escaped. The escape grew from the fortunate missing of Lt. Keller at roll call. He came back and unlocked our doors. A long time elapsed between the time of escape and the search of the rooms by the guards. Changed rooms to across hall in afternoon. Locked in. Searched rooms. Confiscated most of extra food they could find."

21 November: "Rumors from Germans is they caught Michael [Foot] and Leo [Léon Spanin]. French turned them over. They are hurt. Other

two still free [Norelius and Keller]. General came. They want to find out how the boys got out."

22 November: "The Captain promised us almost everything if we would tell how the boys got out. He tried to trick us all kinds of ways. He even promised us a taxi ride to Paris. We refused. He gave us back some of the things that were confiscated in the earlier search. Evening passed normal except for the very alert guards. They have been alert since the escape."

23 November: "We were allowed to move back into our old rooms this morning, but our move was under very careful scrutiny from guards who watched all our movement. But we were able to get extra food unnoticed. New room has changed a bit. Skylight is boarded. There is a new heavy-duty lock on the door. All the planks have extra and heavier spikes in them. Our ventilation holes in the shutter were blocked by metal. The outside house door had a heavy lock on it. Besides all these escape precautions, they have strung lights all over the factory and lit it all up. Things are getting more difficult. Léon [Spanin] is back locked up in the little shack where we used to live. Some of the fellows got a glimpse of him, and he is in terrible shape. They won't let us near there. I tried to find out how he was. It was impossible. Germans rumor they have caught the others. We don't believe them."

26 November 1944, 94th Infantry Division Headquarters, Châteaubriant

Andy Hodges prepared for the next day's trip to St. Nazaire to meet with German officers and finalize the details for the November 29 POW exchange at Pornic. He requisitioned Red Cross supplies to take with him to the prisoners—medical necessities, food, cigars, cigarettes, and toiletries—and stacked the boxes high in his jeep.

In his satchel he carried Major General Malony's letter of November 21, typed on American Red Cross stationery, and addressed to "*An den Deutschen Kommandanten*, St. Nazaire."

No right-thinking German would mess with the guy carrying this letter . . . I hope.

He also carried the 1938 Michelin map, identifying the next day's meeting place as well as the site for the Pornic exchange, with the tissue overlay appropriately marked and Hauptmann Schmuck's hand-signed note: "In confirmation of our agreement made on 23 November 1944."

What Landser troops would intercept the mail of Generalleutnant Hans Junck and ignore the note of Hauptmann Schmuck, his chief of intelligence?

Andy reviewed once again the list of agreements he and Hauptmann Schmuck had discussed earlier. Hodges had added an extra sentence to the list—"It is requested that your concurrence to the above terms be indicated by indorsement [*sic*] hereon"—and left a space for Oberst Pinski to sign:

"*Für den Festungskommandanten St. Nazaire*

"*Der Chef des Stabes und l. Generalstabsoffizier.*"

With Pinski's concurrence on behalf of his general, Andy concluded and said aloud: "Okay, the hay's in the barn."

Well almost. I've seen enough wrangling between Allies to imagine how crises could arise between combatants. How this exchange drama will play out is anybody's guess.

Hodges folded his Red Cross flags to later drape on his jeep.

That afternoon he had a telephone call from Bergquist.

"Andy," Bergquist said. "I presume everything is ready for your meeting tomorrow with Schmuck and Pinski?"

"Yes, sir," Hodges said. "Everything's ready."

"What about Müller?" he asked. "Everything on schedule with his flight from Scotland?"

"Yes, sir," Andy said. "Müller will be arriving here at headquarters tomorrow. We'll take him with us to Pornic the day of the exchange. We're all set to go, sir."

"Good work!" Bergquist said. "I knew you'd have things under control! Just keep it that way."

FORTY-THREE

THE DISAPPOINTMENT

St. Nazaire, Early Morning, 27 November 1944

Andy stuck the Red Cross flag in the jeep's front holder and set out for St. Nazaire. He stopped frequently to check his map, turning the thin tissue overlay round and round until it fit over the map's proper coordinates. A penned note in English on the overlay stated: "X marks meeting place—main road (GC5)—between Chauve and to Saint-Père-en-Retz. St. Père-en-Retz to second road to left up to X."

This is so confusing! I have no idea where I'll end up.

He studied the handwritten English notations once more, making sure he was reading the markings correctly.

The cold November winds blew rain from the Atlantic as Andy motored slowly along narrow roads, keeping an ever-watchful eye out for some trigger-happy German soldier with a machine gun. Every rustling bush or swaying tree limb threatened to shelter the enemy. He licked his lips; his mouth was so dry.

As he drew closer to enemy lines, Andy thought about Mary Louise and their toddler son, Gerry, back at home in Alabama.

Is this prisoner exchange worth the huge risk I'm taking? I'm purposely putting myself in a dangerous situation that could end my life at any minute. Is that fair to my family?

He shook his head, took a deep breath, and felt glad Mary Louise was so many miles away.

Why, that woman of mine would have a fit if she saw me right now! Where'd she and the boy be if someone loosed off a few rounds at the guy in the jeep wearing the weird uniform?!

Then Andy envisioned the young British patient, Michael Foot, his head bandaged, his neck broken, his eyes reflecting a mixture of terror, pain, and pleading.

Sure. It's worth the risk. Not only for Foot, but for all the fellows in that camp. They're cold, hungry, and sick. Yep, it's definitely worth it. Someday, in some future war, one of those soldiers wasting away in a foreign POW camp might be my own Little Gerry. I sure hope some guy would risk his neck to save him.

Andy was still thinking about his son when he reached the designated meeting place on the edge of St. Nazaire. It was nothing fancy, just an intersection in the middle of nowhere with an old building nearby. After stopping the jeep, he reached for his satchel, stepped out, and stretched. He checked to make sure all the Red Cross flags were clearly visible.

Okay, Germans! Here I am! Well protected and heavily armed with my briefcase and flags.

Hauptmann Schmuck met Andy Hodges by the old building and led him inside a large room. When Hodges entered, Pinski and a group of German officers stood up from their chairs and gave the customary *Hitlergruß.* Andy gave a halfhearted wave of the hand that could pass for a salute.

"Do you have the necessary paperwork, Herr Hodges?" Pinski asked impatiently.

Hodges withdrew the documents from his satchel and handed them to Pinski. "Yes," he said. "Please check them and make sure they meet with your approval."

"You may rest assured, Herr Hodges, we will do exactly that," Pinski said, giving a thin smile to the others.

After Pinski read the papers line by line, occasionally stopping for a point of clarification with Schmuck, he asked: "Herr Hodges, have you found a volunteer with the *Ritterkreuz* to exchange for Captain Foot?"

"Yes, I have," Hodges responded. "His name is Kapitanleutnant Karl W. Müller, a member of the Kriegsmarine. Do you know who he is?"

"Of course, we know of Kapitanleutnant Müller!" Pinski said. "A naval hero! The Führer will be most happy to know 'The Tiger' will soon be back in action."

"Kapitanleutnant Müller will fly in from Scotland tomorrow," Hodges said. "He will travel with me to Pornic on 29 November to be exchanged for Captain Foot. Just like we agreed."

Pinski passed the papers to Schmuck. After he'd made a further review, Pinski signed his name opposite that of the American colonel.

"It is now official," Pinski said. "The exchange will take place at Pornic on 29 November between the hours of 0900 and 1800."

"Just one more thing," Andy said. "Let me make sure that you have made the necessary arrangements to transport Captain Foot safely by ambulance to the exchange site on 29 November. He will need skilled medics to accompany him to Pornic."

Schmuck glanced at Pinski.

"Herr Hodges," Schmuck said, clearing his throat. "We have encountered a most unfortunate problem we must discuss with you."

The Hauptmann handed Hodges a typed letter with his signature at the bottom.

"Please read this letter," Schmuck said, "so that we may discuss the details with some intelligence."

Andy took the letter and silently read its message. After he finished, he laid the letter on a nearby table and frowned.

"Hauptmann Schmuck," Hodges replied. "This is not acceptable, and we have nothing more to discuss."

Andy Hodges stood silently, still frowning, and looked at Schmuck.

I should have expected something like this. He expects me to believe that

Captain Foot can't be transported because of his 'shaked brains' and 'para-lysed bowels and bladder'? And he has the gall to ask me to release three of his POWs taken by American troops near St. Omer: Ehlfeldt, Engler, and Mager? Unbelievable!

"Take me to see Captain Foot," Hodges demanded.

Michael Foot could barely open his eyes when Schmuck, Hodges, and the German doctor walked into his hospital room at La Baule.

"His condition has declined significantly," the doctor said. "He is not able to be transported."

Michael looked up longingly at Hodges, his eyes begging him to inter-vene, to take him home. The Red Cross field director patted Michael's shoulder: "Michael, in two days I will come back and take you to a British hospital and to your father. You're going to make it, Michael, just hold on for a couple of days. Can you do that?"

Michael tried to nod, but he couldn't move his head. The pain proved too intense. Instead he managed to blink his eyes several times in response.

"I promise you, Michael, I'll be back for you," Hodges said, then smiled and softly squeezed the young Englishman's shoulder.

Hodges said little to Schmuck on the drive back from the hospital. When they returned to headquarters, Pinksi greeted them.

"You have now seen for yourself," Pinksi told Hodges. "Captain Foot is much worse, and he certainly cannot be moved."

"Yes," Hodges said. "His condition has grown considerably worse. But, Oberst Pinksi, as we agreed, you will bring him to Pornic on the day after tomorrow, and at that time, I will take him with me. He needs medical treatment that you are unable to give him at La Baule—"

"But the Brit is dying," Schmuck interrupted. "He will not live until the 29th, and if he does, he certainly cannot survive the transport to Pornic!"

"We made an agreement and I intend to fulfill my promise to you,"

Hodges stated firmly. "I will deliver Kapitanleutnant Müller to you on 29 November at the Pornic exchange. Now I expect you to honor your word as a German officer regarding Captain Foot."

"If he is moved and he dies," a red-faced Pinski blurted out, "his death shall be on your head, not ours! We will not take responsibility for your foolish decision!"

"Oberst Pinski, Hauptmann Schmuck, once you deliver Captain Foot safely into our hands at Pornic—as we agreed—we will take full responsibility for his well-being. You will be released from any further liability for his welfare."

The room became uncomfortably quiet as the Germans exchanged glances. Andy said nothing more, but waited patiently and unyieldingly to receive an answer. Pinski and Schmuck excused themselves, stepped out of the room, and walked down the hall—still within Andy's viewing distance. For several minutes, Andy watched them as they talked, sometimes appearing quite angered and animated. When they returned, Pinski spoke directly to Hodges.

"When you deliver to us Kapitanleutnant Müller on 29 November at Pornic, if Captain Foot is still alive, we will release him to you as we agreed," he said.

"If he is still alive"? I don't like the way that sounds.

"Herr Hodges," Schmuck said and attempted a smile-turned-sneer. "I mentioned in my letter three additional German POWs in your prison camp, and I asked for their release. Did you see that request?"

"Yes, I saw it," Hodges said. "I will present your request to Colonel Bergquist. You will have an answer from him on 29 November."

"I have brought Red Cross supplies for our prisoners," Hodges added. "Can they be delivered to Camp Franco today?"

"Certainly," Schmuck said.

"Will you kindly sign a receipt listing the items and distribute them to our men?" Hodges asked.

The Hauptmann nodded his head and signed the list. Hodges was glad the meeting was finally over.

. . .

Colonel Bergquist called Hodges into his office when Andy returned to headquarters that afternoon.

"How did the meeting go, Andy?" Bergquist asked.

"As well as could be expected," he said. "They are still hesitant about giving up Captain Foot. It's a good thing we have Müller as a bargaining tool. Without him, they'd never agree to release Foot."

"Andy," the colonel said. "I've got some bad news. Very bad news."

"What is it, sir?" Hodges asked. "Does it concern the exchange?"

"I'm afraid so," he said.

"Please don't tell me Müller's backed out of the agreement!" Andy said.

"No," Bergquist said. "But I've just gotten word that bad weather has closed in throughout the UK and Scotland. Unless the overcast clears, no planes will be allowed to fly."

Andy rubbed his forehead and sighed. "That is bad news, sir," he said. "Müller's supposed to fly in from Scotland tomorrow so I can drive him to Pornic for the exchange on the following morning. If Müller doesn't show, the Germans will refuse to release Foot. In Foot's poor condition, I don't know how long he'll last at the German hospital."

"I know, son," Bergquist said. "But planes can't fly in this weather. Maybe, if the skies clear, he'll make it by the 29th. But weather's one thing this army can't command."

FORTY-FOUR

THE DILEMMA

28 November 1944, St. Nazaire

When U.S. Army Air Force pilot Second Lieutenent James Silva first heard about the possibility of a prisoner exchange, he wrote in his diary:

24 November: "High ranking officers came this morning. They brought good news. There would be an exchange of all prisoners, except Michael [Foot]. Michael might not be well enough to make it. This came after they fired questions at us about how we were living. Were there any beefs we had to bring up? A sudden change to kindness. We were told it was strictly voluntary. Anyone not wishing to be exchanged could go to the commandant before three o'clock that afternoon. I lined up the men outside while the Krauts told them. Were they happy! But I was afraid of a trick. I tried to calm the men down and have them take it in stride. It was difficult. Practically impossible. No one volunteered to remain. Sleeping was difficult. Leo [Léon Spanin] came and got his stuff. We got the story of his escape."

27 November: "Another day of wild discussion. It is difficult to calm everybody down in case this is a trick."

28 November: "Commandant called a formation. Explaining we will take our own clothes, leave what we wish, and we will look as good as possible. Told us it is foolish to escape now. I'm still suspicious. I don't trust him."

Corporal Onald Nelson, sitting on his wooden bunk at Camp Franco, made a quick note in his diary:

28 November: "The exchange—it's tomorrow, for sure."

On the day of the exchange, November 29, Lieutenant Silva wrote in his daily logbook: "Sergeant Iannone woke us up. . . . I shaved and got ready. I counted the men; they were more than ready. We decided to leave the [Red Cross] medical supplies and cigars behind, as well as some of the clothing. The guards put us on a bus with the camp commandant. We were blindfolded as we got close to the front line. We later dismounted and were put into a couple of small boats, one for the French and the other for the Americans and the British. We crossed the Loire River and two other buses were waiting for us on the other side. As we got close to the exchange point, we got out of the bus, formed up in ranks, and marched to the exchange point."

Andy Hodges checked the UK weather report early that morning.

All flights still grounded. May be grounded for a while. How will I ever explain to Pinski that Kapitanleutnant Müller won't be here today, tomorrow, or maybe all week?

Hodges knew the German officer wouldn't release Michael Foot if Müller didn't show up for the exchange that day at Pornic.

Pinski will think I'm pulling a fast one. He and Schmuck want to keep Captain Foot anyway. This will give them the perfect excuse. If Michael stays at La Baule, he won't live long in his poor condition. He may already be dead.

Hodges bathed, dressed, gathered his maps and documents, and packed his small travel bag. He prayed that the prisoner exchange would go smoothly, maybe as well as the swap at Lorient. But he had lingering doubts.

Andy Hodges and Colonel Bergquist traveled the straight, flat, rural roads, conversing like old friends, and arrived at the exchange site—the La Rogère crossroads near Pornic, early on 29 November.

National and international news reporters were already there. They immediately pounced on the colonel, bombarding him with questions. Also surrounding the colonel were photographers—the official German naval photographer with a 35 mm Leica, and two U.S. Army Signal Corps cameramen, one with a triple turret Bell & Howell motion-picture-film Eyemo—for newsreel recordings—and the other with a press camera—a Speed Graphic camera and flash. Scores of unofficial photographers with cheap Kodak box and Brownie cameras also swarmed around Bergquist, popping flashbulbs and recording the events. Hodges looked at the reporters swarming around the colonel.

Looks like flies on a mule! Where did they all come from?!

Bergquist waved them away in order to make an official statement:

"At 0900, in the vicinity of Pornic, France, the Germans and Americans called a truce here at the crossroads," he began. "The cease-fire will last until 1800 hours, at which time the fighting in this area will resume. Soldiers from the 93rd French Infantry Regiment are here to defend the vicinity and to help keep the peace while the exchange takes place."

Bergquist also outlined the conditions of the exchange, the details that had been approved by both sides. When he finished speaking, the reporters overwhelmed him with questions, all the while flashing camera bulbs in his face. With a considerate and seasoned dignity, Bergquist answered each question. At one point during the noisy madness, the colonel paused, took a deep breath, and turned to Hodges.

"Remember this moment, Andy," Bergquist said and smiled. "Thanks to you, this event will go down in history."

FORTY-FIVE

THE PORNIC EXCHANGE

29 November 1944, Pornic, France

Andy Hodges stood waiting in the quiet morning with the American and French officers, photographers, and civilians, approximately one mile east of Pornic, France, at the bullet-pockmarked concrete road sign stating the location—Road Junction D6 on road D14b.

He watched soft rain drizzle on the French troops from the 1st FFI Battalion of the Vendée, as they stood along the long, isolated, muddy stretch of road, armed and ready. The troops controlled the sector La Bernerie-en-Retz to the La Rogère crossroads, where the exchange was to occur.

Escorted and surrounded by American military police, Hodges and Bergquist stood with the fifty-four German prisoners to be exchanged for the equal number of allied POWs. Under overcast skies, they waited patiently on one side of the barbed wire concertina for the rest of the German officers and guards to arrive with the prisoners—nineteen Americans, thirty-one Frenchmen, two Brits, and the injured English captain, Michael Foot.

The air seemed a powder keg of tension.

One stray shot, one misfired bullet, one restless German POW starting a scuffle with an American military officer—and this whole thing could blow up in our faces!

Andy bit his bottom lip. An American jeep armed with a 30-cal. machine gun pulled up and stopped on the road near him. He noticed how tightly the military police held their M1 rifles. They, too, seemed to expect trouble.

This is a disaster just waiting to happen. With Pinski's quick temper and sharp, uncontrolled tongue, I reckon things couldn't go smoothly.

Several minutes passed. Bergquist checked his watch. The German POWs shuffled their feet. Andy worried that the German officers and guards, and French, British, and American prisoners, would be late—too late to complete the exchange during the brief hours of the cease-fire. He also felt great concern over the state of Michael Foot. No ambulance had yet arrived.

I hope Michael is still alive. And if so, that Pinski keeps his word and brings him today.

He remembered Pinski's last words to him about Captain Foot at their 27 November meeting. "*When you deliver to us Kapitanleutnant Müller on 29 November at Pornic, if Captain Foot is still alive, we will release him to you as we agreed.*"

"*If Captain Foot is still alive.*" *I didn't like the way that sounded then, and I don't like the way it sounds now.*

Andy wondered what might have happened in the two days since his conversation with Pinski and Schmuck.

They could have shot and killed Michael, and so conveniently blamed his death on his "shaked brains and paralysed bowels and bladder." The German doctor's report would falsely confirm that his death was due to injuries received on 21 November during his escape attempt. And there's not one thing we could do about it.

The sounds of engines interrupted Hodges's concerns. A caravan of vehicles pulled up at the Le Rogère crossroads, splashing muddy water as they raced through puddles and came to an abrupt stop. From the cars emerged Oberst Pinski, Major Kerrl, Hauptmann Schmuck, and a host of other officers. Following salutes all around, Hodges introduced the German officers to Bergquist. Hodges, Bergquist, and the German officers stood stiffly side by side and posed for cameras as photographers encircled them and snapped pictures, preserving the event for posterity.

After a few minutes of necessary and obviously uncomfortable conversation, Bergquist turned to Schmuck. "You requested that we release three additional German prisoners: Lieutenant Ehlfeldt, Sergeant Engler, and Corporal Mager," he said. "As a token of good gesture, we are willing to do this. They are here and ready to be exchanged."

"Thank you, Colonel Bergquist," Schmuck replied, his sharp chin held high, and his hands clasped tightly behind his wasp-thin waist.

Bergquist looked over the sea of drab, colorless uniforms—a mix of khaki, green, and gray. He watched the exchange take place as one would watch a well-choreographed Broadway play. The actors looked tired and ragged, thin and weathered. But the various stages of the POW swap were coordinated and perfectly timed, like they had been repeatedly rehearsed. Everything happened smoothly, as if synchronized to a predictable rhythm. The Allied and German combatants never came within close contact with one another lest they have opportunity to jeer, insult, or taunt. Each part of the operation and maneuver came across as hoped and intended. Doctors examined troops; prisoners waited patiently. Lists were checked and rechecked; roll was called and answered. When ordered to move, newly freed prisoners marched quietly and obediently toward their respective lines.

When the exchange was half completed, Bergquist turned to Hodges and asked: "Andy, has Pinski or Schmuck mentioned Captain Foot or Kapitanleutnant Müller to you today?"

"No, sir," Hodges replied. "Not a word."

Bergquist furrowed his brow. "That's not a good sign. I've not seen an ambulance all morning. I wonder if they're planning to bring Foot."

"Neither have I, sir," Hodges said. "I hope Captain Foot is still alive and able to travel, and that Pinski will keep his word."

"I wonder what Pinski's reaction will be when he finds out Kapitanleutnant Müller isn't here," Bergquist said. "He may not allow Captain Foot to go with us."

"I've been thinking about that, sir," Hodges said. "I hope he'll agree to our proposition."

"I would strongly advise you, Andy, to reconsider that proposition," Bergquist warned. "It's far too dangerous to go ahead with your plan."

"With your permission, sir, I still want to do this," Hodges said. "Captain Foot—if he's still alive—won't last much longer in his condition. We've got to get him out of there."

"It's your choice, Andy," Bergquist said and exhaled deeply. "I don't like it, but I won't stand in your way."

A few minutes passed as the two men watched the prisoner exchange proceed.

"Andy," Bergquist said. "I want you to notice something about the POWs. Look at the American prisoners."

Andy looked at the group of Americans cheering and laughing, bubbling over with excitement as they marched toward the Allied boundary. Several men looked directly into the moving picture camera, smiled showing all their yellowed teeth, and flashed the "V" sign.

"They look happy to be free," Andy said.

"Now look at the German POWs," Bergquist said.

Andy watched the newly freed volunteers as they moved toward German lines. They said nothing. They lowered their heads and looked at the ground, their faces downcast or without expression.

"See the difference?" Bergquist asked. "The Germans know they're headed back to combat. No doubt, most of them are aware that their Fatherland can't last much longer. I wonder if any of them will still have homes or families left—if they ever get back to Germany."

Andy looked at his wristwatch: 1700 hours. In sixty minutes the cease-fire would end, and the muddy stretch of road would once again become an active battleground. Andy saw a white ambulance pull up. German medics opened the vehicle's rear doors and carefully lifted out a blanket-covered patient on a stretcher. Andy walked to the ambulance and knelt beside the young Captain Foot.

"Michael, I'm real glad to see you!" he said.

The young English captain opened his eyes and smiled.

"Like I promised," Andy said, "we're taking you to receive medical treatment and then back to your father. He'll be so glad to have you home."

"Thank you," Michael whispered. "Thank you."

When U.S. medics approached the stretcher to take Michael to another ambulance that would transport him to Allied lines, Andy heard a German voice shout: "Wait! Not so fast!" He turned around and saw Pinski standing behind him.

"Herr Hodges," Pinski said. "As we agreed, and against the doctor's advice, we have delivered Captain Foot to you. We are ready to make the exchange with Kapitanleutnant Müller." Pinski turned his head and searched the area. "Where is Müller?"

Andy took a deep breath. "Oberst Pinski, the weather has closed in over Scotland, and Kapitanleutnant Müller's plane was unable to take off yesterday or this morning. He won't be coming here today. No one can say when the weather will clear. But let me be honest with you, it doesn't look promising for the next few days."

Oberst Pinski narrowed his eyes and focused them on Hodges's face. He was careful to control his quick temper, to keep his face expressionless, acutely aware that photographers were snapping pictures of the German officer's every move.

I trusted this man, Hodges, and he has deceived me, making a mockery of our agreement. He lied when he claimed Kapitanleutnant Müller had agreed to be exchanged for Captain Foot. And I was fool enough to believe this Yank!

"Herr Hodges," Pinski said through gritted teeth, his face becoming various shades of crimson. "We had an agreement. Without Kapitanleutnant Müller, there will be no exchange with Captain Foot."

"Oberst Pinski," Hodges said. "I'm afraid the weather in Scotland is beyond my control. However, I am prepared to stay as your prisoner in place of Kapitanleutnant Müller, until the weather clears, his plane can arrive, and he can be delivered safely to you at St. Nazaire."

What?! Surely I misheard Hodges. Did he say . . . no . . . of course not! He is not a stupid man!

"Herr Hodges," Pinski said, a questioning look on his face, "I did not hear you correctly. Would you repeat yourself?"

"I am now your prisoner, Oberst Pinski," Hodges said louder and more clearly. He reached down and picked up a small travel bag. "I'm packed and ready to go with you as soon as we complete the exchange."

". . . I . . . I . . . don't . . . under . . . stand," Pinski stuttered. "Why . . ."

"Captain Foot desperately needs medical attention in a properly equipped hospital. I promised his father I would see that he received it, and then send him home to England. And I gave you my word I would have Kapitanleutnant Müller here at Pornic today to exchange for Captain Foot. Since the weather has prevented me from keeping my word to you, Oberst Pinski, I am offering myself as the exchange prisoner for Captain Foot."

This man, Hodges, is offering himself in order to save the life of the Brit, Captain Foot?! Does he not understand the danger he invites by doing so? Would he be risking his own neck if he were trying to deceive us? Perhaps he has made an arrangement with Kapitanleutnant Müller after all. Maybe he is telling the truth about the weather closing in.

"You . . . you . . . will do that . . . for Captain Foot?" Pinski asked, still somewhat stunned.

"Yes, I will," Hodges answered. "I have received permission from Colonel Bergquist, and I have prepared to do so." Hodges patted his travel bag. "I'm ready to go as soon as we finish up here."

After a time of silence, Pinski spoke. "You may go ahead and take Captain Foot with you, Herr Hodges. And it will not be necessary for you to become a prisoner at Camp Franco. You may go back today with the rest of your division."

Pinski paused and looked Hodges in the eye. "Oberleutnant Schmitt and Hauptmann Reick judged you correctly when they told us that you are an American with unusual integrity!"

"Thank you, Oberst Pinski," Hodges said. "And I give you my word, as soon as the weather clears and Kapitanleutnant Müller's plane is able to take off in Scotland and land in France, I will drive him to you in

St. Nazaire myself. That's a promise—on my honor as an American Red Cross representative."

"I believe you, Herr Hodges," Pinski said and nodded. "Yes, I believe you."

"One more thing, Oberst Pinski."

"What is it, Herr Hodges?"

"You may call me Andy."

At the end of the day, a few minutes before 1800 hours, after the American, French, and German POWs had been officially released and welcomed by their respective military parties, the officers from each side met together in the middle of the road: the American Red Cross's Andrew Hodges; division chief of staff Colonel Earl Bergquist; German chief of staff Oberst Harry Pinski; Major Karl-Heinz Kerrl, adjutant to Generalleutnant Hans Junck; Hauptmann Heinz-Roland Schmuck; Oberleutnant-zur-See Joachim-Hans von Reibnitz, public relations officer; Captain Hochstetter, 94th Infantry Division interpreter; and French officers, representatives, and the swarm of press. All proclaimed the November 29, 1944, St. Nazaire exchange a triumphant success.[1]

The night before the exchange, Corporal Nelson and the other POWs had left the Germans at St. Nazaire a small remembrance of them. On a wall of the camp, they drew a large five-point star with an American flag in the middle and "U.S.A." lettered beneath it. Then each man wrote his name and hometown around it.

Late that night after the exchange, Nelson made an entry in his diary:

29 November: "No one slept last night—this morning we were up at 0500 for the bus; we crossed the Loire two hours later—at one point the Germans made us blindfold ourselves. Then the exchange. Brass heats everywhere. All this was covered by war correspondents and newsreel cameras. The correspondents took all our names and told us it would be in the United States papers in four days. Hope Mom reads it so she'll know I'm safe. Later, we've

been treated like kings. For the first meal—steaks! Pork chops for supper! A show tonight, and this afternoon—a shower. . . . All this I'll have to sleep on."

In mid-December Mary Louise Hodges received a phone call from a friend.

"Mary Louise!" her friend exclaimed. "It's unbelievable! I just saw your husband in a newsreel at the Alabama Theater!"

Hodges's young wife grabbed her coat and took the next bus to the Alabama Theater. She impatiently endured the picture show, waiting for the Movietone newsreel always shown at the end. She beamed when she saw her smiling husband standing among the newly freed French, American, and British soldiers and airmen. She heard brief details of his negotiations resulting in the historic prisoner exchange at Pornic, France. After it ended, Mary Louise sat through another showing of the same movie—*And Now Tomorrow*, again watching Loretta Young and Alan Ladd perform, just to see her husband smiling once more in the newsreel. The next day the young mother took her toddler son, Gerry, to see the short news film. Again she had to watch rich, deaf Emily Blair (Loretta Young) fall in love with the handsome Doctor Merek Vance (Alan Ladd) who struggled to develop a new serum to cure Emily's deafness. After a fully hearing Blair and Dr. Vance finally wed at the end of the film, Mary Louise pointed to her husband's face on the big screen's newsreel, and said: "Look, Gerry, that's Daddy!"

When Mary Louise told the owner of the theater her husband was Andrew Gerow Hodges, he gave her sections of the film to keep.

As the word spread, she received phone calls from her friends: "Mary Louise," one friend told her, "the newspapers are calling your husband a 'diplomatic wizard' and an 'exchange artist.'"

She began to clip the articles about him that appeared in local and national newspapers, even in the *New York Times*.

"Birmingham Red Cross Aid Negotiates Captive Exchange," wrote the *Birmingham Age-Herald*; "Prisoner Swap Makes 'Em Smile," proclaimed the *Stars and Stripes*. Others included "Former Grid Star Negotiates Prisoner Swap," "Nazis Free 53 Allied Men," and many more.

FORTY-SIX

THE REPORT

29 November 1944, Allied Lines, France

Colonel Bergquist and men of the 94th welcomed the American ex-POWs to Allied lines with loud music, hot meals, showers, clean uniforms, and all the Lucky Strikes they could smoke.

Bergquist tasked Lieutenant Colonel R. Love, division G-2, with interviewing all the prisoners to learn the scoop about German defensive positions in St. Nazaire. On December 2, he reported to Bergquist:

"The repatriated prisoners estimate that approximately thirty-eight thousand men occupy the St. Nazaire section. Among them are Russians, Poles, Czechs, Italians, and Romanians. They're employed in various trades and many as soldiers. The Germans have basic training camps with firing ranges in the city of St. Nazaire."

"How is morale?" Bergquist asked.

"Very low. The prison guards believe St. Nazaire will fall by Christmas, and that the war will end by spring. They have little food, perhaps only enough to last until spring. They plan to surrender without a fight."

He continued: "They have one Tiger tank armed with an 88, obviously in poor condition, an armored car with an 88, and an American half-track—

pulled by horses. They claim to have several large ships with guns fore and aft and anti-aircraft weapons on some. They also spotted two or three four-thousand-ton ships in the port, many armed patrol boats, minesweepers in the sub pens, and a single U-boat. Most of the everyday transportation is done by horses—thousands of them, underfed and bone-thin."

"What about communication and supplies?" Bergquist asked.

"They receive mail from Germany every four days. They have radios, and soldiers can speak to their families in Germany. Our men saw a hydra-plane land one night. They noticed it was heavily defended by anti-air weapons. A four-car train arrives in the morning and leaves in the afternoon transporting troops and workers.

"Supplies have reached a critical state. Coats are thin and dirty; boots are in bad shape; no laundry service; munitions are low; not enough oil supplies to light lamps; electricity only three nights a week; wood is rationed; can only bring in food and cigarettes. They can't send money home; they keep it to buy food from local farmers and merchants."

"How do the Germans defend the area?" the colonel inquired.

"Mostly by barbed wire and mines. They have mined the water, roads, and beaches. They post 'Mine Warning' signs where they place no mines, and hide the mines where they put no signs. Guns are mounted on trucks; bunkers, marked with a red cross, contain machine guns and powerful anti-aircraft guns. Large floodlights are placed along the riverbank. By the roadsides, they have barrels used to create smoke screens during air attacks. Despite the shortages, they are ready and well prepared for battle."

"What about medical supplies and care?" Bergquist asked.

"They have three or four hospitals, with two to three hundred beds in at least two of them. The medical supplies are limited and inadequate. No medicine to treat even common illnesses and infections. They are dealing with polluted water, fleas, and no new bandages. Surgeries are performed with local anesthesia, if any. Ether, if available, is used only for amputations."

"Very informative, Colonel," Bergquist said. "Hopefully the German guards are right and this fight will be over by Christmas."

FORTY-SEVEN

GROUNDED STILL

30 November 1944, 94th Infantry Division Headquarters, Châteaubriant

On Thursday morning, November 30, Andy Hodges checked the United Kingdom's weather forecast. It was not encouraging.

Overcast. All aircraft still grounded in Scotland.

Hodges was growing concerned about Kapitanleutnant Müller's arrival in France, and the promise he had made to Pinski.

Another day with overcast skies and grounded flights. How many days— or even weeks—before the weather clears and planes can take off?

Andy worried that Müller might renege on his agreement to be exchanged.

With all this extra time to mull it over, will "The Tiger" come to his senses and change his mind? If that happens, the fat will hit the fire! What would ole Pinski think about that?!

Hodges could just imagine Pinski's reaction to that disastrous news: his pale face and bulging ears burning brick-red, his squinting eyes becoming ophidian, his Mount Vesuvius temper erupting and spewing everywhere.

How that burr-headed, unimpressively statured man with the narrow shoulders and sunken chest can elicit such terror—I have no idea! But I certainly don't want to deal with him if Müller backs out!

Hodges had no Plan B if Müller chickened out of the agreement. He knew that without the Kapitanleutnant, the cupboard would be bare.

Hodges kept a check on the weather until late that evening. But nothing changed.

FORTY-EIGHT

"TAKE ME HOME"

Thursday, 30 November 1944, Lorient

On that same day, flying above the Lorient sector, Lieutenant William Sullivan's B-17 took a direct blow from German ground fire.

"We've been hit!" shouted Sullivan, the USAAF pilot of "Take Me Home," on mission from Kimbolton, England, sent to destroy a factory in Zeitz, Germany, south of Berlin.

Sullivan's heavy Flying Fortress took another burst of flak. From where he sat, he saw the direct strike on one of the bomber's four engines.

"We've lost an engine!" he called to his crew as anti-aircraft shells began exploding beside the plane. The B-17 shook as shells blasted all around it. Sullivan heard the sickening sound of shredding metal as flak repeatedly impacted the plane's wings.

"Sir, we should abort this mission," Second Lieutenant Henry Heerman, the B-17's copilot, shouted to Sullivan above the noise. "We have only three engines left. If we lose another one, we'll have to put her down. Hard. And we're carrying a five-thousand-pound bomb load. If we're forced to crash-land, not one of us will make it out of this plane alive before it hits the ground and explodes."

"I am aware of that," Sullivan told Heerman.

"Lieutenant Sullivan," Tech Sergeant Victor Stark reported, "we've lost all radio contact with the other thirty-five planes in our formation. Flak must have knocked out our radio and navigational system."

"Do you know our location, Stark?" Sullivan asked.

"No, sir. I think we're somewhere over Germany, but I can't be sure. I suggest we turn around and head back to Kimbolton. We're also running seriously low on fuel."

"We couldn't be far from our target, Stark," Sullivan said. "I would estimate we are only minutes from Zeitz. We'll go ahead and drop our bombs on the benzene factory, complete our mission, and then head back."

At that moment, Sullivan heard a loud crunch and felt the plane vibrate violently. The cockpit filled with smoke.

"We've lost another engine!" Heerman shouted.

Second Lieutenant Hamilton C. Platt, the B-17's bombardier, sat huddled in the nose of the plane. He felt the Flying Fortress shake with every direct flak hit. The sound of each engine's death knell sent shivers down his spine. Platt had flown thirty-four previous missions on B-17s. He knew the signs and sounds of an impending crash.

My final mission. Then I could've gone home. Why did this have to happen on my very last flight?!

Platt thought about his wife waiting at home for him, counting the days until his honorable discharge.

I promised her I'd be home by Christmas, just in time for the birth of our first baby. Our Christmas baby. But now . . . my child . . . growing up without a father . . . never knowing me . . .

Platt heard a shell explode in the air outside the plane's nose.

Why was I assigned to this mission—Sullivan's first mission as a lead pilot?! Why, he's only twenty-one. Too young for such responsibility. I certainly hope Sullivan knows enough to turn this plane around and take us back to England! If not, well . . . we're doomed. And I'll never meet my little son or daughter.

• • •

Somewhere over Germany, Sullivan assessed the situation: *We've lost the formation, we have no navigation equipment or radio, we don't know exactly where we are, two engines are out, we don't know the extent of the plane's damage, and we're almost out of fuel. Choices? Not many. Can think of just one: Drop the bombs. Find some place to land.*

"Heerman," Sullivan said. "Try to figure out where we are. I don't want to unload these bombs on the Allies."

I hate to abort this mission and fail on my first chance to prove myself as pilot of a B-17. And that benzene factory in Zeitz needs to be destroyed. But I have no choice.

"Sir, I believe we're in Germany," Heerman said.

Sullivan gave orders to Platt, the bombadier, to drop the bombs. Sergeant Henry Kritzer, the waist gunner, helped him. The bombs were released from the bomb-load located behind the cockpit.

"Let's head back to England," Sullivan told his copilot. But the pilot found the damaged B-17 almost impossible to guide. "We won't make it," he said.

"I see the coast, sir," Heerman said. "It could be England's coast, but I'm not sure."

"Look for an airstrip, some place we can land," Sullivan said.

One of the crew spotted a small airstrip near the coastline. "Let's bring her down there," Sullivan told the crew. As the plane circled and began to descend, Take Me Home took more anti-aircraft fire. Sullivan noticed the airstrip had been heavily pockmarked by bombs.

The airstrip's almost too damaged to land the plane, and this has to be German-occupied France—not England. But we have no choice.

Ground shelling continued as the B-17 dropped to a low altitude and prepared for a wheels-up landing. Sullivan began quickly destroying all the important information in the cockpit.

"We've got bullet holes in the turret," nose gunner Sergeant Lawrence Archer shouted. "Sergeant!" he screamed. "A 20 mm round just went through the front of the plane, right between me and Platt!"

"We're behind Nazi lines! Everyone! Go to the radio room and stay there!" Sullivan shouted. "And hold on! We're in for a rough landing!"

The pilot brought the bomber down hard on the old airstrip[1] just inside the Lorient pocket. German soldiers shot at the plane as Sullivan struggled to make the belly landing. After the pilot brought the plane to a halt, he called to his crewmen: "Is everyone okay?"

Sergeant Archer responded: "Everyone is okay, sir, no injuries."

Before the pilot could check on his crew, he and his men were surrounded by Germans and ordered from the plane.

Oberleutnant Schmitt watched the B-17's crew gather in a single file, their hands high in the air, as German guards marched them into a Lorient jail for overnight keeping.

"More Americans," Schmitt said, rolling his eyes heavenward when he saw them.

"What is your name? What was your mission?" he asked each man in English.

The pilot and each crewman gave his name and rank. Nothing more.

The next day Schmitt ordered them transported by ferry to Fort Surville on the Île de Groix.

"We have little heat here," Schmitt told them. He saw they wore heavy flight suits and jackets, and assumed they had on the standard long underwear. "But you are wearing warm clothes, so you will be warm enough."

The prisoners did not stay at the fort for long, however. Schmitt moved them to a wooden facility nearby.

"As you will notice," Schmitt said, "these facilities are surrounded by double rows of barbed wire and guarded by armed sentries and dogs. I would advise you not to try to escape.

"You will be given coffee, bread, and soup twice a day, as well as some items from old Red Cross packages. You are not to accept food from the French civilians on the island. Violation of this order will result in severe punishment for you and the civilians."

• • •

Several days later, back in St. Louis, Missouri, the pilot's mother, Mrs. Lillian M. Sullivan, received a dreaded Western Union telegram. Her hands trembled as she opened and read it:

> THE SECRETARY OF WAR DESIRES TO EXPRESS HIS DEEP REGRET THAT YOUR SON SECOND LIEUTENANT WILLIAM J SULLIVAN HAS BEEN REPORTED MISSING IN ACTION SINCE THIRTY NOVEMBER OVER GERMANY IF FURTHER DETAILS OR OTHER INFORMATION ARE RECEIVED YOU WILL BE PROMPTLY NOTIFIED. DUNLOP ACTING THE ADJUTANT GENERAL.

She caught her breath and held it.

Missing in action? What does that mean? Is he alive? Or is he dead? How could he be missing?

Mrs. Archer, in Detroit, Michigan, received the War Department's telegram about her son, Larry, during the third week in December 1944.

Missing in action? She, too, pondered the meaning of those three terrifying words.

She remembered an incident Larry had written to her about—something that had happened to him just a few months before, on October 2. Larry and three others had had to bail out of a plane just after takeoff. A fire started in the cockpit area, destroying the intercom. Sergeant Archer, the nose gunner in the front of the plane, walked back to the cockpit to check out the smoke and found no one there—not the pilot or the copilot. Larry and the crew bailed out only seconds before the B-17 bellied in on a Royal Air Force field. The crash landing destroyed the plane. Larry and the crew had survived, but Mrs. Archer's son had seriously injured his back during the hurried bail-out.

Mrs. Archer wrote her other son, who at that time served in the South

Pacific, and told him the news about his brother, Larry. He immediately wrote back, assuring his worried mother that Larry would be fine.

One afternoon shortly after their capture, Sullivan and Platt were allowed to take a walk around the grounds of Île de Groix.

"I'm worried about the men," Sullivan said. "If they don't die of starvation, they'll die of dysentery."

"Me, too. Dark bread and lard won't keep any of us alive and well for very long," Platt said.

"I know you're anxious about your wife and baby," Sullivan said.

"Of course I am. I don't know if the child's been born or not, or if he's a girl or boy or doing well or—" Platt said and stopped abruptly.

"Look!" He pointed to the edge of a small farm surrounded by a fence. "A live chicken."

Sullivan saw it, too. "Grab it when the guard turns his head," he said. "I'll help you."

When, for a split second, the guard looked the other way, Sullivan and Platt seized the chicken by its head and somehow wrenched its entire body through a small chink in the fence. Sullivan hid the fowl in his armpit, and without alerting any attention, the two men crawled to the nearby latrine. Sullivan killed the chicken with one quick twist of its neck, and the two starving men ate the entire bird raw before the guard realized they were gone.[2]

FORTY-NINE

THE WARNING

Friday, 1 December 1944, 94th Infantry Division Headquarters, Châteaubriant

Andy Hodges lay awake during the early hours of Friday morning, December 1, after a long, restless, and sleepless night. At dawn, he dragged himself from bed and checked the weather report. He expected to hear that the heavy veil of murky mist continued to blanket the UK, and all planes were still grounded.

But to his surprise, during the night the dark clouds had lifted and planes were flying once again out of Scotland. Dressing quickly, he made arrangements for a military aircraft to fly that morning from Scotland to the Châteaubriant area near the 94th headquarters in France.

Hodges telephoned the Scotland POW camp commander to inquire about travel plans for Müller.

"We will speak with Kapitanleutnant Müller and return your call," the commander told him. "We must ask him if he is still open to the exchange and willing to come."

Andy paced the floor for the next thirty minutes, waiting for the phone call that would confirm or renounce the Kapitanleutnant's decision. Finally the telephone rang.

"I'm sorry, Mr. Hodges," the camp commander said. "I'm sorry to make you wait so long for my return phone call. I know a lot depends on this answer."

"How did Kapitanleutnant Müller respond?" Hodges asked, trying to keep his growing impatience from reflecting in his voice.

"Kapitanleutnant Müller is still willing to come and has agreed to board the plane this morning. He will expect to meet you in France when the aircraft lands."

Hodges smiled, let out a deep breath of relief, and headed for Colonel Bergquist's office with the favorable news.

Bergquist welcomed Hodges's news and exclaimed elation that the unpredictable Scottish weather had finally cooperated with the U.S. Army and that Müller would soon be arriving.

"Andy," Bergquist said, "I'll arrange to send a caravan of armed guards with you for Müller's transport to St. Nazaire. I don't need to warn you about the multiple potential dangers of such a trip."

"Thank you, sir," Hodges said. "But that won't be necessary. I've made that trip several times without incident."

"You'll be traveling into enemy-held territory, and since you're a Red Cross representative, we aren't allowed to send weapons with you," Bergquist said. "And I also don't trust Müller. He's the enemy, remember? He could turn on you, and you'd have no protection. The man's a trained fighter, and from what I hear, he is vicious—a skilled killer."

Bergquist took a deep breath and continued. "There are Germans with machine guns hiding behind every bush on those roads to St. Nazaire. They wouldn't hesitate to shoot you in order to release a decorated German officer, especially a recipient of the prestigious *Ritterkreuz*. They wouldn't give you a chance to explain that you were taking him to Pinski in St. Nazaire. And if they did allow you to explain, they wouldn't believe you.

"If the Germans didn't stop you, some green GI roaming around out there with a weapon might. A young new recruit might see the German officer, react with terror, and shoot him without waiting to hear your explanation."

Hodges stood still and listened as the colonel continued the warnings.

"The worse of all possible scenarios, of course, I haven't even mentioned. You could be attacked by members of the French Resistance! Those hotheads like to shoot first and ask questions later. Feelings run high with those people. Can't blame them. They've been under the Krauts' deplorable brutality for over four years now. It's been tough on them—their family and friends tortured, killed, or sent away to camps. They are a roaming ragtag bunch, great in number, rough and ruthless, and ready for their sufferings to end. They are highly dangerous, and they are everywhere. They'll take one look at that haughty medal-wearing German, and he's a dead man. And so are you! Those Red Cross badges and white flags won't stop that gang of thugs."

"I appreciate your concern, Colonel," Hodges said. "But I think an army caravan with armed guards might draw more attention from the Germans and members of the French Resistance than a lone American Red Cross rep and a single German slipping quietly down the road. And surely, Müller won't be fool enough to wear his uniform and medals! He knows he'd become 'target practice' for our GIs. If it's okay with you, sir, I'd rather make the trip with Müller by myself and skip all the fanfare. I believe it might be safer."

"I don't recommend it, Andy," Bergquist stated. "But I will acquiesce and support you in your decision. Just be careful, son."

"Thank you, sir. I hope I won't regret this decision."

"I'll send a signed letter with you in case you need it," Bergquist said. "It'll be in your office within the hour. Let me know whatever you need. And thank you."

The colonel shook his head from side to side like an anxious father and looked Hodges squarely in the eye. "Andy, be careful. You've got a wife and baby back home that need you."

Hodges walked back to his office and sat down at his desk. He mulled over Bergquist's warnings about the Germans "with machine guns hiding behind every bush on those roads to St. Nazaire" that "wouldn't hesitate to shoot . . . in order to release a decorated German officer, especially a recipient of the prestigious *Ritterkreuz*."

Bergquist is right. No German soldier would understand why an American and a German officer would be riding together in a jeep—two sworn enemies—combatants—traveling in Allied territory, and both of them unarmed. I don't know enough German to explain the reason why. And I don't know if Müller speaks English or not. He could tell his fellow Germans anything—any sort of lie—in their native language, and I'd have no idea what he said.

Andy also thought about Bergquist's cautions about the French Resistance members—"those hotheads" who "like to shoot first and ask questions later . . . a roaming ragtag bunch, great in number, rough and ruthless . . . highly dangerous . . . and everywhere."

Yes, those poor people have suffered under the Germans in ways I can't even imagine.

Hodges had heard rumors about the Resistance movement and how strong it had become since the Germans first invaded France. Just that October, he'd learned that its membership had grown from one hundred thousand to over four hundred thousand. He knew the FFI (French Forces of the Interior) members came from all classes of people, from many different occupations and political parties, and that they helped the Allies by sabotaging the Germans' power grids, transportation facilities, and communications networks. They were serious, angry, and dedicated brutes.

I have no illusions about my ability to protect Müller—or myself—from the FFI. They would consider me a traitor for driving a German officer, and instantly overpower me. There's nothing I could do to save us.

He also pondered Bergquist's warning about "some green GI roaming around out there with a weapon," who might feel tempted to have a crack at Andy and his charge.

Must by all means avoid "friendly fire." Maybe I should decorate the jeep with some "invasion stripes" to identify me as a "good guy," like the Allies painted on the planes at the Normandy landings last June.

But Hodges thought deepest that morning about the words Bergquist said at the end of their conversation: "Andy, be careful. You've got a wife and baby back home that need you."

I can't imagine not going back home, and not seeing Mary Louise and Gerry again! Am I being fair to them by taking this risk? I know they could manage without me. Our families would love and support them. But my wife would lose her husband, and Gerry would grow up without his father.

Andy took pen and paper from his desk and addressed a letter to his wife.

"Golly! Darling! I'll be so awfully happy when we can be together again! Tell Gerry I miss him, too, and I can hardly wait until he and I start doing a few of the things I have planned for us. I love you, Dutchess!"

At least if something happens to me, my wife and son will know how much I love them. And I sure hope I've made the right decision about making the trip to St. Nazaire alone with Müller.

A few minutes later, a messenger delivered Bergquist's letter to Hodges's office. Andy quickly read the letter:

Headquarters
Allied Forces, St. Nazaire
1 December 1944

Subject: Exchange of Prisoners of War
To: Commanding General, German Forces, St. Nazaire.

In accordance with the agreement previously made in connection with the exchange of Prisoners of war this Headquarters offer Captain-Lieutenant Mueller, who wears the Knight's Cross, in exchange for the British Captain Foot. Six German officers, all of them decorated with the Knight's Cross or the Iron Cross First Class, were obtained from an officers' prison camp in order to select one as an exchange for Captain Foot. When these officers were told that they were to go to the Fortress St. Nazaire, five declined to volunteer. The above statement can be confirmed by Captain Mueller who was the only volunteer.

This Headquarters has made every effort to comply with the original agreement insofar as providing a suitable officer exchange for Captain Foot.

Acknowledgment of this letter is requested by indorsement [sic] hereon. This acknowledgment will serve as a receipt for the exchange of Captain Lieutenant Mueller for Captain Foot.

The Allied Commander:
E. C. Bergquist
Colonel, Chief of Staff

Hodges tucked the letter and the note to his wife inside his blouse pocket.[1]

FIFTY

THE MISUNDERSTANDING

Early Afternoon, 1 December 1944, an Airstrip Near Châteaubriant

After Hodges posted the note to his wife, he draped the white Red Cross flags on the jeep, doubled-checked the security of his uniform's ARC pins and left shoulder badge, and waited for Kapitanleutnant Müller's plane to touch down on the airstrip.

The more he thought about the upcoming trip to St. Nazaire with Müller, the greater the knot in his stomach grew. Colonel Bergquist's words about the duo traveling alone ran through his mind, and each time the warnings became louder and more frightening.

What if . . . No! I won't think about the "what ifs"! Too many and too scary!

When the aircraft landed and the pilot killed the engine, Andy walked to the plane to meet Müller. After a moment or two, the Kapitanleutnant stepped from the door. The German officer was dressed in full uniform; the *Ritterkreuz* hung prominently from his throat, and his chest sparkled with a garden variety of awards and decorations. Müller stood straight and erect, his neck positioned high, his short, proud nose flaring and pointing skyward. When he stepped forward, he almost seemed to prance, to strut quick-stepped toward Andy.

Müller reminds me of one of Dad's stallions during mating season! I halfway expect him to rear up on his hind legs! Or give me the ole "lip curl" or "horse laugh." If he starts stomping and biting and "marking his territory," I'm outta here!

Andy managed to silence the cockamamie comedian in his head and subdue an impending smile.

Seriously, I hoped he would downplay his pride and his German-ness. Maybe wear overalls or lederhosen or something. Anything but a full officer's uniform with all those glittering trinkets dangling from his chest. But I guess not—after all, he is the "Tiger of the Channel." I hope his gaudy baubles don't get us both killed.

Andy politely introduced himself to the German officer and escorted him to his jeep.

"I trust your flight went well and your trip was uneventful," Hodges said as he motioned Müller inside the vehicle and into the passenger's seat.

The Kapitanleutnant ignored him, looked straight ahead, chin held high, and said nothing.

"Well," Andy said. "I guess you don't speak English. That's okay. I don't speak German." Hodges smiled.

This is going to be one long, quiet journey. At least I hope so!

Kapitanleutnant Müller expected more pageantry when he stepped from the plane that afternoon in France.

Where is the convoy of vehicles, the caravan of soldiers to escort me safely to Germany?

When one lone American, driving a white flag–covered jeep, greeted him, Müller felt humiliated.

Does the United States Army not realize who I am? Do they not understand my importance?

Müller sat stiffly in the jeep's passenger seat, secretly inspecting the interior of the vehicle.

Where are the weapons? How do they plan to protect me from hostile enemies we might encounter on this journey?

Keeping his head pointing forward, he cut his eyes to the left and tried, inconspicuously, to scan Hodges.

The driver carries no visible weapon?! Surely they have arranged for armed guards to accompany us on this trip? But, if so, where are they?

The driver started the engine and drove away, and to his shock the German saw no armed troops follow them.

Just the two of us? Surely the Americans must think me a weak fool! What is to stop me from breaking this Yank's neck, stealing his vehicle, and escaping to the Fatherland? I could easily overtake him. But I'll be patient. For now. Either way, I'll end up back in Germany.

The Kapitanleutnant stared at the road in front of him as the young driver passed between rows of thick hedgerows, trekking silently and slowly down the narrow road. They traveled through open fields and small villages, and saw French civilians walking or shopping or talking with friends. Müller enjoyed watching the citizens' confused expressions as they stopped and stared at the American and German officer traveling side by side in the flag-covered jeep.

Andy Hodges drove slowly, cautiously, and attentively scanned the roadsides all around him. He watched for possible machine gun nests tucked behind the camouflaging hedgerows and manned by patiently waiting, trigger-happy German soldiers. Every time a tree branch moved or the wind swept through and shook a bush, Andy braked slightly, expecting to be ambushed by German opposition.

So far, so good.

They had driven only a few miles on the way to St. Nazaire when Andy noticed Müller looking up at the sky, his eyes seemingly searching for the afternoon sun. Suddenly, with great force, Müller grabbed Hodges's right arm. The jeep veered sharply to the left. Andy struggled to keep the vehicle on the path and out of the deep roadside ditch.

"*Nein! Nein!*" Müller shouted. "Stop! Stop this vehicle!"

Andy slammed on the brakes, brought the jeep to a hard stop, and turned off the motor.

"You have tricked me!" Müller shouted and jumped out of the jeep. "You have tricked me!"

"What are you talking about?!" Andy asked. "What in the Sam Hill is wrong?!"

"You should be driving northeast to Germany!" Müller roared. "I was told I would be returned to the Fatherland. But instead you are heading southwest—toward the Atlantic coast! What is the meaning of this?!"

Andy noticed the look of extreme agitation on the German's face and saw angry fire burning in his dark round eyes. Beads of sweat broke on his forehead, his nostrils flared, and his whole body shook with rage. The stallion looked ready to bolt. Or fight.

If he takes off in those woods, I'll never catch him. Or if he chooses to turn and attack me, he'll win. No doubt about that! But I have one advantage I just learned I have—Müller speaks English! At least I can communicate with him!

"Kapitanleutnant Müller," Hodges said. "I have not tricked you. Our destination was never Germany, but Oberst Pinski's headquarters in St. Nazaire. The Oberst and other high-ranking German officers are waiting for you there. The 94th has promised them your safe deliverance."

Andy retrieved Bergquist's signed letter from his blouse pocket. "Look," he said and handed him the paper. "Read this."

Müller skimmed through the letter, returned to the jeep, and sat down in the passenger's seat.

"I see," he said quietly. "St. Nazaire. Not Germany."

"I can understand why you were upset, Kapitanleutnant," Hodges said. "I would've felt the same way. Can we continue our trip now?"

"Yes, Herr Hodges," Müller said. "Certainly."

FIFTY-ONE

THE LONG TREK

1 December 1944, En Route to St. Nazaire

Andy Hodges approached each bend in the road cautiously as he and Müller motored mile after mile toward St. Nazaire. He expected at any moment to be stopped, searched, captured, or shot by a German soldier hiding behind a bush. Andy knew he had no way to protect himself or his charge from an attack. A brisk, cool breeze blew in from the Atlantic coast, not cold, but filled with mist and just warm enough to feel refreshing. A light rain followed.

"We are fortunate, Kapitanleutnant Müller, to have the canvas top covering our jeep," Hodges said in an attempt to make conversation. "I've made this trip to St. Nazaire in the rain without it. It's much nicer with it."

The Kapitanleutnant furrowed his brow and looked directly at Hodges. "You've made this journey before? For what reason?" he asked.

"To meet with Oberst Harry Pinski and Hauptmann Heinz-Roland Schmuck, and to negotiate the release of our Allied prisoners in the St. Nazaire POW camp," Hodges explained. "The exchange of a large number of Allied and German prisoners took place on 29 November in Pornic."

"One man negotiating the freedom of many? That is highly unusual,"

Müller said. "Are you responsible for bringing about the release of the Englishman . . . the Captain Michael Foot for whom I am being exchanged?"

"Yes, Kapitanleutnant. Your willingness to offer yourself in place of the captain has saved Michael Foot's life. He is currently in a hospital receiving medical treatment. Five other German officers, each one a recipient of the *Ritterkreuz*, were not as brave as you and refused to volunteer. We are most grateful that you agreed to the exchange."

"Zank you, Herr Hodges. My greatest ambition in life is to honor the Fatherland," Müller said.

"Do you have family back home in the Fatherland, Kapitanleutnant?" Hodges asked, seeking to continue the conversation, but being careful not to pry into the officer's personal life. "A wife, children?"

"No, Herr Hodges. Not yet. But one day."

"I have a wife, Mary Louise, and a toddler, Gerry, back home in Alabama. I miss them very much. Can't wait to get back! I had hoped I'd be back by Christmas this year, but it doesn't look like it. Maybe by this fall for Gerry's third birthday, or maybe by next Christmas."

"Yes, Herr Hodges."

Kapitanleutnant Müller felt the tight tension in his gut start to ease a bit after the brief and informal dialogue with the American. The pain was still there, however—sharp and stinging—but the knot? Not tied quite so tightly; the lump not quite so hard. He felt somewhat less suspicious now of the Yank driver and his possible motives. He looked forward to reaching the German pocket of St. Nazaire and meeting Oberst Pinski, Hauptmann Schmuck, and the other officers who anxiously awaited his anticipated arrival.

At least I will be out of enemy territory and safe from the impending peril that could happen at any second as I travel unarmed through this dangerous no-man's-land. I look forward to the warm welcome from my comrades.

He turned his head to the left and took a long, hard look at his driver. The expression on Hodges's face looked calm; his body seemed composed, unruffled.

How can he be so relaxed in these uncertain and nerve-racking circumstances? Is he not terrified, as I am?

Then he noticed the driver's hands, how firmly they gripped both sides of the steering wheel, and how white his knuckles appeared.

Ah . . . he, too, is terrified. As he should be.

As Andy drove closer to the St. Nazaire enemy barrier, he grew more concerned about a possible German ambush. He knew the enemy closely guarded the perimeter of their boundaries. He wanted to step on the gas, accelerate faster to more quickly reach enemy lines, and make this nightmare end. But instead, for safety's sake, he slowed the jeep, looking right and left, front and back, watching for the slightest movement of body, bush, or branch.

"Not much farther, Kapitanleutnant Müller," he said, as if he was a father sensing a child's anxiety and trying to reassure him. "We're almost there."

"Zank you, Herr Hodges. I am glad. It has been a long and unsettling journey. I know we will both be relieved to be back on our respective sides."

"We aren't out of danger yet, Kapitanleutnant. And I trust if we're stopped by your comrades, you'll explain our mission and encourage them to allow me to continue our trip to Oberst Pinski in St. Nazaire. They'll, no doubt, want to release you and shoot me."

"Herr Hodges, I . . ."

At that moment, on the edge of the right side of the road several yards ahead of them, Andy saw a small piece of a broken twig move an inch or two from its place. His heart skipped.

The wind?

But the movement seemed to be unnatural, to make no sense.

An animal?

He slowed the jeep to a crawl, and then brought it to a complete stop. Holding his breath, he motioned for his companion to be quiet, and then he pointed with his index finger at the road's right side. Müller froze. For the next few seconds, the two men sat still, alert, and scarcely breathing.

Andy noticed Müller's hands visibly tremble. Hodges heard a sharp, loud crack. Müller flinched and audibly sucked in his breath. A large limb had broken off from the top of a tree beside them, hitting hard every bare branch as it toppled down, and finally crashed on the ground.

Andy exhaled loudly, and after a second, he chuckled. "Well, Kapitanleutnant, we were almost ambushed by an assailant tree limb! I'm too wound up, on edge. I should try to—"

At that split second, the right roadside's bushes parted. From behind the hedgerows jumped a gang of dirty, raggedly clad ruffians. Each rogue carried a weapon—some had clubs and knives; others held German machine guns and World War I rifles. They surrounded the jeep, pointing their various weapons at its two occupants.

"Bergquist warned me about the French Resistance," Hodges whispered to Müller. "I hope you speak French."

"*Nein!* Not a word of it," Müller replied. "Do you speak French, Hodges?"

"*Nein!*" Andy said. "Only two words of it."

FIFTY-TWO

THE ATTACK!

Andy raised his arms in the air. Müller followed his example. The thugs banged on the vehicle with their fists and clubs, shouting and screaming in confused unison a jumble of French words Andy couldn't hope to interpret.

"*Sortir du véhicule!*" the hoodlums ordered and motioned the men out of the jeep. "*Placez vos mains! Expliquez-vous et votre mission!*"

Through their body language, tone of voice, and clumsy pantomimes, Andy guessed the vandals wanted them to get out of the jeep, explain who they were, where they were going, and why. His arms still in the air, he stepped from the vehicle and motioned Müller to do likewise.

"*Mon nom est* Andrew Hodges," Andy told them. "I . . . *Je suis avec la* . . . Red Cross . . . ah . . . *Croix Rouge*. U.S.A. *Comprenez-vous* you?"

Andy glanced at Müller, who he thought looked slightly impressed. Having exhausted his entire knowledge of the French language, and then some, Andy repeated: "Red Cross! *Croix Rouge! Croix Rouge!* 94th Division—American. Colonel Bergquist. Prisoner exchange. I am taking this German to St. Nazaire. *Comprenez-vous* you?" He pointed to the ARC pins attached to his blouse and his left shoulder badge. "*Croix Rouge!*" he said. He opened his blouse to show he carried no weapon. "Unarmed. No weapon!"

I hope at least one or two of these guys get the drift of what I'm trying to say, 'cause that's all the pidgin French I know.

The man who appeared to be the leader shouted, motioning angrily to another member of the group: "*Vérifier les hommes d'armes!*"

A tough-looking man, wearing baggy blue denim trousers and a French Army helmet, stepped toward Hodges and Müller and patted down both men roughly, checking them for weapons.

"*Pas d'armes!*" he shouted back to the leader.

Müller said nothing. He focused his eyes straight ahead, almost unblinking, and looked as if he were preparing to die. His face became steel and showed no expression.

The French leader ordered: "*Shot l'officier allemand! Nous devons tuer Hitler mal les hommes!*"

I'm not sure what the French gang leader just said, but it looks and sounds like they're planning on shooting Müller. There's no reason for them not to kill him.

Andy stepped quickly and directly in front of Müller, pressed his back against the German's beribboned and iron-crossed chest, stretched out his arms on each side, and positioned his body like a shield to protect the Kapitanleutnant from the Frenchmen's weapons.

"This German officer is my prisoner!" Hodges shouted to the FFI leader. "I am the Red Cross senior field officer of the U.S. Army's 94th Division. I have orders to deliver this prisoner, alive and unharmed, to German officials at St. Nazaire. He is part of a prisoner exchange program. If you want him, you'll have to shoot me first! Otherwise you need to move aside and let us pass!"

A puzzled look crossed the French leader's face.

"*Croix Rouge?*" he asked.

"Yes! *Croix Rouge!* Red Cross! U.S. Army's 94th Division! Colonel Bergquist! Prisoner exchange! St. Nazaire!" Andy shouted. He reached into his blouse pocket and retrieved Bergquist's letter. "Read this letter! Here are my orders!"

The FFI leader took the letter, scanned it, and handed it to a nearby member to read. After a moment, the French Resistance member, most likely able to read some English, nodded his head, and the leader returned the letter to Hodges.

For a few intimidating seconds, no one moved and no one spoke.

"So," the FFI leader finally said to Hodges in badly broken English. "You speak truth. You are . . . ah . . . *sous les ordres* . . . Colonel Bergquist . . . 94th Division—*échange de prisonniers.*"

"Yes," Hodges said. "I have direct orders from Colonel Bergquist to deliver this German officer to St. Nazaire. If you harm him, you'll start another war!"

"*Abaisser vos armes!*" the leader ordered his troops. "*Leur permettre de quitter.*"

The FFI members obeyed, lowered their weapons, and allowed Hodges and Müller to continue their journey to St. Nazaire.

After Hodges drove away, the Kapitanleutnant was visibly trembling.

Kapitanleutnant Müller said nothing else during the rest of the trip. He could think of no English words that would adequately express his respect for this American, or his appreciation to Herr Hodges for so gallantly saving his life.

I am awestruck. Speechless. Words fail me. Rarely have I witnessed such courage, such a heroic act! And it came from a Yan . . . ah . . . an American!

When the two men arrived at the sentry outpost in St. Nazaire, Hodges stopped the vehicle, handed Bergquist's letter to the German guard, and asked for a receipt stating that Müller had been "safely delivered to St. Nazaire as promised."

Before the Kapitanleutnant stepped out of the jeep, Müller extended his right hand. Andy took it in his and smiled. Then without saying a word, the "Tiger of the Channel" looked deeply into Hodges's eyes, returned his smile, and firmly shook his hand.

You are a brave man, Herr Hodges. I have never met such a courageous man—on either side of the battlefield. I owe you my very life.

But as hard as he tried to speak them aloud, to convey his deep appreciation to Hodges, the English words would not come out. They formed in his head, but stuck in his throat. He opened his mouth to speak, but was only able to say:

"Zank you, Herr Hodges. Zank you much."

PART THREE

THE REST OF THE STORY

To the Director of the American Red Cross: I desire to invite your attention to the outstanding character of service rendered by Mr. Andrew Hodges, who was the American Red Cross representative attached to my Division until I left it on 26 June 1945. . . . He was under fire many times and acquitted himself with distinction. His intelligence and devotion to duty under all conditions of combat were a great credit to his unit and to himself.

—HARRY J. MALONY, MAJOR GENERAL, U.S.A.

Near the end of November 1944, Colonel Bergquist summoned a group of men from the 94th Reconnaissance Troop to work with British rapid patrol boats and set up an observation post on Houat, a small island in the Quiberon Bay, in order to observe German shipping routes from St. Nazaire to the Lorient sector. The Americans needed to cut off the German's supply route between the pockets. On December 15, Germans attacked Île de Houat, wounding, killing, and capturing Americans and Frenchmen, and incarcerating them at Fort Surville at Île de Groix and at the Lorient hospital. Staff Sergeant Orval L. Love was seriously injured and hospitalized in Lorient. Several dozen POWs joined the earlier captives of the crashed B-17 Take Me Home's crew at Fort Surville on Île de Groix.

On December 18, Bergquist handed Hodges a letter he had received the day before. It read: "Dear Sir: There are 12 American soldiers being held prisoners of war here [Fort Surville]. Food is very scarce here and we would greatly appreciate it if you could send us some rations. We are very hungry. Greatfully [sic] yours, The Americans."

Bergquist requested that Hodges negotiate the release of these prisoners immediately, by Christmas if possible. Two days before, Hitler had launched a massive counteroffensive in northwest Europe, and Bergquist indicated that the 94th Infantry might soon be moving to that area.

Hodges packed his jeep with Red Cross supplies and headed for Lorient to discuss a prisoner exchange with Oberleutnant Schmitt. Hodges and Schmitt met, agreed to the terms of the swap, and scheduled it for December 24, Christmas Eve. Hodges promised to return to Le Magouer with sixteen healthy German volunteers to trade with Schmitt for an equal number of American POWs being held at Lorient and Fort Surville. But Bergquist and Hodges could find no German volunteers willing to return to front battle lines—not one single volunteer. Hodges returned to Le Magouer on Christmas Eve with fresh supplies for the Allied POWs, but no German volunteers for the exchange. No prisoners were exchanged, except one: Sergeant Love. Due to Love's serious injuries, Schmitt allowed Hodges to take the sergeant back with him late that night. Andy drove him to an Allied hospital for emergency medical treatment.

On Christmas Day, Schmitt delivered the Red Cross supplies to the Allied prisoners on Île de Groix. The next day, December 26, Hodges and the 94th Division began packing up and heading for the Ardennes. Hodges drew up the necessary prisoner exchange papers reflecting his verbal agreement with Oberleutnant Schmitt. Colonel Bergquist decided to stay behind at headquarters in order to locate German volunteers, and to make sure the exchange took place in Etel and Le Magouer just as Hodges had planned. Hodges put together comfort article packages to be given to each American prisoner after the exchange—a welcome back gift upon reaching Allied lines.

The fourth and final POW exchange took place on December 29, 1944, negotiated and planned by Andrew Gerow Hodges, but attended and orchestrated successfully by Colonel Bergquist, Oberst Borst, and Oberleutnant Schmitt. Hauptmann Reick sent a gift to be given to Herr Hodges—a hand-carved pipe. Fifteen German POWs, and a Hodges-promised two extra German prisoners for the Christmas Eve release of Sergeant Love, were exchanged for fifteen Americans. A small boat made its way across the river from Etel to Le Magouer and back again, as it had in the first

POW exchange. That evening after the exchange, Colonel Bergquist radioed Andy Hodges.

"Andy," Bergquist said. "We got our seventeen German POW volunteers. The final exchange took place today with Schmitt and Borst without a hitch. All fifteen Americans came back with me. And each man received his welcome gifts from you. Both Schmitt and Borst send you their greetings, and Reick sent you a hand-carved pipe. Everybody behaved himself, and you would've been proud."

"Thank you, sir!" Hodges said. "Thank you so much!"

Colonel Bergquist couldn't be absolutely positive, but he felt pretty sure that on the other end of the radio, one American Red Cross captain was grinning.

THE HERO COMES HOME

By December 31, 1944, Major General Herman Kramer's 66th Infantry Division had relieved the 94th Infantry Division at Châteaubriant, France. The 94th Division moved to the Ardennes, where it became heavily engaged in the Battle of the Bulge. Among the division's numbers were former prisoners: Privates First Class George Boyd, Harry Glixon, George Brady, Wayne Stewart, and Morris Shulman, and Sergeant Roy Connatser. For its courageous fighting, the 94th Division was awarded the Presidential Unit Citation.

Based on the precedent-setting negotiations of Andy Hodges, the 66th Division exchanged four of its captured POWs at Lorient on April 11, 1945.

In May 1945, Oberst Otto Borst stepped into the small café at Etel and officially surrendered Festung Lorient to the Allies. The German commander of St. Nazaire also capitulated.

That summer the American Red Cross offered Hodges a job as Red Cross field director of a zone in France/Belgium. He wrote to his wife about this position on July 19, 1945:

"Darling . . . I think I wrote you about being offered a job . . . as Field Director of a zone. If I thought there was a possibility of you and Gerry getting to come over before the division could get back to the states, I would take it. But not having that assurance, I'm not going to jeopardize the chance of seeing you as soon as I possibly can, because, darling, I need you and want you. I love you always!"

Hodges turned down the position, and completed his service with the American Red Cross. In 1946, he returned home to his wife and son in Birmingham, Alabama. He once again was called by his middle name, "Gerow," instead of the army's "Andy." He told few people about his wartime accomplishments. He returned to Liberty National Life Insurance Company, eventually becoming its executive vice president, and retired in 1984. During his long lifetime, he supported numerous charitable organizations and financial campaigns, and won many local and national awards for his work with the Boy Scouts and other charities. As a life trustee, and former chairman of the Board of Trustees, of Samford University, Hodges was intimately involved in Dwight and Lucille Beeson's, and Ralph and Orlean Beeson's, $100 million gifts to Samford. In recognition of his five decades of devoted service, the university conferred on him the honorary degree doctor of humane letters (1987) and named the new campus Beeson Divinity School chapel the Andrew Gerow Hodges Chapel. (It is interesting that the chapel faces Samford University's football field.) He and Mary Louise had two sons, six grandchildren, and nine great-grandchildren. Andrew Gerow Hodges died in 2005 at the age of eighty-seven.

It is said that courage has many faces. One of those was Andrew Gerow Hodges. It took courage, persistence, and imagination for the lad from the small town of Geneva, Alabama, in the Deep South, to make fifteen or more forays behind German lines, alone and armed only with his wits and a Red Cross badge. A hundred and forty-nine Allied soldiers and airmen, the former prisoners of Lorient and St. Nazaire, are glad that courage had the face of Andy Hodges.

THE REUNION: JANUARY 25, 2002

The program's headlines on January 25, 2002, read:

THANKS TO HODGES, WE SURVIVED:
WWII POWS AND THE MAN WHO GAINED THEIR FREEDOM

Samford University presents a salute to members of The Greatest Generation, Americans who are surviving prisoners of war from St. Nazaire and Lorient sectors of France, and whose release was won by A. Gerow Hodges.

During his long life after the war, Andrew Gerow Hodges rarely mentioned his WWII experiences. In 2000, Hodges's fellow Samford trustee Harlan Hobart Grooms, Birmingham attorney, past president of the Birmingham Bar Association, and retired marine colonel, heard about the POW negotiations and became deeply interested in Hodges's role in the exchanges. Grooms got to know Michael Foot while the historian was teaching a January term course at Samford University, but it wasn't until Grooms delved into Hodges's files that he saw the possibility of a documentary.

"Here were the original German POW lists, photos, correspondence, receipts for Red Cross parcels, cease-fire agreements," Grooms recalled, "even a 1938 Michelin map with an overlay showing coordinates where Gerow would meet the German officers who'd escort him blindfolded to enemy headquarters."

Having prepared a notebook of his discoveries with a story outline, Grooms presented them to Dr. Tom Corts, Samford's president. Dr. Corts liked the idea enough to locate an award-winning director, T. N. Mohan, who reviewed the material and asked to do the film. Samford's funding made the project possible.

Locating the POWs was a daunting task, but Grooms found thirteen in the U.S. and helped organize a film session and POW reunion with Hodges in Birmingham.

"We shot eleven interviews in two days. It was a killer," Grooms recalled. Grooms shot a total of twelve interviews. Filming also occurred in England, Paris, and Brittany.

Grooms and Mohan spent days at the National Archives in Washington, D.C., discovering more photos, footage of the exchanges, and even a 1944 newsreel of the St. Nazaire event.

On January 25, 2002, Samford University hosted a dinner/reunion with twelve of the former POWs from the St. Nazaire and Lorient sectors, and two hundred guests and family members. In a special program—"Thanks to Hodges, We Survived"—each ex-prisoner shared his story of capture and rescue, and personally thanked Hodges for his courage and timely intervention.

The reunion was the idea of Samford University president Tom Corts after Grooms described the need to interview the ex-prisoners who were spread across the country from Washington State to New England. The reunion could give the men a chance to tell their stories and thank Hodges. Most of the servicemen never knew who had orchestrated their release, nor had they had the opportunity to express their appreciation.

"It was therapeutic to talk to men we hadn't seen since the war," Wayne

Stewart said. "It was a wonderful service the school [Samford University] performed."

"Who knows what another six months [in the POW camp] would have meant?" James Silva asked when he addressed the group of honored veterans.

"Four of the twelve men who came to the reunion were Jewish," Private Harry Glixon's wife, Lorraine, said after returning home from Birmingham. "This was a Christian college, but there was such an outpouring of love from everybody. They were interested in the stories, in the POW exchanges, and in what Mr. Hodges had done. They made us feel very, very important. It was just incredible."[1]

Wayne Stewart described his POW experience: "Supplies were low, and we survived on two slices of bread, two spoons of lard, and a cup of thin soup a day. I weighed one hundred and sixty pounds when captured, and about one hundred thirty when I got out. I'm certain we would all have died or had our health seriously impaired had we remained in captivity. Thanks to Hodges, we survived."

Those attending the reunion were Dr. William J. Reynolds, Bernard I. Rader, Harry Glixon, Jim Silva, Harold M. Thompson, David Trachtenberg, Wayne Stewart, Gerow Hodges, Morris Shulman, Roy Connatser, George Boyd, Kermit Harden, Jr., and George Brady. Michael Foot, unable to attend, sent a letter:

After many years' work on the history of the war against Hitler, I remain proud of our record as prisoners of war in St. Nazaire. For us the war was not over, as the Germans told us it was. We remained a tiny thorn in the hide of the Nazi beast.

Quite how nasty the beast was only became clear later, when much worse camps than ours were freed. It remains a task for all honest men to be ready to stand up against tyranny; as no American needs reminding, after 11 September [2001] last year.

And all of us who survived from the St. Nazaire camp owe a lasting debt of gratitude to Gerow Hodges for having got us out of it; I above all. When first I met him, I was dying quietly in a German military hospital, and was so confused (I had a broken neck and a cracked skull) that I took him for a Gestapo nark, till he slipped a message from my father into what he was saying. And when the man for whom I was to be exchanged failed to turn up, Gerow volunteered to become a prisoner himself until he did.

I much wish I could have been with you all to celebrate our debt to him. I trust you are doing so in something more appetizing than turnip soup and acorn coffee!

Every possible good wish to you all. Michael Foot. [January 25, 2002]

Several of the veterans at the reunion said they appreciated the opportunity to meet Andrew Gerow Hodges.

"I want to hug his neck," Roy Connatser said.

"I'm convinced you saved my life," Wayne Stewart told Hodges.

"I've been waiting fifty-five years to shake your hand," George Boyd said.

ACKNOWLEDGMENTS

First and foremost a special thanks to Colonel Harlan Hobart "Hobie" Grooms, Jr., Marine Corps Reserve (retired), and past president of the Birmingham Bar Association, who persisted in getting this story from my father and worked tirelessly to first tell it in a 2002 documentary. Without his vision, this book would not have been written. Indeed, Hobie worked tirelessly, endlessly reviewing my collaborator's extensive research, confirming the facts, and elaborating on military matters from his significant grasp of WWII history.

Secondly, the idea for this book originated with my collaborator, author Denise George. She saw the depth of the drama in numerous situations. Her deep devotion to historical research was matched by her talent as a writer and her tenacity to see the project to completion without letting up. She counted the cost this major effort would require, and she paid it relentlessly and always with a smile on her face.

Dr. Elizabeth Wells, Dean Kim Herndon, Assistant Dean Laurie Northcutt, and Lisa C. Imbragulio, J.D., as well as other archivists and librarians, and the library and special collections staffs at Samford University, which houses the archives on my father's WWII materials and also Colonel Hobart Grooms's research, deserve my gratitude. Thank you to Diane Dill who also greatly assisted Denise George as she tirelessly unearthed fascinating facts to flesh out my father's story.

I'm grateful to my family, especially my mother, who provided many details of my father's military service. My brother, Greg Hodges, knew the story well and my niece, Jane Latham Hodges, also researched the entire story as her senior thesis at the University of Virginia.

A special thank-you to the late Dr. Thomas Corts, Samford University, and Beeson Divinity School, as well as to Michael Foot and the former POWs and their families, especially Bernie and June Rader, who so generously shared their WWII documents, photographs, and stories included in this book. My gratitude also goes to French author Luc Braeuer, who generously offered assistance, information, and photographs to this project, and to Lieutenant Colonel Mary Walsh, USAF (retired) for transcribing Braeuer's helpful book *Les Incroyables Échanges* into English.

Several discussions with Michael Foot, a former POW and a central character in the book, were illuminating on different trips when he visited the States. Also my discussions with several of the former POWs at the 2002 reunion in Birmingham were helpful in providing new information.

Additionally, several readers were kind enough to read the unpublished manuscript and offer their valuable suggestions. These included Colonel Harlan Hobart Grooms, Jr.; Dr. Lucien Coleman; Dr. Frank Limehouse; Dr. Matt Tomlin; Mr. Robin Skipper; and Mrs. Willene Wyse.

With his extensive knowledge of WWII books and great vision for Dad's story, our literary agent and the president of WordServeLiterary, Greg Johnson, provided a steady guiding hand. A special thank-you to the editors and staff at Penguin Random House, New York, who contracted with us to publish this book.

On behalf of my father and my family, I thank you all for helping to bring this story to light.

A WORD BY
HARLAN HOBART GROOMS, JR.

"Gerow" (he was called after the war) Hodges was at once a devout, persistent, compassionate, and humble person. Because of the last trait, his unique story from World War II was almost destined to be forgotten. As a fellow Samford University trustee, I'd heard secondhand fragments of his adventures. I tried over two years to get him to share them with me. Gerow always demurred, saying what he'd done was "unimportant . . . no one would be interested" and "others did much more" during that bloody conflict.

Finally, tiring of my persistence, he loaned me his copy of the 94th Division history, adding that he had "some old photos and papers," but hadn't seen them in years. The division history devoted an intriguing chapter to describing Gerow's part in the exchanges of Allied prisoners, enough to warrant renewed efforts to see what he had tucked away. Easier said than done. Personal affairs and conflicts always interfered. Months passed until, one day, he confessed he'd "found a few things," and I was welcome to drop by and see them.

Late one afternoon in Hodges's sunroom, I began a journey that was to consume years of my life after retiring from the practice of law. Before me was a large cache of U.S. Signal Corps photos, military records, correspondence between Gerow and German officers, letters from POWs, German receipts for Red Cross goods, and original German prisoner lists. And there was the large 1938 Michelin map given to Hodges by the Germans, which detailed the coordinates leading into Festung St. Nazaire. The German markings of respective parties' positions for the exchange at Pornic were also indicated.

After so many years had passed since the war, Hodges knew the location of only one former prisoner, Harold Thompson, a former Alabamian. Locating others was a challenge. Hodges's reticence was nothing compared to the Department of Defense, which jealously guards personal information of all personnel, active or retired. Contacts with veterans' organizations produced a few names that eventually led to other names. British SAS captain Michael R. D. Foot, whose life was saved by Hodges, had stayed in touch with a fellow escapee, Léon Spanin. In all, more than two dozen ex-prisoners were eventually located and interviewed.

Hodges's wife, Mary Louise, recalled a 1944 newsreel of the November 29 Pornic exchange. She had sat through several showings of the main feature just to catch a few seconds of her husband conferring with German and Allied officers. The newsreel was discovered at the National Archives and was highlighted in a television documentary *For One English Officer*, funded by Samford University and coproduced by T. N. Mohan. The award-winning film was shown on our Public Broadcasting System.

Andrew Gerow Hodges passed away October 13, 2005, but his mark on his Birmingham community and the causes he loved still endures. And the former prisoners of Lorient and St. Nazaire fondly recall the quiet Alabamian who, although physically disqualified from military service, volunteered for overseas duty. Armed with only his wits and a Red Cross badge, he made his way fifteen times through German lines and into the hearts of those desperate prisoners. Despite Gerow's protestations, they would argue that his story was one that *had* to be told. It is a heart-warming account of perseverance, compassion, trust, and honor seldom seen during that terrible conflict. It is the story of the soft-spoken Southerner who stood up to the Germans by declaring that there would be no exchange if one English officer, or a single French soldier, were omitted.

HARLAN HOBART GROOMS, JR., COLONEL,

U.S. MARINE CORPS RESERVE (RET.),

PAST PRESIDENT OF THE BIRMINGHAM BAR ASSOCIATION,

BIRMINGHAM, ALABAMA

HOW THE BOOK CAME TO BE WRITTEN

Harlan Hobart Grooms, Jr., was ten when the Japanese bombed Pearl Harbor in December 1941, plunging the United States into the Second World War. Due to its industry, Birmingham, Alabama, his home, became a beehive of activity in the war effort due to its aircraft and steel industry. While a youth, Grooms did his part to help in the war, selling war bonds door-to-door in his neighborhood.

After graduating from the University of Alabama with a law degree and earning a major in history, Grooms joined the Marines, serving as legal officer. Returning home, he practiced with the Birmingham firm Spain & Gillon LLC, where he spent forty-one years before retiring as a senior partner in 1999. He is a former president of the Birmingham Bar Association. Having spent thirty years in the Marine Reserves, Colonel Grooms retired in 1985.

Grooms never lost his passion for history, especially military history. When he heard his friend Gerow Hodges's story, and eventually saw his treasure trove of museum-quality WWII memorabilia, he was amazed. "Here were the original German POW lists, photos, correspondence, receipts for

Red Cross parcels, cease-fire agreements, and even a 1938 Michelin map with an overlay showing coordinates where Hodges would meet the German officers who'd escort him blindfolded to enemy headquarters," Grooms recalled.

Grooms did the research, wrote a story outline, and approached Samford University's president, Dr. Thomas Corts. Together, with Samford's help and funding, they hired award-winning director T. N. Mohan, from Huntsville, Alabama, and created a documentary, *For One English Officer*.

During the research stage, Grooms prepared a "trial notebook," (attorney's workbook) containing documents and photos that became an invaluable tool in preparing the documentary and in writing this book.

Grooms and director Mohan spent three days searching files at the National Archives, uncovering useful information and rare film clips, photos, and documents. Grooms drafted the script, and mounted a search for the Americans involved in the 1944 POW exchanges. He located twelve POWs living across the United States, and found Lieutenant Léon Spanin, the French Resistance fighter who had joined Captain Michael R. D. Foot in his last abortive escape attempt.

Samford University brought twelve surviving POWs* to Birmingham, Alabama, for a reunion dinner for two hundred people to honor the surviving POWs and Andrew Gerow Hodges. While at Samford, Grooms interviewed each about his war experiences. For the next three years, he worked on the film project. When *For One English Officer* was released, it caught the attention of Alabama Public Television. They aired it twice in January 2004, and it later aired nationally on PBS on Memorial Day, 2004. The award-winning film has also been shown in Europe.

Birmingham author Denise George had collaborated with a number of authors on books about significant historical events. Married to the founding dean of the Beeson Divinity School, Dr. Timothy George, Denise knew Gerow Hodges and his family and had had many delightful dinners and conversations with them. She had attended the celebration of the naming of the Beeson chapel—the Andrew Gerow Hodges Chapel—as well as Gerow's funeral. Denise had been invited to the 2002 reunion, but had been unable to attend.

In 2013, Denise asked Gerow's older son, Gerry, if a book had ever been written about his father. He said no. Why had she waited so long to inquire about writing a book about Hodges's WWII experience? "We are losing 'the greatest generation' day by day," she told him. "I thought it was a great story that needed to be told."

Denise knew that Gerry himself was the author of six books, had heard his father's WWII stories all his life, met the POWs in 2002, and personally knew Michael Foot. She then asked if Gerry would be interested in the two of them working on a book together—Gerry as author, Denise as collaborator.

Gerry and the rest of the Hodges family agreed. Denise met with Gerry and Hobart Grooms, borrowed the bulging "trial notebook" Grooms used in preparing the documentary film, and wrote an extensive book proposal. Her book agent, Greg Johnson, president of WordServeLiterary, received an immediate offer from New York's Penguin Random House to publish the manuscript. After much hard work, and with a huge, incalculable debt owed to Grooms's extensive research, gracious guidance, and military history expertise, the book honoring Andrew Gerow Hodges was born.

[*By 2011, Grooms had located twenty-three ex-prisoners or their next of kin.]

ANDREW GEROW HODGES'S LETTER OF 22 MARCH 1945, WRITTEN FROM PARIS, FRANCE

[Written to his wife, Mary Louise (Shirley) Hodges]

My darling, I wrote you last night about Phil coming in from Paris, and that he was going to spend the night with me. We had a wonderful time just talking about you, Gerry, Camp McCain, the few parties we [all] had together. . . . I always enjoy talking to someone that knows you, because they always remind me what a lovely and charming wife, and wonderful little son I have. No one knows that better than I, but it is always music to my ears to have someone tell me. I love you —G.

ANDREW GEROW HODGES'S LETTER OF 21 OCTOBER 1945, WRITTEN FROM GERMANY

[Written to his wife, Mary Louise (Shirley) Hodges]

Darling, I have spent all the day typing up the evaluations on the men I visited in Czechoslovakia, and I found typing long reports on eight men just is not fun, especially when one uses the method of typing I do. You have heard of the hunt-and-peck method, haven't you? Well! That is the method I use. I do darn well on the pecking, but I am still plenty slow on the hunting end. . . .

Darling, I think you know I miss you very much. Give Gerry my love. I love you, G.

ANDREW GEROW HODGES'S LETTER OF 7 JULY 1945, WRITTEN FROM CZECHOSLOVAKIA

[Written to his wife, Mary Louise (Shirley) Hodges]

Dearest Shirley:

Colonel Hendrixson, Colonel Brown—the division surgeon, Colonel McGlucklin—the division chemical warfare office, and I played bridge tonight. Col. McGlucklin and I were partners. We had a close game until the last. Col. Hendrixson and Col. Brown beat us 3,000 points. I enjoyed playing very much, and it was a good way to while-away a lonely Saturday night.

Sunday is about the only day in the week that I change my routine, and that is changed because I go to church. I have gotten to where I hate to miss one of the chaplain's services. He is a wonderful minister and a prince of a fellow. He and I have our offices together here, and I enjoy having an opportunity to talk with him often. We also go fishing together frequently.

Darling, due to a change in the salary of field directors, which became effective July 1, 1945, I have increased our war bond purchase $50.00 per month to become effective August 15. What has happened is that the Red Cross has stopped the flat maintenance fund we were given each month, and has given us a $75.00 per month increase in pay. Frankly, the old method was more profitable, but we have no choice. My salary breakdown beginning August 15th, will be per month:

[Money sent] to you: $100.00
[Money] for me: $25.00
[Money to buy] bonds: $150.00 [Bond face value: $200.00]
[Total each month: $275.00]

I may not be able to make it on $25.00 per month, but I believe I can. Anyway I am going to give it a big try, because the raise in salary will mean more income tax I will have to pay. I also want to save as much as I possibly can to enable us to have the many things we shall need and want after this war is over.

I miss you more than you could ever imagine. I love you.

ANDREW GEROW HODGES'S LETTER OF 19 JULY 1945, WRITTEN FROM CZECHOSLOVAKIA

[Written to his wife, Mary Louise (Shirley) Hodges]

Darling,

. . . We have had a lot of changes in officers since General Malony was transferred from the division [94th Infantry Division]. Our G2 and G4 have been replaced, and today our Chief of Staff, Colonel Bergquist, left to take an assignment in Washington. I hated to see Col. Bergquist leave, however, Colonel Gaddis, former assistant to Col. Johnson, is taking his place and we get along well. The division really doesn't seem the same since these changes have been made, and since the officers and men with over 85 points were transferred out of the division.

I honestly don't think the division will ever fight the Japs, unless things get rather critical, but you never can tell. . . .

BACKGROUND INFORMATION ON CAPTAIN MICHAEL R. D. FOOT

Michael Foot joined the Officer Training Corps (OTC) in 1934 while a student at Winchester College. He later passed the Certificate A examination that deemed him fit to command a platoon.

Foot said that in 1912, his grandfather, who had been a commanding officer in the Territorial Army Hartfordshire Artillery Regiment, told his father that it looked as if a war was going to occur, and that he should enlist. History repeated itself in the winter of 1938–39, when his father repeated the same words to Michael. Michael joined the Territorial Army in 1939 as a second lieutenant. Mobilized while still in the university, Foot was assigned to a searchlight battalion in Anti-Aircraft Command. He spent the first half of the war in that duty. In 1942, a friend of his managed to leave the AA and asked Michael if he would be interested in getting into Combined Operations Headquarters. Foot quickly agreed. He spent the next eighteen months involved in the planning of Operation Torch (North Africa) and Operation Husky (Sicily). He was promoted to major in January 1944.

Foot was later approached and asked if he would be interested in going with the Special Air Service (SAS) as an intelligence officer, having been assured that he would get much "closer to the Germans" in that position. As was customary, he had to drop a rank to get into the Special Air Service. He spent six months as a British intelligence officer with the SAS. He was involved in the planning phases of various aspects of D-Day operations in France and subsequent operations.

Captain Foot was sent into Brittany on an SAS mission on August 22, 1944, to capture an officer in the SD. On August 24, 1944, he was captured by a German parachute battalion, interrogated, and later taken to a POW compound in St. Nazaire. Seriously injured when he tried to escape from the POW camp, Foot was later exchanged for a German POW. He spent many months in a hospital in Rennes, unable to move his body for months, but he recovered from his injuries. Foot was one of only six (out of one hundred SAS officers) who survived the war.

KAPITANLEUTNANT KARL W. MÜLLER'S HILARIOUS MISUNDERSTANDING!

Kapitanleutnant Karl W. Müller, dubbed the "Tiger of the Channel," the German *Ritterkreuz* recipient, and the commander of *Schnellboot* S-52 in the 5. *Schnellbootflottille*, was captured on September 18–19, 1944. He later volunteered to be exchanged for the British SAS captain Michael R. D. Foot. Andy Hodges drove him by jeep from the 94th Division's headquarters to St. Nazaire on December 1, 1944.

After Müller's release, he joined the staff of Admiral Karl Dönitz, the man who succeeded Adolf Hitler. Dönitz led Germany for only a short time before the May 1945 German surrender.

For years after the war, Kapitanleutnant Karl W. Müller boasted at dinner parties about having been swapped for Michael Foot, the highly acclaimed British Labor Party leader. "The Allies had to cough up one of their top politicians to buy my freedom," the German bragged for years, unaware of his error. He experienced something of a comedown—his bubble was burst!—when he discovered the man wasn't *that* particular Michael Foot, but Michael R. D. Foot, the British scholar, not the famous politician. German records still attest to the false information, however.

A LETTER TO HODGES FROM MICHAEL FOOT, 1975

[More than thirty years had passed since Andrew Gerow Hodges negotiated Michael Foot's release from the St. Nazaire German POW hospital. In 1975, Hodges was planning a company trip to England. He decided to see if he could locate Michael Foot. With the help of some people in England, he found him and received this gracious letter from Foot in response.]

My dear Mr. Hodges:

It was an equal surprise and delight to be put back in touch with you, out of the blue, yesterday; and I enormously look forward to seeing you when you come over to England next month.

My father, Brig. R. C. Foot, whom you knew much better than you can have known me, died five years ago in Australia; age 75, of a sudden heart attack. He repeatedly told me how your efforts saved my life in November– December 1944, when you were negotiating a prisoner-of-war exchange at St. Nazaire. I remember your visiting me in a German hospital at La

Baule; but was far from being in full command of my thoughts or my speech at the time. A sane talk with you would be splendid. . . .

Come and spend an April weekend with us. It's absurd not even to know whether you are married; anyhow, our spare room sleeps two and you would be thoroughly welcome, single or a deux. Failing that, have a meal at least in London. Every possible good wish from your continually grateful, Michael Foot.

[Andrew Hodges and Michael Foot met in England in 1975 and stayed in contact as long as they lived. In the 1990s, Michael Foot traveled to Birmingham, Alabama, and taught a January term course at Samford University. The two veterans spent time together recalling the war.]

A LETTER FROM MICHAEL R. D. FOOT

[On November 11, 2002, after viewing *For One English Officer*, the documentary sent to Michael Foot by Andrew Gerow Hodges, Foot wrote Hodges a letter. He referred to the Armistice Day remembrance at Camp Franco, St. Nazaire, on November 11, 1944.]

Fifty-eight years ago, to the day, I had just begun a spell of a few days' solitary confinement, for the impertinence of having organized that morning a two minutes' silent parade in memory of both sides' war dead from the Great War of 1914–18. I still remain permanently grateful to you for having rescued me from the deplorable prisoner of war camp in which I and several score others were confined; and have just had my gratitude confirmed by a sight of T. N. Mohan's film about the rescues you arranged from the Ile de Groix and from St. Nazaire. I hope you liked the film too. It was a delight to see your face in it again, as well as the faces of several of my fellow-prisoners; one of whom, Léon Spanin (then using the cover name of Rollin), I had dinner with at his home near Paris last spring. . . . Your most affectionate Michael.

A LETTER FROM MICHAEL R. D. FOOT

[On January 13, 2004, Michael Foot received a package of photographs and papers from the Special Collections Department of Samford University that Colonel Hobart Grooms, Jr., had put together and sent him. This is Foot's reply from Hertfordshire, England.]

Dear Department:

A few days ago I got a packet from you . . . including a mass of photographs and papers about the prisoner-of-war exchange that Gerow Hodges organized in 1944. I have known for almost sixty years that I owe my life to him (I have now turned eighty-four), and am most grateful to you for having bothered to put the package together and to send it to me. . . .

Again, a few days ago, I spoke by telephone with Dr. Léon Rollin (as he was called at the time: it was a cover name), my fellow-escaper . . . [who] lives just outside Paris in France, and we meet when we can. You will have seen him in the Mohan film. I was Mohan's 'one English officer.'

There are a few faces [in the film] . . . that I had hoped I would not have to look at again this side of Doomsday; you have sent me three photographs of the German officer who interrogated me, who bears one of them. (Had he discovered who I was and what I was doing, he would have shot me on the spot.) So I went through your package with a certain frisson; but want to send my warmest thanks for it, and to you. With every warm wish, Yours most sincerely, MRD Foot.

(Note: In an interview for *For One English Officer*, WWII historian Michael R. D. Foot said about Andrew Gerow Hodges: "It was quite remarkable . . . he literally saved my life . . . [Andrew Gerow Hodges was the] only one I know of to have personally negotiated an exchange of prisoners [during WWII].")

A LETTER FROM MICHAEL R. D. FOOT TO COLONEL HARLAN HOBART GROOMS, JR., NOVEMBER 6, 2005

[When Michael Foot, in England, learned of Gerow Hodges's death, he wrote Hobart Grooms a letter dated November 6, 2005.]

I have of course written to Gerow's widow, as well as to President Corts; but you will let me send you a word as well, to say how sorry I am that Gerow is dead. Had it not been for him, I would not be here to write; I would have faded out quietly, from exhaustion and starvation, in a German military hospital. He [Hodges] was the very best sort of practical Christian, with a degree of obstinacy in a cause he knew to be just that would have done credit to any early father of the church; both Samford, and the whole Birmingham Baptist community, must still be mourning for him.

K301 VETS HONORED IN BRITTANY

On May 7–8, 2000, several towns in Brittany honored the 94th Division and its men during their World War II Liberation Day celebrations. Wayne Stewart, Bernard Rader, and Bob Higgins represented K Company. A commemorative plaque was placed on an Etel building in memory of KIAs Lieutenant Thomas J. Leone and Sergeant Loray E. Thornton, who died in Etel on December 4, 1944. On May 8, ceremonies were held on Île de Groix, at the prison where Stewart and the other K Company men were incarcerated.

Stewart visited the room in Fort Surville where he was imprisoned. Local children presented him and his wife, Vivien, with flowers.

The mayor officially changed the name of the road connecting the fort and Port Tudy to "Rue de la 94th Infantry." Three elderly women, who were teenagers at the time, were pointed out. They had sneaked apples to the hungry prisoners on their walks outside the fort. The mayor presented Stewart, Rader, and Higgins with American flags, and they were given a wreath by the French to place on the monument to honor the men of the 94th killed in action on October 2, 1944.

More than four hundred people filled the Catholic church in Etel to honor the guests. The tribute paid the 94th Division and the men of K Company by the French on that May day, more than fifty-six years later, was described as "overwhelming and deeply appreciated."

BIOGRAPHICAL INFORMATION ON ANDREW GEROW HODGES

Andrew Gerow Hodges was born on June 14, 1918, to Jesse T. Hodges and Lee Ola (Hayes) Hodges. On November 14, 1941, he married Mary Louise Shirley. Hodges graduated from Howard College (now Samford University) with his B.S. degree in 1942. During college, he worked as manager of the Birmingham Athletic Club and as an auditor of the Brown-Service Insurance Company. After his WWII Red Cross representative service as a senior field director (1944–1946), Hodges became the superintendent of agents, Ensley Distributors, with Liberty National Life Insurance Company (1946–1947), then manager of Cullman Distributors (1947–1950), manager policyholders' service, home office (1950–1952), assistant secretary (1952–1957), assistant vice president (1957–1959), and vice president (until retirement).

Andrew Gerow Hodges also held other important positions, including:

Board of directors of Brown-Service Funeral Homes Company, Jefferson County Red Cross, and Junior Achievement of Jefferson County, as well as serving on the Board of Trustees with Samford University; vice chairman of the Birmingham Salvation Army; the general co-chairman of Birmingham First United Appeal; and the Business Division chairman of Highland Baptist

Hospital Campaign Memorial. Mr. Hodges also was a member of the Metro YMCA, Birmingham Kiwanis Club, Monday Morning Quarterback Club, Vestavia Hills Country Club, The Club, and the Boy Scouts.

His honors and awards include: Bronze Star (military); Birmingham Citizen of the Year (1978); Silver Buffalo Award (1988); William Boothe Award (1998); International Red Cross Award (2002); Alabama's Men's Hall of Fame (2012, induction posthumously).

WHAT HAPPENED TO THE MEN

THE POWS AT LORIENT

Private First Class George C. Boyd: K Company, 301st Regiment, 94th Infantry Division. Private First Class George Boyd, imprisoned at Fort Surville after the October 2, 1944, ambush, was exchanged at Etel/Le Magouer on November 16, 1944. He later fought with the 94th Division in the Battle of the Bulge. He holds the Bronze Star. After the war ended, he returned to the United States, married Gladys Gertrude Gates, worked for thirty years for the Efland Hosiery Mills, and was later employed by a television cable company. Private First Class George Boyd attended the Samford University reunion on January 25, 2002. His wife, Gladys, died on January 27, 2014. George still lives in Efland, North Carolina. He is the father of three sons, grandfather of six, and great-grandfather of eight.

Private First Class George M. Brady: Headquarters Company, 3rd Battalion, 301st Infantry, 94th Division. Private First Class George Brady, from Baltimore, Maryland, was involved in D-Day and landed on Utah Beach. Captured during the October 2, 1944, ambush and imprisoned at Fort Surville, he was exchanged at Etel/Le Magouer on November 16, 1944. He later fought with the 94th Division in the Ardennes and the Rhineland. After the war, he graduated from John Hopkins University and the University of Maryland Law School. Brady became a leader in real estate and mortgage banking. Founding director of the James W. Rouse Co., he became president and later board chairman of the National Corporation of Housing Partnerships, retiring in 1988. Brady attended the Samford University reunion on January 25, 2002. Until his death on August 24, 2009, at age eighty-seven, Brady and his wife of thirty-eight years, Maria Nomita, resided in Bethesda, Maryland.

Sergeant Roy Connatser: K Company, 301st Regiment, 94th Infantry Division. Sergeant Roy Connatser was born in Louisville, Tennessee, on January 19, 1920. He was drafted into the army in December 1942. He received his basic training at Camp Phillips, Kansas. Sent to Northern France, he joined General Patton's 3rd Army, 94th Infantry Division. He was captured in the October 2, 1944, Lorient ambush and imprisoned at Fort Surville for forty-five days. Connatser was exchanged at Etel/Le Magouer on November 16, 1944. During his military service, he was awarded the following medals: Expert Rifleman, Good Conduct Medal, the French Medal for Bravery, the Purple Heart, Prisoner of War, and Service in the European Theater. He was discharged at Camp Shelby, Mississippi, in December 1945. After returning to the United States, he resumed his job at Alcoa Aluminum and stayed there until he retired in 1982. He and his wife of sixty-eight years, Mary Ruth White, settled in East Tennessee. Connatser attended the Samford University reunion on January 25, 2002. He died on January 9, 2013, at age ninety-two.

Private Harry Glixon: K Company, 301st Regiment, 94th Infantry Division. Private Harry Glixon, imprisoned at Fort Surville after the October 2, 1944, ambush, was exchanged at Etel/Le Magouer on November 16, 1944. Glixon served as the field radio operator during the ambush, and for his bravery during battle, he was awarded the Bronze Star with Oak

Leaf Cluster and V for Valor, the Combat Infantry Badge, and the Purple Heart with Oak Leaf Cluster. After his release from Île de Groix, he moved with the 94th Division to the Ardennes and fought in the Battle of the Bulge, where he was again wounded and received his second Purple Heart. Glixon was also the recipient of the POW Medal, Good Conduct Medal, American Campaign Medal, European-African-Middle Eastern Campaign Medal with four Bronze Service Stars, WWII Victory Medal, Army of Occupation Medal with Germany Clasp, Expert Infantryman Badge, and Expert Marksman Badge with Automatic Rifle Bar. After the war, Glixon returned to the States and earned an electrical engineering degree from New York University. He became the founder and president of Consolidated Avionics Corporation of Westbury, New York. At age thirty-three, he was elected to the Young Presidents Organization. He and his wife, Lorraine, had four children. Glixon attended the Samford University reunion on January 25, 2002. He died on December 10, 2007, at his home in Sarasota, Florida, at age eighty-two.

Sergeant Charles E. Hanson: 301st Regiment, 94th Infantry Division. Sergeant Charles Hanson, captured by the enemy in the October 2, 1944, ambush, was imprisoned with injuries at the Lorient Naval Hospital and exchanged at Etel/Le Magouer on November 16, 1944. After his release, Hanson was sent to the hospitals at Rennes and Paris, assigned to a replacement depot at Versailles, and received an assignment to S.H.A.E.F. Discharged from the army on December 7, 1945, Hanson married, started classes at the University of Kentucky, and worked part-time for Greyhound, retiring after forty-one years. He and his wife reared two daughters, five grandchildren, and six great-grandchildren. Sergeant Charles Hanson was unable to attend the Samford University reunion in 2002.

Private First Class Kermit L. Harden, Jr.: K Company, 301st Regiment, 94th Division. Private First Class Kermit Harden, imprisoned at Fort Surville after the October 2, 1944, ambush, was exchanged at Etel/Le Magouer on November 16, 1944. After Harden's release, he was sent to a military hospital for medical treatment. He fought with the 94th Division in the Battle of the Bulge and received the Purple Heart, the Bronze Star, and the Silver Star for his gallantry in action in Germany. While holding a hill with a dozen men, Harden suffered frostbite in his feet and required medical treatment. After the war, he returned to the United States, earned a degree in mathematics, and later an Ed.D. from the University of Illinois. He and his wife, Ann, settled in Urbana, Illinois. Harden held many administrative positions during his career in education, including superintendent of Urbana schools, and has served on the boards of Urbana Rotary, the Reading Group, the Boy Scouts, and the UI Alumni Association. He devoted many years of volunteer service to the library in leadership roles on the board of trustees and the foundation board. Mr. Harden attended the Samford University reunion on January 25, 2002. In May 2004, Harden (along with Bernie Rader and his friend, Bob Moore), traveled to Groix and presented a memorial plaque to the French people on behalf of the 94th Infantry Division. The Hardens still reside in Urbana, Illinois.

Private First Class Bernard Rader: K Company, 301st Regiment, 94th Division. Private First Class Bernie Rader, captured by the enemy in the October 2, 1944, ambush, was imprisoned with injuries at the Lorient Naval Hospital and exchanged at Etel/Le Magouer on November 16, 1944. He received the Bronze Star. After the war, Rader returned to the United States, completed college, and became a CPA, practicing with his father until retirement. Rader became a leader in the New York State Society of Certified Public Accounts. In 2003, he contacted his former fellow prisoners at Fort Surville and requested they contribute to a commemorative plaque to thank the people of the Île de Groix for their kindnesses to the POWs during their 1944 imprisonment. Bernie and June Rader attended the Samford University reunion on January 25, 2002. Rader, along with Bob Moore and Kermit Harden, traveled to Groix in May 2004 and presented the memorial plaque to the French people. On November 5, 2007, Rader was decorated by French president Nicolas Sarkozy with the Knighthood of the Legion of

Honor at the French Embassy in Washington, D.C. Bernie and June Rader live in New York, and attended the seventieth D-Day anniversary remembrance in Normandy, France, in June 2014. (The author is greatly indebted to the Raders for their gracious assistance with information during the writing of this manuscript.)

Sergeant James Sarsfield: 6th Armored Division. Sergeant James Sarsfield was captured by Germans on September 19, 1944, in the Lorient sector. He was imprisoned at Fort Surville on Île de Groix. He penned the first letter to the American Red Cross that alerted Colonel Bergquist of the prisoners in the Lorient POW camp. Sarsfield was exchanged at Etel/Le Magouer on November 16, 1944. Originally from Lucerne, Pennsylvania, James Sarsfield returned to the United States after the war, settled in Los Angeles, California, and became a successful banker. He died [date unknown] before the Samford reunion in 2002.

Private First Class Morris Shulman: K Company, 301st Regiment, 94th Division. Private First Class Morris Shulman, born on September 28, 1925, in Elizabeth, New Jersey, enlisted in the army upon graduation from high school. Captured during the October 2, 1944, ambush, he was imprisoned at Fort Surville and exchanged at Etel/Le Magouer on November 16, 1944. He moved with the 94th Division and fought in the Battle of the Bulge. After the war, he returned to the United States, graduated in 1950 from New York University with a degree in business and advertising, and worked with his brother in the family business, operating retail stores in the New Jersey area. He retired in 1996. He and his wife, Dr. Valerie Lowitz, settled in West Orange, New Jersey. Shulman attended the Samford University reunion on January 25, 2002. He died on October 27, 2012, in Boca Raton, Florida, at age eighty-seven.

Private Wayne A. Stewart: K Company, 301st Regiment, 94th Infantry Division. Private Wayne Stewart was born in Clark, South Dakota, on April 14, 1925. He was imprisoned at Fort Surville after the October 2, 1944, ambush and was exchanged at Etel/Le Magouer on November 16, 1944.

After his release, Stewart participated in the recapture of German coastal fortifications, including Etel, where he had been exchanged earlier. He was awarded the Silver Star for heroism during the capture of Etel. Stewart moved with the 94th Division, fought in the Battle of the Bulge, and was later wounded there. He was awarded a Bronze Star and Purple Heart. When he returned to the United States, he studied at South Dakota State University, earning a degree in electrical engineering. He worked as director of system, planning, and design for the Chelan County PUD. He and his wife, Vivian, settled in Wenatchee, Washington. They became parents of four children and had eleven grandchildren and thirteen great-grandchildren. Stewart attended the Samford University reunion on January 25, 2002. He died on April 10, 2013, at age eighty-eight.

Private First Class David Trachtenberg: K/301, 94th Infantry Division. Private First Class David Trachtenberg, from Wurstboro, New York, was wounded and captured during the ambush on October 2, 1944, in the Lorient sector of France. He was imprisoned at the Lorient Naval Hospital (along with Bernie Rader) and exchanged at Etel/Le Magouer on November 16, 1944. After the war, Trachtenberg and his wife, Selma, settled in Lake Worth, Florida. Trachtenberg attended the Samford reunion on January 25, 2002.

THE POWs AT SAINT NAZAIRE

British SAS Captain Michael R. D. Foot. Captain Michael Foot was the most well known of the prisoners exchanged by Andrew Gerow Hodges in the fall/winter of 1944. After the second POW exchange at Pornic, France, on November 29, 1944, Foot received surgical and medical care at an American hospital in Rennes. He was ordered to lie in bed with his head on a pillow until February 1945. Afterward, a friend flew him back to England. British doctors evaluated Foot and determined not to allow him to return to military duty for reasons of physical health. He taught at Oxford University for eight years and became a professor of modern history at the University of Manchester, England. A British specialist in the resistance movement in Europe, he earned himself the nickname "Mister Resistance." He authored many best-selling books on the history of World War II. He was decorated commander of the Order of the British Empire and awarded the French *Croix de Guerre* for SAS service in Brittany.

A world famous historian and also a scholar on the life of British prime minister William Gladstone, Foot edited the first four volumes of the Gladstone diaries between 1968 and 1974.

Captain Michael Foot was unable to attend the Samford University reunion on January 25, 2002, but sent a letter to Andrew Gerow Hodges and the group, read by Colonel Hobart Grooms. Foot died on February 18, 2012, at the age of ninety-two. He is survived by his wife, Mirjam, emeritus professor of library and archive studies at University College London, and by his daughter and son. [Note: Captain Foot was one of only six SAS men—out of one hundred captured by the Germans—who survived the war. Some of the information gleaned from an August 2, 2001, phone conversation between Michael Foot and Hobart Grooms. Some information also found at: http://www.theguardian.com/world/2012/feb/21/mrd-foot. Accessed: April 4, 2014.]

British Brigadier Richard Cunningham Foot (Captain Michael R. D. Foot's father), during WWII, directed the anti-aircraft defenses of London that were successful in knocking down German V-1s over the British capital. He served as a captain of the Royal Artillery in WWI and was such a formidable shot that he received the Military Cross of Gallantry in Action. Before the war and after, he built a career as an export-import merchant and worked at it until his seventy-seventh birthday. At the end of his life, he moved to Australia with his third wife. He died in 1969.

Lieutenant Dr. William Reynolds: 29th Field Hospital. Dr. William Reynolds served for a year and three months as part of the U.S. Army Dental Corps, with the 29th Field Hospital in Europe, assisted with D-Day invasion preparations, accompanied troops ashore at Omaha

Beach in Normandy, and participated in the capture of the Port of
Brest. On October 28, 1944, Dr. Reynolds (accompanied by Lieutenant
Norman Le Barre and Private Orville Spencer) was scouting out a location for a new field hospital in the St. Nazaire Allied area when his
vehicle hit a land mine and exploded, throwing him into a ditch and
severely wounding his foot. He was captured by the enemy, imprisoned
at the French Naval Hospital in Lorient, and released in the second
POW exchange at Pornic on November 29, 1944.

After the exchange, Reynolds was transported to a hospital in Rennes,
from there to Cherbourg, then by boat to England with other wounded
soldiers—Americans and Germans—most of them suffering with frostbite.
Several of the German wounded died during the voyage and were given
burials at sea. From England, Lieutenant Reynolds was sent to New York
City, and finally to the William Beaumont Army Hospital in his home, El
Paso, Texas. Following the war, Dr. Reynolds earned a master's degree in
orthodontics from the University of Missouri, Kansas. He practiced orthodontics in El Paso and was an active Catholic layman. He and his wife, Ruth,
were married for sixty years and became parents of thirteen children, who
gave them forty-one grandchildren and nineteen great-grandchildren. Dr.
Reynolds was a recipient of the Purple Heart, POW Medal, Victory Medal,
American Theater Medal, European Theater Medal, and Liberation of
France Medal. Dr. Reynolds kept his old smelly boot as a souvenir all his
life. And he never left home without his spare pair of eyeglasses. His life-
long limp reminded him every waking hour of his experience in the Lorient sector of France, 1944. Dr. Reynolds attended the Samford University
reunion on January 25, 2002, at which he told the story about his boot. He
died on September 18, 2009, at age ninety.

**Second Lieutenant James Silva: 160th Tactical Reconnaissance Squad-
ron, 363rd Tactical Reconnaissance Group, 9th Air Force.** A P-51
pilot, Second Lieutenant James Silva bailed out of his plane after taking
direct flak over the St. Nazaire sector on September 19, 1944. Silva,
twenty years old, a native of Lexington, Massachusetts, joined the air

force during his freshman year at Northeastern University. Imprisoned at Camp Franco in St. Nazaire, Silva was released during the second POW exchange in Pornic on November 29, 1944.

After the exchange, Silva requested to remain in Europe with his old outfit, the 160th. In that role, he flew planes to depot for overhaul, ferried aircraft, and checked them out after maintenance. After the war, he was stationed at Wiesbaden. He was discharged and returned to the U.S. in May 1946. He moved to the Boston area, where he received an engineering degree from Northeastern University. In August 1950, during the Korean conflict, he was recalled into the air force and stationed at Langley Field. During the following seventeen months in Korea, he flew twin-engine B-26 Night Fighters and completed thirty-three missions before returning to the States and marrying Dorothy Louise Peppard. The couple had three girls. Silva worked as an engineer for Sylvania (later GTE) until he retired in 1982. Silva attended the Samford University reunion on January 25, 2002. He resides in Peabody, Massachusetts. His wife, Dorothy, died on July 2, 2013.

French Lieutenant Léon Spanin (Rollin). Lieutenant Léon Rollin was the French name that the Russian Léon Spanin used during his work with the French Resistance. After Léon Rollin's parents left Russia, Rollin lived in Berlin for five years of his adolescence. He then moved to France with his parents and was drafted by the French Army in 1940 while attending a French medical school—only eight days before the Germans took Paris. His regiment retreated to Bordeaux and then to Toulouse. When the army discovered his Russian origins, they interned him and made him a cook in a Pyrenees quarry. Rollin escaped, joined the French Resistance, helped liberate Rodez and the South West, and fought on the Atlantic front. Captured by Germans near Vannes, Rollin was imprisoned at the St. Nazaire POW camp. He was released during the second POW exchange in Pornic on November 29, 1944.

After the war, Rollin did not resume his medical education, but settled in Paris and became a teacher. He and friend Michael Foot stayed in close touch throughout their lifetimes. At age eighty-two, Rollin gave an interview in French for the documentary *For One English Officer*. Lieutenant Léon Rollin/Spanin was unable to attend the Samford reunion on January 25, 2002.

Sapper George H. Tegg: 676th Construction & Ordnance Company of the British Royal Engineers at Dunkirk. Sapper George Tegg, from Birmingham, England, was captured by the Germans on August 4, 1944, when he was commissioned (without official permission) by Lieutenant G. Goss to serve as his driver. Tegg was imprisoned at the German POW camp in St. Nazaire. (For his unauthorized actions, Lieutenant Goss later received a court-martial.) Several POWs spoke of listening to Tegg's beautiful tenor voice on dark nights as he sang "Danny Boy." Sapper Tegg was released during the second POW exchange in Pornic on November 29, 1944. After the war, Tegg stayed in the British Army part-time for 7 years, 117 days. He died in 1998. (The author is indebted to Sapper Tegg's grandson, Kevin Bywater, in Australia, for information on his grandfather.)

Sergeant Harold Thompson: 31st Regiment, 83rd Division. Sergeant Thompson, from Mobile, Alabama, eagerly joined the army at age eighteen. He arrived in Normandy on July 4, 1944. Thompson and his twelve-man patrol were returning from an intelligence mission behind German lines in Festung St. Nazaire, on September 13, 1944, when he was injured and captured by the enemy. Imprisoned at the POW camp at St. Nazaire, Thompson was released during the second POW exchange on November 29, 1944.

Following his discharge, Thompson returned to the United States and was employed by the U.S. Air Force as a civilian employee, finishing as chief of the Program Management Branch, Electronic Warfare Management Directorate, Robbins AFB. Thompson held the Bronze Star, Combat Infantry Badge, Purple Heart, Ex–Prisoner of War Medal, European-Africa-Middle Eastern Medals with two Bronze Stars, World War II Victory Medal, American Campaign Medal, and other awards. He settled in Hawkinsville, Georgia, with his wife, Eddie, and worked in Baptist life. Thompson attended the Samford reunion on January 25, 2002. He died on May 21, 2002, at age seventy-seven.

THE AMERICAN OFFICERS

Colonel Earl C. Bergquist was born on April 8, 1902, in Grand Forks, North Dakota, and was raised in Minnesota. He graduated from the Infantry School in 1934, the Signal School in 1935, the Command and General Staff College in 1939, the Industrial College of the Armed Forces in 1947, and the National War College in 1951. As chief of staff during WWII, Colonel Bergquist worked closely with Andrew Gerow Hodges in orchestrating the prisoner exchanges. After the war, Colonel Bergquist worked as secretary and instructor of the Command and General Staff College; assistant chief of staff, Seventh Army; commander, 4th Infantry Division; chief of the Army Section of the Joint United States Military Group in Spain; and assistant division commander, 3rd Infantry Division. Colonel Bergquist retired in 1959. He and his wife settled in McLean, Virginia, where he was active in the March of Dimes. Colonel Bergquist died on January 9, 1983. Some of his many awards include the Legion of Merit, Bronze Star, and *Croix de Guerre*. [Some of this information found at: http://cdm16635.contentdm.oclc.org/cdm/compoundobject/collection/p16635coll16/id/73/show/64/rec/8. Accessed: November 24, 2013.]

Major General Harry J. Malony, commanding officer of the 94th Infantry Division, was born on August 24, 1889, in Lakemont, New York. He graduated from the United States Military Academy at West Point, New York, on June 12, 1912. Assigned to the 10th Infantry Regiment, he was stationed near the Mexican border during WWI. On January 29, 1941, he was promoted to the rank of brigadier general. After WWII, Major General Malony returned to the U.S. on February 6, 1946, was appointed the director of the Historical Division within the Department of the Army, and served until his retirement on March 31, 1949. He died on March 23,

1971, at age eighty-one. Some of Major General Malony's many awards and citations include the Army Distinguished Service Medal (World War 1 and World War II) and the Silver Star. [Some information found at: http://projects.militarytimes.com/citations-medals-awards/recipient .php?recipientid=17874; http://www.94thinfdiv.com/faqsheet.html; and http://en.wikipedia.org/wiki/Harry_J._Malony. All accessed: November 24, 2013.]

THE GERMAN OFFICERS

Oberst Otto Borst, Atlantikfestung Festungskommandant Lorient, was born on October 10, 1897, in London, England. Borst worked with Andrew Gerow Hodges in negotiations to release the allied POWs imprisoned at Lorient and Fort Surville on Île de Groix. Oberst Borst remained at Lorient until the end of the war. He was then arrested for war crimes, spent time in prison, and was released on February 18, 1948. His last known address was in Germany. No records of Borst could be found after 1957.

General der Artillerie Wilhelm Fahrmbacher was born on September 19, 1888, in Zweibrucken, Germany. Fahrmbacher served as the German commander in Brittany from August 1, 1944, to May 10, 1945—when he surrendered to the Americans in Fortress Lorient. Americans handed him over to the French, who held him as a prisoner until 1950. When the French released him, he became a military advisor to the Egyptian Army from 1951 to 1958. Fahrmbacher died on April 27, 1970, in Garmisch-Partenkirchen. [Found at: http://www.geocities.com /~orion47/WEHRMACHT/HEER/General/FAHRMBACHER _WILHELM.html. Accessed: November 17, 2013.]

Generalleutnant Hans Junck, commandant, Fortress St. Nazaire. Generalleutnant Junck was born September 16, 1893, in Leipzig, Germany. Active in WWI as an Oberleutnant, he served as adjutant of the

Mounted Battalion of the 12th Field Artillery Regiment. He became commandant of Fortress St. Nazaire in September 1944 and stayed there until May 8, 1945. After Germany's surrender, Junck was held in French captivity for three years. When tried for war crimes in September 1947, he was acquitted and released on March 15, 1948. Highly decorated during WWI and WWII, he died on November 28, 1966, in Berlin-Zehlendorg. [Information found at: http://www.geocities.com/~orion47/WEHRMACHT/HEER/Generalleutnant2/JUNCK_HANS.html. Accessed: November 24, 2013.]

Kapitanleutnant Karl W. Müller was born in Essen-Borbeck-Mitte, a small village in northwest Germany. At age twenty-eight, dubbed the "Tiger of the Channel," he was a German *Ritterkreuz* recipient and the commander of *Schnellboot* S-52 in the 5. *Schnellbootflottille*. On September 18–19, 1944, his S-boat was destroyed, and he was captured by Lieutenant John Humphreys, the senior British naval officer of the frigate *Stayner*, in North Sea waters near Ostend, off the Belgian coast. Imprisoned at an allied POW camp in Scotland, Müller later volunteered to be exchanged for British SAS captain Michael R. D. Foot. On December 1, 1944, Andrew Gerow Hodges personally drove the Kapitanleutnant to St. Nazaire and released him to Oberst Pinski.

Before the end of the war, Müller joined the staff of Admiral Karl Dönitz, the man who succeeded Adolf Hitler, and served briefly before the May 1945 German surrender. At the war's end, Müller became the Kriegsschauplatzbearbeiter West (commander, surface operations, Western Front). After the war, Kapitanleutnant Müller headed the firm of Metallguss Sulingen. He received numerous awards and medals in his military career, including the *Ritterkreuz*, Iron Cross, Sudetenland Medal, Destroyer War Badge, Minesweeper War Badge, Fast Attack Craft War Badge, and more. He died on May 19, 1989, in Celle, Germany, at age seventy-two.

Dr. Alfons Theo Schmitt, Oberleutnant Lorient, was born in Stuttgart, Germany, on October 24, 1905. Schmitt studied in Britain, earned a degree in history from Oxford University, taught English and German at the University of Rennes, and traveled the world, spending time with a cousin in the United States. He forfeited his academic career when WWII broke out, serving as Oberleutnant in the Lorient sector of France. Schmitt was instrumental in negotiating the first, third, and fourth POW releases (November 16, 1944; December 24, 1944; December 26, 1944). After the Christmas Eve 1944 release of Sergeant Orval Love, Alfons Schmitt never saw Andrew Gerow Hodges again. Schmitt negotiated the final (December 26, 1944) exchange with Hodges, but Colonel Bergquist orchestrated the exchange at Etel/Le Magouer.

After the war, Alfons Schmitt was convicted of war crimes and incarcerated by the French government. He suffered immensely during his imprisonment. When released in 1957, he returned to Germany and lived with his nephew. Oberleutnant Schmitt never discussed his season at Lorient. Due to poor physical health caused by the years of prison abuse (according to a relative), Schmitt died six months after his release.

Hauptmann Heinz-Roland Schmuck, **Festungskommandant,** was chief of intelligence at the St. Nazaire sector. Schmuck, along with Oberst Harry Pinski, negotiated the second POW exchange at Pornic, France, November 29, 1944, with Andrew Gerow Hodges. After the war ended, Schmuck was arrested for war crimes and interned by the French government. He was believed released between 1948 and 1950. He was last heard of in Germany in 1954.

ETEL, 28 DECEMBER 1944

POWs EXCHANGED WERE:

94th Division POWs Held in Belle Ile:
Daniel A. Brosman, New York
Jesse C. Jones, North Carolina
Alfred G. Winkler, Colorado
George Glader, New York
Elmer J. Sparagna, New York
Albert C. Ponellit, California

The Crew of the B-17 "Take Me Home"—527th Bomb Squadron 379th Bomb Group (crash-landed on Kerlin-Bastard Airfield on 30 November 1944):
Second Lieutenant William J. Sullivan, Jr. (pilot)
Second Lieutenant Henry L. Heerman (copilot)
Second Lieutenant Hamilton C. Platt (bombardier)
Staff Sergeant Lawrence V. Archer (nose gunner/togglier)
Tech Sergeant Victor P. Stark (radio operator/gunner)

Sergeant Rudolph R. Rust (engineer/top turret gunner)

Sergeant Wayne O. Shelton (ball turret gunner)

Sergeant Henry R. Kritzer (waist gunner)

Sergeant William H. Endsley (tail gunner)

NOTES

CHAPTER 2: THE SPY

1. In August 1931, the Nazi Party created its own intelligence and security body: the SD (*Sicherheitsdienst*). In 1933, Hitler gave the SD extra power to deal with all opposition to the Nazi government. During WWII, the SD and the Gestapo became part of the Reich Security Administration (RSHA). Found at: http://www.jewishvir tuallibrary.org/jsource/Holocaust/sd.html. Accessed: September 18, 2013.

2. In the summer of 1944, *Operation Bulbasket* was one of the missions the SAS was called on to perform. A large party of SAS men were dropped into occupied France, with orders to cut railway lines, delay German reinforcements, etc. The operation was located to the east of Poitiers in the Vienne department of southwest France. The SAS men were captured, and on July 7, more than thirty men were executed by a German firing squad. Found at: http://www.historyofwar .org/bookpage/mccue_sas_operation_bulbasket.html. Accessed: September 18, 2013.

3. Note: The driver, Caplan, got away. According to Michael Foot, Caplan was later killed during the French conflict in Indochina. The German SD (Bonner) that Captain Foot hunted, disappeared and was never seen again. Information taken from a phone conversation between Michael Foot and Hobart Grooms.

CHAPTER 10: THE AGREEMENT

1. Found at: http://uboat.net/flotillas/bases/lorient.htm. Accessed: October 8, 2013.

CHAPTER 16: ON THE EVE OF THE EXCHANGE

1. Found at: http://projects.militarytimes.com/citations-medals-awards/recipient.php ?recipientid=17874. Accessed: October 18, 2013.

CHAPTER 19: THE EXCHANGE, PART 3

1. Quoted from: Luc Braeuer, *The Unbelievable Exchanges (Les Incroyables Échanges)* (5 Chemin des Grands-Pres, 44510 Le Pouliguen), p. 34.

CHAPTER 20: THE AFTERMATH

1. Found at: http://wwii-washingtoncountymo.com/taxonomy/term/1436. Accessed: March 3, 2014.

2. Note: Sent to author by Bernie Rader, January 2014. Some of the factual information in this letter about the October 2 ambush differs from other reports.

CHAPTER 21: THE "TIGER OF THE CHANNEL"

1. Some of the information found at: http://www.telegraph.co.uk/news/obituaries /1469276/John-Humphreys.html. Accessed: November 2, 2013. Also http://issuu .com/penandsword/docs/german_s_boats_pdf_katic/4. Accessed: November 2, 2013.

CHAPTER 23: CAMP FRANCO

1. Quote from: Michael R. D. Foot, *SOE 1940–1946* (London, England: The Folio Society, 2008), p. 69.

CHAPTER 30: THE PIT OF DESPAIR

1. Found at: http://www.theatlantic.com/national/archive/2012/08/rhythm-repetition -and-the-book-of-common-prayer/261573/. Accesssed: December 1, 2013.

CHAPTER 33: THE REQUEST

1. Found at: *Features*: "The man who knows all the dark secrets," *Daily Telegraph*, Thursday, December 6, 2001, p. 23.

CHAPTER 45: THE PORNIC EXCHANGE

1. Note to reader: International newsreels recorded the event. The silent five-minute, nineteen-second St. Nazaire POW Exchange 1944 video can be viewed at: http://www.britishpathe.com/video/st-nazaire-pow-exchange. Hodges can be seen at the 3:48–3:55 point.

CHAPTER 48: "TAKE ME HOME"

1. The Kerlin-Bastard airstrip was a French naval air base before the German occupation.

2. For more information about the 379th Bomb Group, see: http://www.379thbga.org/history.htm. Accessed: November 25, 2013.

CHAPTER 49: THE WARNING

1. Some information on French Resistance from: http://www.historylearningsite.co.uk/french_resistance.htm. Accessed: November 18, 2013.

POSTSCRIPT 2: THE REUNION: JANUARY 25, 2002

1. Found at: http://donmooreswartales.com/2010/05/12/harry-glixon/. Accessed: November 24, 2013.

INDEX

Index

343

Malony's letter to German commander at
St. Nazaire, 189–190, 193, 194, 196, 222
Michelin map (1938), 206–207, 222, 278
misunderstanding (Müller, St. Nazaire vs.
Germany), 256–259, 301
Müller's life saved by, 265–267
newsreel of Pornic exchange, 239
Pinski and, 194
Pornic exchange, 232–239, 260
request for help from Richard Foot
(Michael's father), 182–187
Ritterkreuz officer to swap for Michael
Foot, 204, 205, 208, 214, 216, 225, 227,
228, 230, 233, 234, 251, 253, 256, 261
terms for, 196–200, 214
Thanksgiving feast missed by, 213
transporting Müller to St. Nazaire,
256–267
warning from Bergquist about taking
Müller to St. Nazaire, 250–255, 256, 263
weather delaying Müller's exchange for
Michael Foot, 228, 230, 236, 237–238,
242–243
Hodges, Andrew Gerow "Gerow" (personal)
Andrew Gerow Hodges, Jr. "Little Gerry"
(Gerow's and Mary's son), 5–6, 54, 76,
223, 224, 239, 252, 253–254, 275
appearance of, 5, 61, 108
background of, 4, 5–6, 7, 75–76, 84, 97,
105, 118, 182, 185, 192, 203, 213, 214,
223, 276, 313
biographical information on, 313–314
brothers, 84
cigars and, 60
death of, 276
family of, 276
father "Old Jesse T.," 6, 7, 75, 84, 187, 202,
204, 207, 257, 259
football scholarship to college, 76
4-F classification from U.S. Army, 6, 76
gifts bought for Mary Louise "Shirley"
(Gerow's wife), 54
hero comes home, 275–276
letters to Mary Louise "Shirley," 54–55, 89,
190–191, 254, 255, 256, 275–276, 291,
293, 295–296
Liberty National Life Insurance
Company, 276
Mary Louise "Shirley" (Gerow's wife), 5,
54–55, 60, 76, 89, 190–191, 223, 224, 239,
252, 253–254, 255, 256, 275–276, 297
mother, 6, 75

mules of Gerow's father, 202, 204, 207
reunion (January 25, 2002), 277–280
Samford University, 276, 277, 278, 279
shoulder injury from football, 6, 76
stallions of Gerow's father, 257, 259
swimming, learning, 84
Holman, H. T., 75
Hotel Hermitage. *See* La Baule hospital,
France
Howard College, Alabama, 76
Humphreys, John (Lieutenant), 131–133,
136–137

Île de Groix, 39, 41–42. *See also* Fort Surville
POW camp on Île de Groix
Île de Houat observation post, 271
Infantry Assault Badge, 102
International Red Cross, 87, 198
interrogations of POWs by Germans, 22,
23, 60–62, 70, 121, 141, 143, 144–145,
247, 248
Iowa, 66
Iron Cross, 102, 112, 119, 135

Jaffré, M. Francois, 95–96, 104–105, 106, 107,
109, 116–117
Jones, Jesse C., 329
journey into darkness (travel to St. Nazaire),
192–195
Junck, Hans (Generalleutnant), 197, 198,
238, 326–327

K301 Vets honored in Brittany, 311–312
K Company, Third Platoon, 24, 26, 28, 30, 33,
35, 37, 38, 39, 42, 43
Keenan, Frank (Private), 121
Keller, Leonard (First Lieutenant). *See also*
Camp Franco in St. Nazaire
Camp Franco, 141–142, 158–159, 166, 167
escape from Camp Franco, 166, 167,
179–180, 199, 220, 221
escape planning, 158–159
"Gooney Bird" crew, 138–140, 141–142
Kentucky, 100
Keroman, Lorient, 16
Kerrl, Karl-Heinz (Major), 197, 206, 213,
214, 233, 238
"killed in action" telegram, 34, 38
Kimbolton, England, 245
kissing stone landing at Etel (Winn), 118
kitchen for POWs, Fort Surville POW camp,
75, 79